Positive Psychology in Business

101 Workplace Ideas and Applications

Sarah Lewis

△ appreciating change

Positive Psychology in Business

101 Workplace Ideas and Applications

© Pavilion Publishing and Media Ltd.

The author has asserted their rights in accordance with the Copyright, Designs and Patents Act (1988) to be identified as the author of this work.

Published by:

Pavilion Publishing and Media Ltd

Blue Sky Offices,

25 Cecil Pashley Way,

Shoreham-by-Sea,

West Sussex

BN43 5FF

Tel: 01273 434 943

Fax: 01273 227 308

Email: info@pavpub.com

Published 2019

A catalogue record for this book is available from the British Library.

ISBN: 978-1-912755-57-8

Pavilion Publishing and Media is a leading publisher of books, training materials and digital content in mental health, social care and allied fields. Pavilion and its imprints offer must-have knowledge and innovative learning solutions underpinned by sound research and professional values.

Author: Sarah Lewis

Cover design: Emma Dawe, Pavilion Publishing and Media Ltd.

Page layout and typesetting: Emma Dawe, Pavilion Publishing and Media Ltd.

Printing: CMP Digital Print Solutions

Contents

This book is dedicated to my father
David Arthur Lewis

Who died before I was old
Yet taught me things that stay with me still

About the author

Sarah Lewis is a chartered psychologist, an Associated Fellow of the British Psychological Society, and a founder and principal member of the Association of Business Psychologists. She holds a master's degree in occupational and organizational psychology, attained with distinction, and a certificate in systemic consultation. She is a specialist Appreciative Inquiry practitioner and an expert at facilitating large group events.

She is the managing director of Appreciating Change and is an experienced organizational consultant and facilitator who has been actively involved in helping people and organizations change their behavior for over 28 years. Her clients include local government, central government, not-for-profit organizations and private sector clients, particularly in the manufacturing, financial and educational sectors.

When positive psychology burst onto the scene, Sarah quickly realized that work in this area both chimed with her practice and offered robust theoretical support to Appreciative Inquiry as an approach to organizational change. She integrates these two approaches in her work and is delighted to be able to share some of her experience of, and thoughts about, applying these approaches in business.

Sarah is a lecturer on the International Masters in Applied Positive Psychology at Anglia Ruskin, and also at the Singapore School of Positive Psychology. She writes regularly for publication, and is the lead author of *Appreciative Inquiry for Change Management: Using AI to facilitate organizational development (2nd edition)* published by Kogan Page in 2016, and sole author of *Positive Psychology at Work* and *Positive Psychology for Change*, both published by Wiley-Blackwell in 2011 and 2016 respectively.

Sarah's work can be viewed on her website: www.acukltd.com, and she can be contacted on ++ 44 (0)7973 782715 or by emailing sarahlewis@acukltd.com.

Acknowledgements

Most of these chapters were originally written as articles for members of my LinkedIn group: 'positive psychology at work'. Every fortnight or so I would write about an experience I'd had, some reading I'd done or something on my mind. I also wrote chapters to support newsletters I sent regularly to clients and colleagues to ensure there were some nuggets of value amongst the shameless self-promotion that tends to find its way into such marketing devices.

Many people were kind enough to say that they appreciated the articles and even looked forward to receiving my fortnightly 'thought piece' in their inbox. In particular a friend of mine who is a team manager, with no formal psychology or management training, would regularly report how useful she found these missives in her day-to-day life as leader of a team. So, my first set of acknowledgements has to go to the folks who took the time to write, or to say kind words, that encouraged me to keep writing into the void that is the internet. Thank you to my readers.

Many of the chapters are reflections on practice based on specific work interventions with clients. As ever I want to acknowledge the courage and grace of my clients in making it possible for me to work with groups of people the way that I do. Sometimes interventions go well and sometimes not so well, but there is always learning to be had and it is the learning that I am keen to share. I am eternally indebted to my clients for experiences on which to reflect and from which to improve my practice. Thank you to my clients.

Other chapters were developed in response to conversations with colleagues at forums like the European Appreciative Inquiry Network or a positive psychology conference. I have acknowledged them as best I can in the text. Even so, there are many other professional colleagues unnamed here who help me develop my thinking through their generosity in wrangling with interesting questions, I am in debt to them all. Thank you to my colleagues.

Both of my sons have worked for me for periods in 'backroom' roles, and one still does. Occasionally I have roped them in to bring a different perspective to the topic I'm thinking about. Jem brings the perspective and knowledge of an economist and Jordan that of a historian. I have credited them as appropriate and am very grateful for the extra breadth their efforts bring to the text. Cheers lads!

Of course, I must mention my other family members, Stewart and Rhia, who despite having a less hands-on role in the production of this text, are always supportive and encouraging of my various interesting projects that intrude on family time and definitively take precedence over shall we say, some of the less interesting household tasks. Thank you.

And finally, my thanks goes to Darren Reed, the editor who helped me with my first 'sole' author book *Positive Psychology at Work* and then *Positive Psychology and Change* and who is also the editor for this text. Without his offer to publish, this book would have remained an unrealized aspiration to bring these chapters to a wider audience. I thank him for his faith that these miscellaneous pieces could add up to something worth reading.

Foreword

Dr Roger Bretherton

Principal Lecturer for Enterprise, School of Psychology, University of Lincoln

'*All books* [writes Sarah Lewis in the chapter, The Habits of Highly Creative People], *are written one word at a time.*'
'*A little done every day adds up.*'
'*Habits of work trump moments of inspiration.*'

And in three pithy points she sums up the essence of *Positive Psychology in Business: 101 Workplace Ideas and Applications*. Read one chapter and you'll be struck by how simple, incisive, and helpful her thinking is. Read two and you'll start to wonder how one person can skip so lightly from making the pains of redundancy a little less painful, to a fairy tale about organisational change. Read them all, and you'll realise that you hold in your hands the distillation of a life's work. When it comes to bringing the insights of psychology to the workplace, Sarah has been there, she's done it, and she has a wardrobe of 101 T-shirts to prove it. In this book we get to benefit from all that she has learned and accumulated little by little over decades.

Two things, in my opinion at least, make this book worth reading. Firstly, Sarah knows the psychology inside out. The short chapters are peppered with academic references and profound scientific insights from the world of positive psychology. She is a good guide. She knows the territory well and can point out the prominent landmarks for those of us who have never delved into this land before. Psychologists call it 'scaffolding', the overall framework we need to make ourselves at home in a new area of learning. We are never lost in the psychological undergrowth, because she is never lost.

This is the second thing I like about this book. One of the worst habits of academics (like me), is to get stuck in abstruse arguments based on technical language that only about three people in the world know or care about – and two of those are usually pretending. This book is erudite and wise and well-informed, but it never loses sight of the fact that most people in the workplace just want to know which bits of psychology will help them, right now. Each chapter addresses an urgent need or a crucial issue in contemporary working life. It's this exceptional amalgam of intelligence and appliance that made me such an advocate for one of her previous books, *Positive Psychology at Work*, much of which made its way onto undergraduate reading lists and PowerPoint slides in teaching the power of positive psychology in the real world of work.

However, if I had to sum up the message of this book for leaders, managers or anyone in the workplace at this strange time in history, it would simply be: don't panic. Avoiding the obligatory reference to Douglas Adams at this point, what I find timeliest about this book is the consistent acknowledgement that we live, work and lead in a milieu that is increasingly VUCA (volatile, uncertain, complex and ambiguous). And yet equally there is a strong emphasis on hope, gratitude, willpower, forgiveness, kindness, civility and so forth as indispensable qualities in a time of crisis, not added extras to be ditched when the going gets tough. Having dedicated my life to the understanding and promotion of character strengths such as these, I couldn't agree more.

This is the perfect book for anyone who at times feels disoriented and bewildered in contemporary organizational life. Certainly I for one now know where to turn next time I'm confronted by a dire change strategy meeting, a difficult conversation, a controversial appraisal or another wave of redundancies. Minutes before the meeting, I'll be nowhere to be found. But I know where I'm likely to be: hiding in the stock cupboard reading Sarah Lewis.

Preface

My hope for this book is that when considering a particular business challenge such as how to improve individual or team performance, how to offer leadership in turbulent times, or even how to downsize, you will find a chapter or two that gives you ideas about how to do it in a positive and appreciative way.

A positive and appreciative way is one that enhances well-being and encourages personal and organizational flourishing while dealing with the issue at hand.

This book pulls together pieces written over the last ten years that address these challenges and others. In this way it is a book designed for dipping into; an informative and useful resource for leaders and managers who are more interested in 'how' than 'why'.

The book is full of ideas, research and theory from positive psychology and guidance to their practical application in business. In addition, it introduces some key change methodologies that fit well with positive psychology, such as Appreciative Inquiry, Open Space, World Café and SimuReal.

Each chapter has a brief summary of content in italics to help you make a quick decision about whether this is for you, although to be honest the titles are mostly of a 'It does what it says on the tin' nature. Not everything will speak to everyone so feel free to move on and find a chapter that does.

This book is designed to be a reference text for the hard-pressed line manager or human resource specialist. Something you can quickly turn to for ideas, direct guidance, or inspiration when wanting to come at something from a positive perspective.

My ambition is that the chapters be quick to read and easy to apply; that they give you ideas about what to do that you can put into practice immediately. As ever I have attempted to write in plain English; if you find any chapter too jargon filled I apologize and suggest you just skip it and move on. I have also attempted to arrange the chapters in a 'flowing' order, however be aware that the reading experience will not be as smooth as a book written to be a coherent piece from the off.

To help with ease of reading I have used footnotes for references rather than in-text citations. For those who want to follow the thread of information back to the source, each footnote will lead back to an academic source. The suggestions and assertions in this book are traced back to over 100 academic references. Rest assured it may be an easy read but it is not an unanchored read; it is grounded in psychology, not snake-oil.

None of the ideas suggested in this book require any toolkits or psychometrics, bar one. All the other guidance needs, if anything, only the usual kit of pen, paper, flipchart and Post-it notes to be put into practice. Having said that, throughout the text I have introduced resources that may enable you to extend the practice suggested in the chapter. Many of these tools we sell in our online shop.[1] However you are well advised to shop around as, depending on where you are in the world, other suppliers may offer the same or similar items at a better price. I am always interested to hear of good value, practical tools to support working in a positive and appreciative way. If you have a particular favourite that I don't appear to know about, please do let me know.[2]

While each of the chapters is unique and I have tried to avoid duplication between chapters, there are some themes that reoccur throughout the text. Positive psychology is strong on the importance of understanding and knowing our strengths and on the importance of attending to mood, as is Appreciative Inquiry. So advice to focus on these two aspects of human life is a running theme in the book. Understanding the organization or business as a living human system, and the importance of questions in producing change, are two more themes that run across the discrete chapters. Similarly, you may find a particular exercise, such as the 'good news round' mentioned in more than one chapter, for the obvious reason that it is applicable in more than one situation.

The chapters are grouped by theme into sections. Those gathered together under *Section One: Introduction to the Key Concepts, Theories and Methodologies of Positive Psychology for Business* start by explaining how positive psychology differs from positive thinking and go on to immediately suggest ways you can bring positive psychology into your business or workplace. This section then takes you through an introduction to four key methodologies that are a good fit with positive psychology, namely Appreciative Inquiry, SimuReal, Open Space and World Café. Along the way we encounter a fairy tale that recounts an appreciative intervention through the metaphor of story. Finally, we look at the evidence base, pulling together the research from positive psychology with the impact of practice and identifying the mediating, psychological factors.

The chapters in *Section Two: Bringing Positive Psychology to the Change Challenge* start by exploding some of the common beliefs about how change can be made to happen in organizations. The section goes on to introduce a more psychologically-based approach to change, looking particularly at the phenomena of co-created or emergent change (as opposed to planned change). Next, we address the challenge of resistance to change and how to address it. There is then a series of chapters considering different aspects of change such as creating urgency or generating energy, or looking at different purposes of

---

1   www.acukltd.com/shop

2   sarahlewis@acukltd.com

change, such as creating a more sustainable environment or working with a project team. Finally, there are three chapters on the challenge of bringing a positive and appreciative approach to cutbacks and redundancy.

Section Three: Positive and Appreciative Leadership starts by addressing the challenge of leading through turbulent times. These chapters reflect a line of thought initially developed following the challenges created by the downturn in 2009 and continuing through the identification of the emerging present as a VUCA environment, that is, one characterized by volatility, uncertainty, complexity and ambiguity. We then move on to look at leadership from the perspective of positive and appreciative practice, including drawing on lessons from economists and from the military. We consider some key questions any business can ask itself to add value to the bottom line, and we end on an optimistic list of ten tips for creating positive and appreciative organizations.

Section Four: Positive Performance Management outlines how to get the best from the practice of performance management. We look at the challenges faced and paradoxical results of performance-related pay from an economic perspective. The section introduces a number of useful approaches such as working with strengths, positive and appreciative coaching, nudging, positive deviance and diamond feedback. There are tips on how to have courageous conversations at work and information on the habits of highly creative people. We also take a look at the dangers of the functioning psychopath in the work place and the factors that predict executive derailment.

Section Five: Positive Psychology for Teams and Groups introduces some information about what helps teams work more effectively. We look at the importance of interdependence and the diversity of group membership. We consider ways to help people work better together and how to create high-performance teams. We also look at specific challenges such as encouraging innovation in team work and working together in a virtual way.

Section Six: The Importance of Positive Emotions at Work makes clear the impact of our emotional state on our behaviour and work performance, while also suggesting many ways to help people feel good at work. We look at how happiness relates to success, performance and productivity. We look at the impact of politeness and rudeness at work. We explore the impact of gratitude and forgiveness on relationships at work. We look at hope and its importance in creating change. And finally we explore the idea of willpower: what affects it and what it affects.

Section Seven: Developing Positive Psychology Skills, Creating Positive Experiences brings together chapters that range from how to run a gratitude exercise to how to run a training session to understanding how to listen appreciatively. Along the way we consider the challenges of getting the best from performance management, strengths-based development, how to have productive meetings, the importance of the quality of our conversation and the challenge of obtaining compliance. We also think about how to apply positive principles to delivering training programmes and to creating effective evaluations. We look at practical activities like the success round and the 'time to talk round'. We focus on how to craft appreciative questions and how to listen appreciatively. We end by thinking about problems from a positive psychology perspective.

The final section *Concluding Thoughts* presents my selection of some of the nuggets of interesting ideas or practice that I have picked up from the major conferences I have presented at and attended over the last few years. We finish with a chapter about eulogy virtues.

This is the path I have tracked through these 101 chapters, grouping them has made more or less sense to me. I fully expect that, bringing your own curiosity and context to them, you would group them differently. Please do read them as makes sense to you.

For those of you who are interested in the 'why' as well as the 'how' my previous three books provide a more in-depth account of how these approaches are relevant to businesses, organizations and the workplace. *Appreciative Inquiry for Change Management*[3] explains how Appreciative Inquiry is different to what went before and how to do it. *Positive Psychology at Work*[4] takes key positive psychology findings and asks, 'So what?' in terms of their applicability to the workplace. While finally, *Positive Psychology and Leadership*[5] focuses particularly on the relevance of positive psychology to leaders.

Finally, I hope you find a few nuggets of your own here that allow you to bring the benefits of positive psychology to your workplace or business.

---

3 Lewis, S., Passmore, J. and Cantore, S. (2016) *Appreciative inquiry for change management: using AI to facilitate organizational development.* 2nd ed. London: Kogan Page.

4 Lewis, S. (2011) *Positive psychology at work: how positive leadership and appreciative inquiry create inspiring organizations.* Chichester: Wiley-Blackwell.

5 Lewis, S. (2016) *Positive psychology and change: how leadership, collaboration and appreciative inquiry create transformational results.* Chichester: Wiley-Blackwell.

Section One:

Introduction to the Key Concepts, Theories and Methodologies of Positive Psychology for Business

This initial section introduces the key theoretical stance that underpins the book: positive psychology. It also introduces the conversation-based approaches to organizational change and development that are referred to throughout the book: Appreciative Inquiry, Open Space, World Café, and SimuReal. If you are not familiar with these approaches then this section is a good place to start.

1: Positive psychology is not positive thinking

This chapter outlines the difference between positive psychology and positive thinking.

Positive psychology and positive thinking are easily confused, not only do they share the word positive in their name but there is also some overlap in their discourse. Both claim to help people improve their lives. However there are also key differences and it is these differences that allow positive psychologists to be ethical practitioners.

1. Science

Positive psychology is subject to the rigours of scientific experimentation; seeking phenomena and effects that are reliable and repeatable. There has been some deserved criticism of the poor quality of some psychological research, even so, many causal[1] relationships, for instance between good social networks and well-being, are being established and explained. Positive thinking on the other hand, is supported by anecdote. It is tautological in its explanations of efficacy: if it didn't work it was because you weren't positive enough.

2. Ethical

Positive psychologists practice within a code of ethics, there are professional bodies to hold us to account. We are discouraged from over-stating our effectiveness or of behaving inappropriately with our clients in any way; we have a duty of care. I find the inferences to be drawn from the extremes of the positive thinking field to be profoundly unethical, e.g. if you didn't manage to stop your cancer it's your fault for not being positive enough, or, if you want to be rich give us your money to attend our courses, put a penny in a jar every day and shout out 'I will be a millionaire' ten times a day.

3. Useful, applicable knowledge

Positive psychology is creating a body of knowledge useful to people about how to live good, long, happy and productive lives: it tells us what we can do to achieve these things, giving guidance on how to live our lives. Positive thinking promotes the belief that you can influence the world just by thinking about what you want. The common and confusing theme here

---

1   N.B. Not casual!

is visualization, which does have an influence on human behaviour but through the medium of the power of our actions not through the medium of the magic of our thoughts.

4. Randomness

Positive psychology accommodates randomness, it is aware that bad things happen to good people, that genetics is a dice game. At its extreme positive thinking suggests that bad things happen to those who deserve them.

5. Rounded view

Positive psychology appreciates the importance and necessity of difficult realities and emotions and recognizes their importance to human well-being (e.g. in the growth of resilience). Positive thinking 'bans' them.

6. Profession

Positive psychology has 'body of knowledge' structures e.g. all the paraphernalia of academia including peer review journals and academic courses and conferences. Assertions made as fact can be verified, challenged and corrected by others.

I hope this helps put some 'blue water' between these two approaches to improving human well-being. For more on all of this see Barbara Ehrenreich's excellent read *Brightsided*,[2] or my book *Positive Psychology at Work*.[3]

---

2   Ehrenreich, B. (2009) *Brightsided: how the relentless promotion of positive thinking has undermined America*. New York: Metropolitan Books.

3   Lewis, S. (2011) *Positive psychology at work: how positive leadership and appreciative inquiry create inspiring organizations*. Chichester: Wiley-Blackwell.

2: Nine tips for getting started with positive psychology at work

This chapter explains how to apply positive psychology to work in general ways.

Positive psychology is the new domain of psychology that burst upon the world when Martin Seligman[4] coined the phrase at his inaugural speech as the President of the American Psychological Association in 1998.

He issued a rallying call for research into human success. He wanted us to know more about what helps us excel, in health, in sport, in achievement. His work, and that of others who responded to the call, has been picked up by institutions as varied as the American military and the education system. We know more now than we ever did about how to help people live happy and successful lives. The ideas have spread to governments, with my own, the UK Government, deciding to take regular measures of national well-being as well as national wealth.

Positive psychology can be applied in the workplace. Its successful application will help you develop an engaged, productive, healthy workforce, and to create a great place to work. Here are some direct and practical ideas of how to apply the best of the results of the research into positive psychology to your workplace.

In 2004 Losada and Heaphy[5] demonstrated that feeling good is beneficial for us: we are more likely to be successful when we are feeling good. In their research the teams that offered each other at least three times more praise than criticism were the most successful.[6] This finding built on Fredrickson's[7] earlier work asking what good emotions do for us. More recently Shawn Achor[8] has brought all the research together in his great book *The Happiness*

---

4   Seligman, M. (1999) *Presidential address*. The American Psychological Association's 107th Annual Convention, August 21st, 1999.

5   Losada, M. and Heaphy, E. (2004) The role of positivity and connectivity in the performance of business teams: a nonlinear model. *American Behavioral Scientist* **47**(6) 740-765.

6   Author's note: while the statistical method in this research has been criticized since I initially wrote this chapter, I stand by the principle of the ratio they established, as this has been supported by research in other domains and is theoretically explained by the established phenomena of negativity bias.

7   Fredrickson, B. (1998) What good are positive emotions? *Review of General Psychology* **2**(3) 300-319.

8   Achor, S. (2011) *The happiness advantage: the seven principles that fuel success at work*. London: Virgin Books.

Advantage, also available on YouTube as a TEDx talk. The result is conclusive: happiness leads to success. So, how can you help your people feel good?

1. Start meetings with a round of success stories

Before you get into the meat of the meeting, usually a litany of problems and challenges, start by giving people the opportunity to share the best of their week.

2. Positive inductions

Build the sharing of great stories about the achievements and success of the organization into your induction programme. Get the owners of the stories to share their best moments of working for your company. Even better, equip your new recruits with appreciative questions about when people have been most proud to be part of the organization, or their greatest achievement at work, and send them off to interview people. This will leaven the dough of getting to grips with the staff handbook and inspire your new recruits.

3. Educate your managers about this research

Too many managers are quick to offer criticism and slow to offer praise, hoarding it as a scarce resource. Explain that they need to keep the ratio of positive to negative comments and experiences above 3:1 and preferably nearer to 6:1 if they want to get the best from people.

4. Give them the tools to do this

Particularly, introduce the concept of 'diamond feedback' and train people in its use. Diamond feedback is when you both report the behaviour you saw that you thought was good and give the praise. e.g. 'I listened to how you handled that customer call. The way you admitted our errors and thanked her for letting us know was really good. I could hear that you saved a customer we might have lost. That's worth a lot of money to us. Well done, that was great work'.

5. Help people use their natural strengths (including you)

Another finding coming through from the positive psychology research is that helping people understand what their natural strengths are and how to use them aids performance. Using strengths is energizing and engaging for people. This means they find work that calls on their particular and unique strengths profile to be motivating. The more you can help people find ways to use their strengths at work, the more likely it is that they will become self-motivated in their work. But first they need to know them.

There are a number of strengths-identifying tools around, particular the Strengthscope[9] psychometric, which also has a great set of support cards. However, in a low-tech way we can just ask people 'When are you at your most energized at work? What feels really easy and enjoyable for you that others sometimes struggle with?' and most interesting of all 'What can you almost not, not do?'

Once you know your own strengths find ways to use them more at work and, equally important, find ways to do less of the work that drains you of energy. Find someone to delegate it to for whom it plays to their strengths. We're not all detail people, but some of us love combing through data with a fine toothcomb. Reconfigure how you achieve the objective so it plays to your strengths. Pair up with someone whose strengths complement yours. Allocate tasks in your team by strengths rather than by role and delegate by volunteer rather than imposition when possible. Make sure other people know your strengths, so that they can call on you for opportunities that play to them.

6. Move towards being an economy of strengths

Find ways to use people's strengths more at work and, equally important, ways to do less of the work that drains them of energy. Encourage strengths-based delegation. Reconfigure how you achieve objectives so the plan plays to strengths.

7. Respond positively to good news

Positivity and strengths are probably two of the headline findings from the positive psychology research that are easily applicable to the workplace setting. However, there are also other emerging findings that are of interest. For example, did you know that how you respond to someone's good news is as important for relationship building as how you respond to their bad news?[10] Apparently so. To encourage positive relationships at work, help people to be actively positive in their response to other people's good news. This means not just saying 'that's great', but actively inquiring into how they did it, how they feel and how they hope to build on it.

8. Find your positive energy network node people

You may have noticed that there are some people that others just like to have around. They give those around them a generally good feeling. People are attracted to them. The research confirms the existence of such people at

9   https://www.strengthscope.com

10 Gable, S.L., Reis, H.T., Impett, E.A. and Evan, R.A. (2004) What do you do when things go right? The intrapersonal and interpersonal benefits of sharing positive events. *Journal of Personality and Social Psychology* **87**(22) 228-245.

the centre of networks of positive energy.[11] They have the knack for giving people little boosts of good feeling in their conversations or interactions with them, and people leave feeling better than when they arrived. These people are gold dust in terms of organizational motivation and performance. Notice who they are, place them strategically in projects and initiatives to which you want to attract other people, for example.

9. Develop a success and achievement strategy

It is very easy during difficult times to lose sight of achievements and successes. All too quickly it begins to feel as if there is no good news, only more bad news. One way to counteract this is to develop a strategy for recognizing, capturing and broadcasting the great things people and teams are still managing to achieve, despite a difficult context.

This chapter has barely scratched the surface of the interesting research and ideas emanating from this field. My book *Positive Psychology at Work*[12] explains these and other ideas in more detail. For these with an aversion to books, we also have a set of development cards[13] that offer bite-sized explanations of twenty core positive psychology concepts, with questions to help understand them and suggestions of how to integrate the concept at work.

We also stock a great game 'Choose Happiness at Work'[14] which offers an engaging, tactile, and easy way to introduce practical positive psychology into discussions of many frequently encountered workplace challenges.

11 Baker, W., Cross, R. and Wooten, M. (2003) Positive organizational network analysis and energizing relationships. In: Cameron, K.S., Dutton, J.E. and Quinn, R.E. (2003) *Positive organizational scholarship: foundations of a new discipline*. Oakland, CA: Berrett-Koehler Publishers.

12 Lewis, S. (2011) *Positive psychology at work: how positive leadership and appreciative inquiry create inspiring organizations*. Chichester: Wiley-Blackwell.

13 https://www.acukltd.com/store/positive-organizational-development-cards

14 https://www.acukltd.com/store/choose-happiness-at-work

3: What is Appreciative Inquiry and how does it work?

This chapter introduces Appreciative Inquiry. It briefly explains what it is, why it works and what it is good for.

What is it?

Appreciative Inquiry is a psychologically-based, revolutionary way of approaching organizational change and development. It is based on an understanding of the organization as a living human system. It calls on all the things that encourage change in people: energy, excitement, imagination, empathy and connection, trust, relationships, understanding, shared goals and concerns and a strong desire to be connected with good things.

It is good for coaching, team development and organizational development. It is excellent for developing employee engagement and motivation, improving performance and achieving change. It is effective when there is a problem, for example with an unmotivated individual, a stuck team, or when the organization is resistant to change. It is also highly effective for devising and implementing strategy within organizations.

Highly adaptable, Appreciative Inquiry can be combined with other approaches or used alone. Almost any organizational activity benefits from an appreciative approach.

How do you do it?

It can take place over a two or three day workshop, or can be incorporated into ongoing organizational life. Either way the key thing is that the whole system is involved. While this can at first appear highly inefficient to an organization, it later becomes apparent that it is highly effective. The benefits become evident as the costs all too often associated with change: resistance, lack of buy-in, poor traction etc are largely absent. Instead, frequently the challenge for the leadership is to keep pace with the energy and enthusiasm for change within the workforce.

What's it good for?

Appreciative Inquiry is good for organizational level issues, questions and challenges. For example:

- Strategy development.
- Product development.
- Improving efficiency or effectiveness.
- Improving organizational relationships.
- Improving work processes.
- Organizational growth.
- Organizational change.

How does it work?

Appreciative Inquiry helps people:

- Get involved.
- Feel engaged.
- Contribute willingly.
- Work together.
- Become motivated to change.

For more on Appreciative Inquiry you can go to my book *Appreciative Inquiry for Change Management*,[15] a great small book by Sue Hammond *The Thin Book of Appreciative Inquiry*[16] or another very well-regarded book by Jane Magruder Watkins and Bernard Mohr, *Appreciative Inquiry, Change at the Speed of Imagination*.[17] Those working in a 'LEAN environment' (LEAN is a technical process improvement methodology related to Six Sigma) might appreciate David Shaked's book *Strength-based LEAN Six Sigma*.[18]

Alternatively, we stock a great set of Appreciative Inquiry cards 'A Taste of AI 2.0'[19] that introduce all the key concepts in a lively and concise way.

15 Lewis, S., Passmore, J. and Cantore, S. (2016) *Appreciative inquiry for change management: using AI to facilitate organizational development.* 2nd ed. London: Kogan Page.

16 Hammond, S. (1996) *The thin book of appreciative inquiry.* Bend, OR: Thin Book Publishing.

17 Watkins, J. M. and Mohr, B.J. (2001) *Appreciative inquiry: change at the speed of imagination.* San Francisco: Jossey-Bass/Pfeiffer.

18 Shaked, D. (2013*) Strength-based lean six sigma: building positive and engaging business improvement.* London: Kogan Page.

19 https://www.acukltd.com/store/a-taste-of-ai-20-appreciating-people

4: Inquiring for a change: an introduction to Appreciative Inquiry

This chapter explains Appreciative Inquiry in more detail, highlighting the importance of language and organizational conversation in achieving change.

Introduction

Appreciative Inquiry is an approach that offers a genuinely different way of working with organizations to achieve change. Initially developed by Cooperrider and Srivastva[20] as a re-invigoration of action research, Appreciative Inquiry has rapidly developed into a recognizably new and innovative approach to organizational development.

This chapter will explain what Appreciative Inquiry is and the thinking behind it. It outlines the key practice model, looks at the skills required, and considers the benefits of working this way.

Growing towards the light

Appreciative Inquiry pre-supposes organizations as 'living systems'. Living systems are heliotropic, that is, they *'exhibit an observable tendency to evolve in the direction of positive anticipatory images of the future'*: in other words, they grow towards the light.[21] Organizations are also human social constructions: we talk them into existence.

The importance of language

Our abilities to jointly create (or co-construct) positive anticipatory images of the future (commonly referred to as visions of the future) are strongly affected by the vocabularies at our disposal, by our linguistic resources. This doesn't mean our personal lexicon of words, it means our shared joint ways of talking. Most organizations have well developed problem vocabularies, they have much less well-developed ways of talking about what has been labelled their 'ultimate concerns' that is, the good, the true and the beautiful. Or to put it in slightly less esoteric language, we're not

---

20 Cooperrider, D. and Srivastva, S. (2001) Appreciative inquiry in organizational life. In: Cooperrider, D., Sorenson, P.F.Jnr., Yaegar, T. and Whitney, D. (eds.) (2001) *Appreciative inquiry: an emerging direction for organizational development.* Champaign, IL: Stipes Publishing.
21 *Ibid.*

so practiced at talking to each other about what is working well, or about the organization at its best.

The Appreciative Inquiry process recognizes that to start to generate or create positive images of the future in a way that will enable growth towards that future, we must first generate, create, or discover a shared, joint vocabulary. We must find an agreed way of talking about the topic we want to address that allows us to do so from a growth perspective (focusing on what we want) rather than the more familiar deficit perspective (focusing on what we don't want).

The affirming topic

To achieve this Appreciative Inquiry encourages us to identify an 'affirming topic'. An affirming topic identifies what we want to affirm and enlarge in our organizational life; in effect, what we want to grow. So, for example, if an organization has a problem with gender harassment, the affirming topic might concern itself with learning more about 'excellent gender relations'. That is, rather than learning more about how to do gender relations wrong, let's learn from what happens when things go right. The inquirers into this topic would then want to inquire into positive experiences of excellent gender relations within the organization, past and present. None of which is to suggest that examples of gender harassment should be ignored, rather that if we want to change the culture to reduce the incidents of gender harassment, then maybe we need to look at situations where the potential is there but something else happens instead. This allows us to identify what enables great gender relationships; a perhaps subtle but highly significant difference to identifying what enables gender harassment.

Key points about the process

There are a few important points to note about the Appreciative Inquiry process.

1. Firstly, it doesn't ignore the problem or try to discredit people's expressed experience, as people sometimes imagine. Rather, it takes the identification of a problem as the expression of a desire for a different future. It then works to find experiences in the present that point towards that future. Experiences in the present, if you like, that give us clues about how to create a positive future.

2. This brings us to the second important point about this way of working: when the process moves on to create the future, that future is grounded in and grows out of present and past lived experience. In other words, it's not 'blue sky thinking', rather it is an imagined future conjured from known best experience.

3. A third thing to notice about this way of working is that it connects people to positive emotions. Indeed, when one practices Appreciative Inquiry with a group it brings those positive emotions very strongly into the present. Good

feelings are energizing, good feelings are inspiring, good feelings increase social bonding. Such experiences create more energy and momentum for achieving change than do councils of despair, wrapped up as they are by 'shoulds' and 'oughts'. Appreciative energy is full of wants and hopes. It's the difference between compliance and commitment.

4. A fourth thing to notice is that the question is the intervention. What we ask and how we ask it is crucially important, for it generates what we find. In this sense language is fateful, it affects fate, and it is impactful.

So how do you do it?

As I hope is becoming clear, Appreciative Inquiry is both a methodology and a philosophical stance that guides appreciative process. As a methodology Appreciative Inquiry offers a five-stage process.

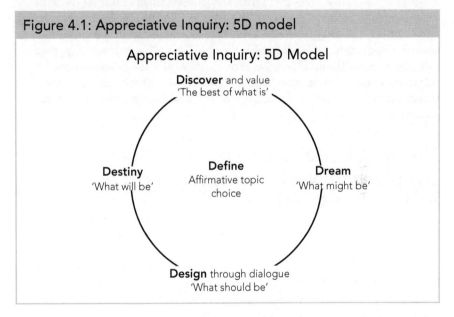

Figure 4.1: Appreciative Inquiry: 5D model

The first stage is **Define**, identifying the affirming topic into which we wish to inquire.

The second stage is **Discover**, appreciating 'the best of what is', examining what gives life to the organizational system. This is done through the inquiry process described previously, that creates a supply of stories about the organization and the people in it at their best.

The third is **Dream**, envisioning results by asking 'what might be' or 'what is the world calling us to become?' By jointly constructing dreams of what might be that are firmly built on the best of the present, attractive and attracting futures can be created.

Fourth is **Design**, co-constructing what should be. In this stage the organization asks itself, 'if that is our dream, how do we need to organize ourselves to make it happen?'

Fifth is **Destiny**, what happens next. At one time it was thought that this was the action planning process and it was known as the 'delivery' stage. More recently faith is being put in the self-organising properties of groups of people joined together in a social action, in this case to change their organization. Planning is still an important part of the stage, but as a servant of energy and collective action.

Appreciative skills

Practitioners have also started to identify what it is that helps make an effective appreciative process practitioner. Bushe[22] notes that interviewers must be able to *'suspend their own assumptions'* and be able to *'attend to others appreciatively'*. He suggests they need *'a poetic ear, an eye for beauty, a keen sense of what others find inspiring and an open heart'*. Yaegar and Sorensen[23] talk about acute listening, positive care, insatiable curiosity, spontaneous reframing of questions and an ability to hold on to the belief that the process is meaningful and worthwhile. Quite a different list to problem analysis and solution formation!

How is it beneficial to organizations and the people who work in them or for them?

To spend more time talking to people about what is good and is going right, and less time going down into the spiral of hopelessness, is a lot more life enhancing for both consultants or leaders and the people they work with. An incidental, yet immeasurable, benefit is that the concept of 'resistance' so often an integral part in people's mind of the concept of organizational change, becomes completely irrelevant, a non-topic. Essentially Appreciative Inquiry works with people as non-rational and emotional beings, rather than ignoring them or trying to deny them their humanity.

Ten key points to practicing appreciatively

1. Think of organizations as living human systems.

2. Be mindful that the inquiry is the intervention.

---

22 Bushe, G. (2001) Five theories of change embedded in appreciative inquiry. In: Cooperrider, D., Sorenson, P.F. Jnr., Yaegar, T. and Whitney, D. (eds) (2001) *Appreciative inquiry: an emerging direction for organizational development*. Champaign, IL: Stipes Publishing.

23 Yaeger, T.F. and Sorensen, P.F. (2001) What matters most. In: Cooperrider, D., Sorenson, P.F. Jnr., Yaegar, T. and Whitney, D. (eds) (2001) *Appreciative inquiry: an emerging direction for organizational development*. Champaign, IL: Stipes Publishing.

3. Be aware that language is fateful.

4. Remember we are drawn towards attractive futures.

5. Re-create positive emotions to produce energy.

6. Treat organizations as socially constructed.

7. Consider every context unique.

8. Trust the simplicity of the Appreciative Inquiry process.

9. See organizational change as a social action movement.

10. Appreciate that hope is motivating.

5: Consultancy fairy tale of using Appreciative Inquiry

I was once commissioned for a piece of work where the story of how the leader came to be in place was, I thought, key to the whole challenge. Here I choose to give an account of this intervention through story. It offers a further account of how Appreciative Inquiry thinking affects practice.

I want to start by telling you all a story, are you sitting comfortably? Then I'll begin.

Once upon a time, in a land not far from here there was a young princess. The princess lived with the king and her ladies in waiting. The princess was a very special and unusual princess; for she was once a lady in waiting with the other ladies in waiting to the queen. The queen was a very powerful queen who had ruled the land and all under her dominion for a very long time.

One day the queen had to go on a long journey, she called the princess to her and told her 'I must go away, while I am away you must look after all I have made for when I come back'. The princess was very pleased to be made a princess and took her charge very seriously: she worked hard to keep everything as it was for the queen's return. But the queen never returned.

After a while the king began to receive reports that all was not well with the ladies in waiting. Stories reached his ears of much wailing and gnashing of teeth. His courtiers also complained that the ladies in waiting were not doing their jobs properly. The courtiers were not happy.

The king began to wonder what he should do, he wondered if he should throw the ladies in waiting out of the palace. While he was wondering he heard of a wise fool. The wise fool was summonsed to court.

The King charged the wise fool with three quests:
'You must make the princess a queen for the queen is not returning.'
'You must make the ladies in waiting happy for they are not happy.'
'You must make them all work, for they are not working.'

The wise fool didn't like to hear of all these unhappy people so promised to fulfil the three quests. She looked in her bag to see what she had to help her. In her bag she found lots and lots of words, she was pleased to see them for they were her good friends. Then in her bag she found four precious things: curiosity, wonder, generosity and appreciation. The wise fool was happy for now she knew what to do.

With her words and her generous appreciation she showed them what good they were doing, and they began to marvel and wonder at all the good things they were doing in these difficult times.

With her words and her curiosity she showed them what hopes they had, and they began to marvel and wonder at all the good things they were doing in these difficult times.

And with her appreciation she helped them ask the princess to be a queen, and the princess said yes and shifted her crown and stood up straight, so they believed her.

And as they began to wonder and marvel they stopped wailing and started working, and as they began to dream they stopped gnashing their teeth and started smiling. And as they began to work and smile they started to make things better. Soon the wise fool's work was done, so she returned to the palace to see the king and get her bag of gold and she said, 'I have done as you asked' and the king replied 'yes, and it is not as I expected'. But that's another story.

6: SimuReal explained

This chapter offers an explanation of a dynamic large group change process that I have used and found very efficacious in the right context.

SimuReal is a technique used to represent an organization to itself by showing its members how the different parts of the organization affect each other in their work. By showing how the behaviour of the constituent pieces of the whole have unforeseen or unappreciated consequences elsewhere in the organization, it allows the participants to analyse and change their ways of working to be more helpful to each other. Here are answers to some commonly asked questions about SimuReal.

Why do organizations need it?

When large organizations are divided into functions, geographically spread and linked by processes that take time to run from beginning to end, it is very easy for them to become a series of isolated functional silos that don't really understand how they connect to the whole. SimuReal brings the whole process or organization together in one space, working on a common issue, to bring into sharp focus the departmental interconnections and interdependencies so the organization can adapt and grow.

How does it work?

SimuReal uses simulation to help an organization become more visible to itself. It enables key members of organizations to work together to become more aware of, and skilled in, dealing with organizational dynamics. Consisting of action periods followed by analysis sessions, the method is used to help organizations explore differences, solve complex problems, work on redesign, determine goals and priorities and engage in future planning. In a large single space the participants work within and between groups to deal with a pre-determined task that is important to the well-being of the organization.

Generally, the room is laid out in a pattern that reflects the structure of the organization. Participants operate in their own functions/departments. Field staff can be located on the periphery. The participants are required to act in role as they address a current issue. In the first hour people work on the issue as they would normally. Then the whole group moves into another space to analyse the learning so far, and to plan improvements. These improvements are put into place in the next round of activity. This cycle is repeated, until the end of the day where decisions are made and further actions are clarified.

What makes it work?

Success depends on the quality of the pre-work. This requires the planning group and the facilitator/consultant to fine tune the chosen issue. They also need to plan how the room is arranged so that it represents both formal and informal groupings in the organization. In addition they need to attend carefully to the process of selecting and inviting participants, clarifying questions and processes for the day and establishing the decision-making processes.

If you want to know more about this methodology I devote a whole chapter to it in *Positive Psychology and Change*,[24] or you can go to the source Klein[25] or Bunker and Alban.[26]

24 Lewis, S. (2016) *Positive psychology and change: how leadership, collaboration and appreciative inquiry create transformational results.* Chichester: Wiley-Blackwell.

25 Klein, D. (1993) SimuReal: a simulation approach to organizational change. *Journal of Applied Behavioural Science* **28**(4) 566-578.

26 Bunker, B. and Alban, B. (1997) *Large group interventions: engaging the whole system in rapid change.* San Francisco: Jossey-Bass.

7: It's a meeting captain, but not as we know it: exploring Open Space

This chapter explains the Open Space process.

A self-organizing meeting

The Open Space process allows people to contribute to conversations that interest and energize them. It ensures that all topics that need to be discussed, are discussed. It allows people to add value to the discussions in a way that works for them. It disrupts established patterns of organizational behaviour, allowing new voices, views, opinions and perspectives to be heard and developed.

How does it work?

People are invited to come together around a topic of key business importance. Once assembled, they are invited to individually put forward ideas for discussions that they believe or feel are of importance to the overall topic. Different rooms at different times are assigned for the different discussions. Each discussion has a host who needs to ensure a written record of the discussion is produced. Once the agenda is created, each person decides for themselves which discussion they wish to join.

Some people choose not to join any discussion, some flit from one to another. This is also fine.

Between rounds of discussion, the group comes back together to share discussions so far and to identify further subjects or questions for discussion. In this way many aspects of a topic can be explored, defined, outlined, or resolved by people who are interested to be in the discussion.

It's that simple?

Yes and no. There are a few key rules that allow the process to work well.

- First, everyone has both a right and a responsibility to put forward things they believe merit discussion. This makes it unlikely that 'the unmentionables' will remain so.

■ Second people have an obligation to ensure that they are somewhere where they are either learning or contributing; if not, they are obliged to take themselves elsewhere. This reduces the abuse of a captive audience scenario.

■ Third the group is formed through voluntary self-selection; there are no disruptive 'prisoners' or 'pressed men'.

Within the sessions there are four key principles: whoever comes are the right people; whatever happens is the only thing that could have happened; whenever it starts is the right time; and when it's over, it's over. These principles make it less likely that time and energy will be wasted on 'might have been'. It also means that when a discussion reaches a natural conclusion, people are free to move on to something else.

If you want to know more about this methodology, I devote a whole chapter to it in *Positive Psychology and Change*,[27] or you can go to the source Owen.[28]

---

27 Lewis, S. (2016) *Positive psychology and change: how leadership, collaboration and appreciative inquiry create transformational results*. Chichester: Wiley-Blackwell.
28 Owen, H. (1997) *Open space technology, a user's guide*. Oakland, CA: Berret Koehler.

8: Why dine at the World Café?

This chapter explains the World Café process.

What's it for?

The World Café process is designed to help people talk together, exchange ideas and develop their thinking about an issue in a relaxed, informal, yet purposive way. In small 'café groupings' of no more than six people, groups discuss particular questions or topics with the aim of expanding their understanding of their own and others' views; and of expanding the sense of possibility. World Café is useful in many contexts. It excels when the main object is to connect and explore around a particular topic. At its best it produces conversation that connects, has energy, is emergent, magic and values not knowing as well as knowledge.

What happens?

The process is one of rounds and themes. For any particular event there will be a number of 'rounds' of conversation. For each round there is likely to be a different theme, or topic. Each round needs to last at least 40 minutes for participants to feel they have had a full chance to both speak and be heard. The themes can be a topic, for example 'increasing teamwork', or more frequently the theme is framed as one or more questions to stimulate discussion. Sometimes each table discusses the same theme, and sometimes different ones. All are introduced to 'café etiquette', some suggestions for how to behave and how to conduct the conversations.

At the end of each round participants are invited to move to a different table with a different group of people for the next discussion. However, one person remains as a host.

How are the conversations connected?

The conversations are connected in a number of ways. In the first instance, after each round, people will disperse amongst the tables. In this way they bring a number of different conversations into contact with each other. Meanwhile the host at each table works to ensure that the conversation at their table is connected with what has already been said. Notes are often kept on paper tablecloths to help people track their conversations. In addition, the facilitator will often seek to have a few minutes 'linking' conversation between tables between rounds.

How does it work?

World Café works on the assumption that very often the knowledge and wisdom needed to move forward on an issue are present and accessible within the organizational system; that intelligence emerges as the system connects to itself in creative ways; and that collective insight evolves from unique contributions, connecting ideas, deep listening, and awareness of deeper patterns. World Café involves the art of 'listening for what is in the middle of our table'.

If you want to know more about this methodology, I devote a whole chapter to it in *Positive Psychology and Change*,[29] or you can go to the source Brown and Issacs.[30]

---

29 Lewis, S. (2016) *Positive psychology and change: how leadership, collaboration and appreciative inquiry create transformational results.* Chichester: Wiley-Blackwell.

30 Brown, J. and Issacs, D. (2005) *The World Café, shaping our futures through conversations that matter.* Oakland, CA: Berret Koehler.

9: The generative power of World Café: strengths and imposter syndrome

Sometimes I get the opportunity to be part of a process rather than being the facilitator. It's always good to experience their power. This chapter gives an account of some generative thinking that emerged from a World Café process.

Last year I ran an evening event I called a Learning Network Event. The purpose of the evening was to provide a space for those interested in positive psychology to share and learn from each other in a gently facilitated way. We used a World Café process to stimulate conversation and to ensure cross-pollination amongst those present.

During the event I had a 'shiver down the spine' moment as I suddenly saw a link between two conversations in which I was involved. I had a really powerful experience of the cross-pollination potential and generative power of the World Café process.

In the first conversation we were discussing 'imposter syndrome': one of our group was doing a PhD investigation into this common yet disturbing workplace phenomena. It's a very interesting topic which resonated with those present.

A short while later I was part of a conversation talking about how knowing our strengths allows us to understand better how we can be a success at our jobs, especially when we don't fit the 'template' for the role. We realized that knowing our strengths allows us to construct an authentic story about how we are succeeding, that may stand in contrast to the dominant story of what is required to succeed in the role.

During this conversation a story was shared by one person who was involved in sales. She talked about how understanding her strengths helped her recognize it was her relational strengths that enabled her to be good at sales even though she didn't see herself as a 'typical salesperson'.

It was around this point of the evening I had my brain tingling moment as I put two thoughts together. I swear I could almost feel the neurons firing as I realized that we can pull these two thoughts together and put forward an argument about how imposter syndrome might arise.

Could it be that part of the reason we experience imposter syndrome is because we don't 'see ourselves' as being like the kind of person who usually succeeds in this role; that we have no understanding of how we might succeed and so see ourselves as 'imposters', getting by on luck and chance?

If so, then understanding our strengths and how they relate to our abilities in our role can help us construct a story about how it is possible for us to be 'good at this' or 'a success at this' that makes sense to us and feels authentic. Might knowing our strengths and understanding how they help us to succeed be an antidote to the debilitating, anxiety-inducing, vulnerability-creating experience of feeling like an imposter liable to be exposed for the fraud we are at any moment?

For me the event demonstrated the power of World Café to produce genuinely generative conversation: I had a new thought and for me that is one of the best feelings in the world.

10: Positive psychology and change: an evidence-based practice

This chapter presents a model of how theory, research and practice in this area pull together to create effective interventions.

We now have enough theory, research and practice from work in Appreciative Inquiry and positive psychology to know how and why these interventions work. We can also work out how to combine them to create robust, effective approaches to change that are suitable for organizations grappling with the challenges of the twenty-first century.

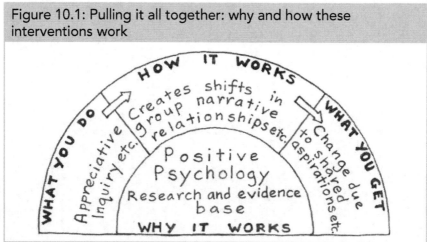

Figure 10.1: Pulling it all together: why and how these interventions work

Why it works: knowledge base

Research in positive psychology over the last 15 years and earlier has given us a robust set of data about what flourishing organizations, organizational practices and people look like, and how to create them.

What you do: practice base

Appreciative Inquiry has extended its methodology from the original 5D summit model to include the SOAR approach to strategic development, appreciative coaching, positive performance processes and many more appreciative practices to tell us how to do it.

In addition, other co-creative methodologies such as Open Space, World Café and SimuReal offer clear processes for applying positive psychology to organizational change.

How it works: process base

An increasing awareness of the psychology of group and human behaviour, and of the influencing factors on that behaviour, means that we know how these co-creative methods work. They have impact through psychological processes such as the creation of new narratives and the reconfiguring of patterns of relationships. Positively applied, co-creative change approaches influence behaviour through socially dynamic processes such as imagination, metaphor, and identity.

What you get: change in the dynamics of a living human system

The application of science through the medium of the conversationally-based, co-creative processes influences group dynamics. This leads to a higher-level organizational transformation. Change occurs through the production of highly-energized shared aspiration, shared hope, keen interdependency understanding, community-level thinking, effortless synchronicity and future-oriented action. Such transformation pulls people over obstacles and set backs towards a better future.

This model is explained more fully in my book *Positive Psychology and Change*.[31]

---

31 Lewis, S. (2016) *Positive psychology and change: how leadership, collaboration and appreciative inquiry create transformational results*. Chichester: Wiley-Blackwell.

Section Two:

Bringing Positive Psychology to the Change Challenge

The chapters assembled in this section start by exploding some of the common beliefs about how change can be made to happen in organizations. They go on to introduce a more psychological-based approach to change, looking particularly at the phenomena of co-created or emergent change (as opposed to planned change). Next, we consider the challenge of resistance to change and how to address it. There is then a collection of chapters considering different aspects of change such as creating urgency or generating energy, or looking at different purposes of change, such as creating a more sustainable environment or working with a project team. Finally, there are three chapters on the challenge of bringing a positive and appreciative approach to cutbacks and redundancy.

11: Myth-busting: five common beliefs about change

This chapter names and explodes some of the common myths about change in organizations.

Leaders and managers are increasingly expected to introduce changes in work practices, routines and structures as part of their management role. Myths abound about the challenges of doing this. Here we lay five to rest.

1. You can't implement the change until you have thought through every step and have every possible question answered

This belief leads to exhaustive energy going into detailed forecasting and analysis of every possible impact and consequence of possibilities: in the worse cases leading to paralysis by analysis. While one group is over-worked another is dis-empowered as they 'wait' for the change. It slows things down, allows rumours to fill the information vacuum, and leads to a downturn in motivation and morale. It is a key contributor to the much-heralded organizational resistance to change.

The ambition is a chimera, it is impossible in a dynamic complex system for one part to map every linkage. In many situations it is sufficient to have a sense of the end goal, or key question, along with some shared guiding principles about how the change will unfold. For example, 'We need to produce our goods more efficiently', or, 'How can we cut our process times?' With these in place leaders can call on the collective intelligence of the organization as it embarks on learning by doing, that is, by creating a shared sense of possibilities, taking the first steps, reviewing progress, learning from experience and involving those who know the detail in their areas.

2. You can control the communication within the organization about change

This belief leads to embargoes on information sharing 'until we have decided everything' (see above) and much investment in finding 'the right words' to convey the story of the change. Meanwhile people are free to make their own sense of what is happening uninhibited by any corrective input from those initiating change.

It is impossible to control interpersonal communication and sense-making, we can only seek to influence it. People are sense-making creatures who constantly work to make sense of what is happening around them. By withholding information we still convey information, usually about levels of distrust or a culture of secrecy. But more than this, in this day and age with so many communication channels instantly available to people, there is no chance of building walls around communication. Instead leaders need to focus on making sure they get to hear what sense is being made of what is going on so that they can contribute a wider, more informed, different or corrective perspective as part of the ongoing flow of conversation.

3. To communicate about change is to engage people with the change

This belief leads to an over-emphasis on communicating about 'the change'. Staff hear managers talking endlessly about how important this change is, how big it is, how transformational it will be, yet no one seems to know what the change actually means for people. To be part of this scenario is to suffer a confused sense of 'but what are we talking about?' This in itself is usually symptomatic of the fact that at this point there is only a fuzzy picture of what this much-heralded change will mean for people: much better to get people involved in finding out.

To believe this (that communicating about the change is to engage people with the change) is to confuse intent with result. People start to engage with the change when they start working out what it means for them, what it 'looks like', where the benefits or advantages might be, how they can navigate it, what resources are there to help them. They find out through exploration and discovery. They become more engaged when they are asked questions, such as: 'How can we implement this here?', and, 'What is the best way of achieving that?', or 'What needs to be different for us to be able to...?', or, 'How can we positively influence this process?' People have to use their imaginations and creativity to start visualising what their bit of the world will be like when 'the change' has happened. Everyone needs the opportunity to create rich pictures of what the words and ideas in the change mean in their context. The answer to the question 'What might it mean for us?' is jointly constructed and evolves as new information emerges.

4. That planning makes things happen

This belief in 'plan as action' fuels a plethora of projects, roadmaps and spreadsheets of interconnection, key milestones, tasks, measures and so on. People can invest time and energy in this fondly believing that they are 'doing change'.

Planning is a story of hope. Creating plans can be an extremely helpful activity as long as we realize that what they do is create accounts and stories of how the future can be. Until people translate the plans into activity on the ground, the plans are just plans. For example, I might develop a really detailed plan about emigrating to Australia, including shipping and packing and visas and job prospects and everything you can think of, but until I do something that impacts on my possibilities in the world, for instance by applying for a visa, then planning is all I have done. Plans are an expression of intention. Things start to happen when intention is enacted in the wider world.

5. That change is universally disliked and resisted

This much repeated and highly prevalent belief leads to a defensive and fearful approach to organizational change, inducing much girding of loins by managers before going out to face the wrath of those affected by the change.

If this were true none of us would emerge from babyhood. Our life is a story of change and growth, of expansion and adaptation, of discovery and adjustment. Do you wish you had never learnt to ride a bike? That was a change. Had never had a haircut? That was a change. What is true is that change takes energy, and people don't necessarily always have the energy or inclination to engage with change. It is not change itself that is the issue, it is the effect imposed change can have on things that are important to us: autonomy, choice, power, desire, satisfaction, self-management, sense of competency, group status, sense of identity and so on. If we attend carefully to enhancing these within the change process, then there is a much greater chance that it will be experienced as life-enhancing growth like so many other changes in our lives.

12: Why we need to do change differently

This chapter outlines why we need a new approach to change.

In the twenty-first century we need to be doing change differently. Whole-system change methodologies such as Appreciative Inquiry and World Café offer alternative ways of creating organizational change.

So why do we need to do change differently?

1. Because the old ways are too slow and hard

Traditionally change has been a top-down, linear compliance process: first designed and then implemented. In today's fast paced world this takes too long and is too hard. People resist the pressure. Instead we need change that is whole-system owned and generated, focused on maximising tomorrow not fixing yesterday.

2. Because the future is created by our actions and our imagination

Forecasting is tricky in an unpredictable world of disjointed and disruptive change. When it's hard to plan a future we need to use our imagination to create attractive possibilities that inspire us, co-ordinate our efforts and pull us forward. Our analytic powers help us analyse data, our imaginative powers create hope, optimism and forward motion i.e. change.

3. Because organizational growth is a systemic phenomenon

The evidence is mounting that good workplaces and profitability can grow together; that beyond a certain point of profitability, greater returns come from investing in social capital features like workforce morale, camaraderie, worker benefits, and community action; and from ensuring that employees feel hopeful, encouraged and appreciated.

Timberland, Merek Corporation, Cascade, Synovus Financial Corporation, FedEx Freight, Southwest Airlines, The Green Mountain Coffee Corporation, Fairmount Minerals and the Marine Corp are all testament to the possibility of doing the right thing and doing well by the people e.g. making a profit and treating people well.

The current edition of *Firms of Endearment* by Sisodia and colleagues[32] lists 28 US publicly funded companies, 29 US private companies and 15 non-US companies that are good organizations and exceptionally profitable.

4. Because relational reserves are key to change resilience

Relational reserves are an expression of the accumulated goodwill and mutual trust that helps organizations bounce back quicker from disruption or trauma. They are as important to organizational resilience, an attribute called on during change, as financial reserves.

5. Because we need to conceive of successful change differently

Pushing change into, down or through an organization takes too long. We need to shift our emphasis from configuring planned change to releasing emergent change. We need ways of achieving organizational change that allows future-oriented action to happen simultaneously in independent yet interconnected ways across the organization; rather than attempting to achieve organizational change through a linear series of dependent actions. To be able to release this wave of emergent change energy, we need to recast our understanding of both change and success. We need to learn to celebrate adaptation, direction shift and even project abandonment as evidence of learning and refinement, rather than viewing these as signs of failure.

6. Because mistakes can be costly

Separating the change shapers from the change implementers and change recipients can be costly, as errors in understanding, judgement and knowledge only come to light when time and money (not to mention hope and commitment) have already been invested. People pointing out such errors late in the day risk being labelled as obstructive or resistant. Better to involve those who will be effecting, or be affected by, any changes from the very beginning.

7. Because change needs more buyers and less sellers

Have you ever walked into a shop, money in hand, keen to buy, only to leave empty handed and frustrated by the salesperson's emphasis on selling rather than listening to you? Maybe they dazzled with jargon, or listed irrelevant features, or tried to push their favourite version onto you despite its unsuitability to your situation? At its worse organizational change can feel like a bad sales job. Good salespeople ask questions and listen before they talk, and so should organizations.

---

32 Sisodia, R.S., Sheth, J.N. and Wolfe, D.B. (2014) *Firms of endearment: how world-class companies profit from passion and purpose*. 2nd ed. Upper Saddle River, NJ: Prentice Hall.

8. Because we need to use our intelligence

The world is a demanding place to do business. Organizations need to be able to access the intelligence of all involved. We need leaderful organizations not leader-dependent ones.

13: Seven helpful things to know about achieving change in organizations

This chapter counters some of the beliefs that can get in the way of achieving change, extending the argument of the previous chapter.

1. The plan is not the change

All too often those involved in creating the plan for change believe this to be the most essential part of the process, worthy of extended time and effort, while implementation is seen as 'just' a matter of communicating and rolling out the plan. Plans are a story of hope. Change happens when people change their habitual patterns of communication and intervention in a meaningful and sustainable way.

2. The map is not the territory

Any map of an organization is going to contain inaccuracies. Therefore any plan based on that imperfect map is going to be subject to corrective feedback where the assumptions of the map proved faulty. Unexpected reactions to, or effects of, implementing the plan should therefore be embraced as giving useful information about how things are, rather than interpreted as a mistake in the planning.

3. A natural response to a burning platform is blind panic

People do not make great team decisions when they are panicking. They don't even make good personal decisions. Creating fear and anxiety as drivers for change can have unhelpful consequences in producing self-orientated, unthinking survival behaviour. Better to create positive emotions in change that encourage creative, complex and group-orientated thinking.

4. The path to the future is created not uncovered

Sometimes in change we act as if the future lies there waiting for us; we have only to uncover the path and follow it. Believe instead that the future is in a constant state of creation, that our actions today affect tomorrow; that how we understand the past affects how we conceive possibilities in the future, and we begin to see the creation of the future as an activity that takes place in a constant present.

5. Resistance is a sign of commitment

Resistance to change is often labelled as problematic. Instead it should be viewed as a sign of engagement, of commitment. There are many truths in organizational life, and they don't always align well. Some people may hold a different view about what is best for the organization. If they are prepared to risk conflict then they care enough to let you know. Be much more aware of unspoken disagreement disguised as compliance; undealt with now, it will surface as soon as the chips are down.

6. Meaning is created not dictated

I cannot dictate to you how you are to understand things; I can only suggest. If I am unable to create a shared meaning with you then we are not aligned. All too often organizations try to dictate how their actions are to be interpreted by all. Better instead to have many conversations that assist groups in the organization to interpret and re-interpret what is happening through the prism of their own many contexts, and to co-create meaning together.

7. There is no correct answer to the challenge of organizational form

Organizations are engaged in an endless challenge to arrange themselves in an optimal form. Since the tensions within organizations are irreconcilable, any solution is only a temporary truce. Constant adaptation within organizational form is healthy, anomalies to the norm may add value for a time, a complexity of forms may aid flexibility. Essentially though, as has been said before, change is a constant organizational activity and continual small changes are usually more adaptive than big lurches every three to five years.

14: The distinct and unique features of co-created rather than imposed change

This chapter looks at the distinct features of co-created, as opposed to imposed, change. The next few chapters are also on this theme.

Co-created change differs from imposed change in its process and effects. Whole-system change methodologies such as Appreciative Inquiry and World Café facilitate co-created change.

Co-created change

1. Builds on past and present strengths to create sustainable change

Co-creative approaches focus on identifying past and present organizational and individual strengths as resources for the change. Using our strengths is energizing and easier than using areas of non-strength. Being able to construct the change in a way that calls on our strengths can be highly motivating.

2. Understands strengths as the key to a new organizational economy

With an awareness of strengths, we can reconfigure our understanding of the organization as an 'economy of strengths'. At its simplest, this suggests that people can spend most of their time doing what they love, within a structure that allows them to easily find people with complementary strengths to their own.

3. Understands social networks as the heart of organizations

Understanding the organization as a social network directs our attention to the importance of relationships in change. It sounds obvious but the language of the organization as a 'well-oiled machine' or 'a bureaucracy' or 'an org. chart' can easily obscure this essential reality. A continual focus on people and their patterns of interaction and communication is a key focus of these approaches.

4. Recognizes the importance of dialogue as words create worlds

It matters both what people say to each other and how they say it. It is easy for people to fall into talking about change in a solely negative way. Creating an opportunity for those concerned to co-create more purposeful, forward-oriented, positive accounts of what is happening, and their role in the change and the future, and creating opportunities to broadcast this new narrative more widely, can be very beneficial.

5. Recognizes the importance of narrative for sense making in action

The accounts we create of the world and what goes on it are our best guides to appropriate action. They are our reality. They aren't immutable. A key factor in the success of these approaches in achieving change is that they facilitate connected, system-wide shifts in narrative, allowing the team or organization as a whole to create new accounts of 'what is going on'. This allows new meanings to emerge, or sense to be made, which in turn liberates new possibilities for action.

6. Recognizes the energizing and resilience boosting effects of positive emotions

Hope and courage are key to the process of change. It is easy for these to be damaged or reduced during change processes. A key focus of all these appreciative and positive methods is the reignition or regeneration of positive emotional states in general, and these two – hope and courage – in particular. Positive emotional states are a key component of resilience, also an attribute much in demand during times of change.

7. Utilizes imagination as the pull for change

We can push people towards change or we can pull them towards change. The former can seem easier and quicker and leads to the desire to create, find or build 'burning platforms' for change. The latter is slower, and since the imagined future is often less immediately available to the imagination than the all too real undesirable present, it can be harder to access. However, it creates a more sustainable energy for change. Appreciative Inquiry as a methodology is particularly alive to and focused on this.

8. Calls on the whole power of systems

Working with the whole system simultaneously is a key way to involve the power of the organization to achieve simultaneous, co-created change.

15: Further distinctive features of co-created change

This chapter highlights yet more ways in which co-created change differs from imposed change.

How is it different, why is it better?

Co-creative approaches to organizational change such as Appreciative Inquiry, Open Space, and World Café have some very distinctive features that differentiate them from more familiar top-down, planned approaches to change.

1. Change is a many-to-many rather than one-to-many process

In co-creative change a lot can happen in a short space of time, as conversation (and change) takes place simultaneously amongst people in various groups, rather than relying on a linear transmission from top to bottom. It can feel messier and less controlled but the benefits of active engagement, participation and commitment far outweigh these concerns.

2. They work on the understanding that the world is socially constructed

By allowing that we live in social worlds that are constructed by interactions in relationships, these approaches recognize that beliefs, and so the potential for action, can be affected by processes or events. The co-creative change processes allow people to experience each other, and the world, differently and so adjust their mental maps of their social world, creating the potential for change.

3. Conversation is a dynamic process

Co-creative approaches to organizational change recognize that conversations and events take place in a dynamic context of mutual and reflexive influence: I act and speak in the context of what you are doing and saying and vice versa. This means that conversation is not a passive process for conveying information but is rather an active process for creation, and so holds the potential to create change.

4. Organizations are about patterns, so changing organizations is about changing patterns

All of the above culminates in the understanding that organizational habits, culture and ways of being are held in place by the habitual patterns of conversation and interaction. Change these and you change the organization.

5. Change can occur at many levels simultaneously

Rather than being focused on rolling out a pre-designed planned change, these approaches are much more focused on growing change from the ground up. A useful metaphor to convey this is that of encouraging lots of different plants to flourish on the forest floor by changing the bigger context, such as clearing part of the canopy to allow more light in.

6. They connect to values to gain commitment

These approaches connect to people's values as well as their analytic abilities. Appreciative Inquiry discovery interviews, for instance, quickly reveal people's deep values about their organization and allow people with divergent surface views to form a meaningful connection at a deeper level that aids the negotiation of difference.

7. They create hope and other positive emotions

Appreciative Inquiry by design, and the other approaches by intention, focus on creating positive emotional states in the participants, particularly hope. Hope is a tremendously motivating emotion and is a key source of energy for engaging with the disruption of change. By building hope in the group that the situation can be improved, these processes create great energy for the journey ahead.

8. They encourage high-quality connections and the formation of high-energy networks

These are two concepts from positive psychology and increasingly research[33] is demonstrating that these phenomena have a positive effect on creativity, problem-solving and performance. The co-creation change methodologies are highly relational and facilitate the development of meaningful relationships, particularly across silo or functional boundaries, increasing the ability of the whole organization to change in synchronization with itself.

---

33 Gittell, J (2003) A theory of relational coordination. In: Cameron, K.S., Dutton, J.E. and Quinn, R.E. *Positive organizational scholarship: foundations of a new discipline.* Oakland, CA: Berrett-Koehler Publishers.

9. They allow people to feel heard

The very essence of the co-creative approaches is the emphasis on voice and dialogue as key components of change. People have an opportunity to input to discussions about the need for change from the very beginning, and are also able to influence the design of change. They feel their voices and needs are being heard by the organization as the change unfolds. This greatly lessens the challenges of overcoming resistance or getting buy-in.

16: Why people resist change and how to encourage them to embrace it

This chapter explores the common challenge of resistance to change.

Resistance to change is seen as a major challenge to organizational initiatives. Before we think about how to reduce it, we need to understand why people resist change.

1. Information about the need for change might not get past the brain's gatekeeper

This is the part of the brain that continually monitors our environment and decides what needs to be attended to and what can safely be ignored. Presented with new information it asks: how is this relevant to me, my needs or my interests? Does this information present me with a challenge I need to engage with? Is it new information? Is it interesting? Fail to stimulate a 'yes' respond to any of these and the information doesn't even register with the conscious brain and therefore no behaviour change takes place. This reaction might be labelled as resistance to change.

2. The information might trigger a defensive emotional reaction

The part of the brain that assesses danger is very sensitive to perceived threat and will trigger an automatic reaction to perceived danger, commonly known as the fight, flight or freeze response. All of these responses can be interpreted as 'resistance to change'.

3. There may be a previous organizational history of change badly done or of ineffectual change initiatives

In this situation the change announcement can trigger a 'they're crying wolf' response of just ignoring the signals that change is coming. Alternatively it might trigger a 'heads down and this too will pass' reaction. Any visible behaviour change is likely to be more of the 'hunkering down' type than active engagement with the change.

4. Organizations and people can suffer from change fatigue

Change takes energy and a group of people overworked and stressed can be incapable of responding positively to a change initiative even if they think it is a good idea. There is no active resistance but there is little volunteering and lots of suggestions about how someone else could take this on.

5. Sometimes there is a good reason to push back against the proposed change

People elsewhere in the organization may be able to see things that the change originators can't. They may be speaking up trying to protect valuable, precious and important things in the organization. They can easily be misheard as protecting their own situation; 'they would say that wouldn't they'. In this case their legitimate objections are discounted and they are labelled resistors.

6. People are emotional

People are emotional beings and sometimes even if the change 'makes sense' in a logical and rational way, people may have an emotional reaction that leads them to delay doing things or making changes. A classic example is the need to deliver bad news, whether it's critical feedback or news of redundancy. People may accept the need but delay the action. This too looks like resistance.

7. They may not have the brain capacity to focus on building new habits

Using the hard drive and RAM analogy, we can imagine the brain as having a lot of hard drive capacity but relatively little RAM. When we are trying to build new habits we are using a lot of the RAM available to us until the new behaviour becomes a habit. If we are using our RAM to cope with fast-changing situations already, it can be hard to systematically also build a new habit. That's why we decide we'll put off instigating that new exercise regime until this mad project rush is over and we have time to think!

So, how can we encourage people to embrace change?

■ Acknowledge the impact. Recognize that change takes time and energy.

■ Acknowledge previous bad experiences of change programmes and use them as a springboard for a positive discussion about what we can learn about how to make this one a better experience.

■ Involve people in identifying the need and designing the response to change. From their point of view this needn't be overly time consuming.

A one-day large group event gives people the opportunity to truly focus on the opportunity, challenge, or need and to have influence at a very early stage in the response design. The benefits of this approach are many. Appreciative Inquiry is a good example of a methodology that creates these opportunities.

- Incorporate their intelligence rather than discount it. By engaging with people who will be affected early in the change process you are able to make good use of their detailed local knowledge, and are in a much better position to assess their motivations in raising different issues. Involving people earlier results in much better solutions down the line, with minimal resistance to them.

- Be sure to engage people's positive future-oriented emotions rather than triggering their blocking ones. Motivation is drawn out of people through the creation of a pull towards an attractive future. Co-creating ideas of how the future could be, based on the best of the past and the present, and exciting initiatives happening elsewhere, releases this pull motivational energy.

- Very actively support the creation of new behaviour habits to make it very easy to do the new thing, and to do it right:

  - Remove as many hurdles as you can between remembering to do the new thing and doing it. Make doing the new thing right the path of least resistance not an effortful feat of memory and resource accessing.

  - Give frequent, small positive rewards for the doing the right thing, especially at the very beginning of the behaviour change process. Initially you want to be right on it, being overly generous with recognition and support for effort made, as well as results achieved.

  - Give this lots of attention. Don't assume that because you've told them you can now switch your attention to something else. They will attend to what you attend to. Make sure they can see in your words and behaviour that this is your primary focus.

  - Make it as routine as possible. We always do it the new way. Have reminders and cues everywhere about the behaviour we want right now. And change these regularly as they quickly become visual wallpaper.

- Switch from a sole emphasis on projects and planned change to incorporate more psychologically-based change approaches such as Appreciative Inquiry, World Café and Open Space.

17: How to avoid triggering resistance to change: five effective strategies

This chapter addresses two of the most frequent concerns expressed by leaders and managers in organizations when they are contemplating or are engaged in change, relating this conversation to the benefits of co-created change. It builds on the previous chapter.

Key change questions

Two of the questions most frequently heard when talking to leaders about their plans for change are:

- How can we get buy-in?
- How do we deal with the resistance to change?

They reflect assumptions about people and change so embedded as to be endemic.

Assumptions about people and change

These assumptions are that 'people don't like change' and that people can be 'sold' change.

It is true that, on the whole, people aren't widely enthusiastic about change that is forced upon them without consultation, particularly if it appears to make their life or working conditions worse. It is also true that people will buy the idea that if they point out the problems that the proposed change will cause, they will be labelled as a troublemaker or worse. Given this, they may stop saying anything. This compliance is often confused with 'buy-in'.

An alternative approach

Co-creation change processes offer an alternative. By working closely, from the beginning, with those who will be affected by any proposed change, these questions become irrelevant. A number of additional benefits accrue.

Benefits of the co-creation approach to change

1. Tapping into collective intelligence

Participative co-creation taps into the collective intelligence of the organization at the point where its application can have the most effective impact at the least cost – at the very beginning. Involved early, before irreversible decisions are made, people can draw on their wealth of localized knowledge about what works and what doesn't while the challenge is still being formulated and considered; at the point at which it can save the organization time and money. They can also road-check solution ideas for feasibility before they have become invested with the weight of being the right and only answer. All of this reduces both resistance and lack of buy-in. **Utilizing the organization's collective intelligence leads to better solutions arrived at in a cost-effective manner, enhancing acceptance**.

2. Creating active participation

When people are involved in the definition of the problem or challenge and the design of the solution, they start to make changes in their behaviour immediately. In addition, once formal plans are issued, or projects started, they already understand why and don't need to be persuaded of, or sold on, the rightness of the action. Being an active participant engaged in understanding the situation, making sense of what is happening and being able to influence decision-making positively affects people's motivation to put ideas into action. Co-creation approaches to change lead to faster implementation. Early involvement effectively bypasses or greatly reduces resistance to change and the need to get 'buy-in' at a later date. **Encouraging active participation in design leads to faster solution implementation through enhanced commitment to the plan**.

3. Direct involvement in decision-making

When people have direct involvement in decision-making, when they feel their views have been genuinely sought, appreciated and considered, and they have been party to the evolving discussions, they are much more likely to accept the outcome and to be able to see their influence on it. Having been actively involved, they experience a sense of ownership and commitment to the outcome.

As long as their views have been genuinely appreciated and considered they are likely to accept the evolving nature of the solution. People can track their particular contributions as the answer evolves. Such involvement inspires a sense of ownership of, and commitment to, the final design. Co-creation leads to a high level of commitment. **Facilitating direct involvement in decisions creates a high level of commitment**.

4. Building social capital

Co-creative methods bring people together across the system and so create greater social capital. People who have worked together in a positive way on something that is important to them form stronger social bonds. Collectively, the strength of these internal relationships is known as the social capital of the organization. High social capital means a high level of trust across the organization; good information-sharing and easy information flow, all of which lower organizational cost and increase co-ordination during the disruption of change. It also facilitates problem-solving at the level of the problem. Investment in social capital helps to ameliorate the well-known problems of silo mentality. Co-creation facilitates low level, quick and effective peer-to-peer problem-solving, which is vital when new and unfamiliar systems are being implemented. **Increasing social capital leads to coherent, co-ordinated action**.

5. Leverage strengths

Co-creation processes that focus on identifying existing strengths and core values as part of the change process help people link the need for change with success and personal integrity. They focus on identifying past and present organizational and individual strengths as resources for the change. Using our strengths is energizing and easier than using areas of non-strength. Being able to construct the change in a way that calls on our strengths can be highly motivating. They also create positive emotion that is energy for the change. Co-creation based on existing strengths and clear values is likely to be implemented with hope and enthusiasm, leading to a smoother implementation process. **Leveraging strengths and values leads to hope and optimism, increasing motivation to make change happen**.

How can you implement change like this?

There now exists an abundance of co-creation change processes that help organizations avoid triggering resistance and all the costs and delays incurred with that. They require organizations to demonstrate a different style of leadership, one that is predicated on an understanding that an organization is a social system, with leadership a privileged position within that system. The role of the leader then becomes to find ways to help the organization continually evolve towards a better future. To do that the leader needs to call on and release the collective intelligence and capability of the whole organization.

18: How to create urgency in positive change

This chapter explores one of the challenges of positive change, where we forgo the creation of a burning platform for change.

How can we create urgency in positive change?

This was the question posed to me recently by a human resources director taking up a new post with a big change agenda. He was attracted to the idea of positive change, but working with an organization with a long and successful history, he was challenged about how to galvanize the workforce into engaging with the necessary changes. I thought it was a great question and it has stayed with me.

It has long been known that negative emotions such as fear, despair or anger can act as a catalyst for change.[34] Leaders and change consultants have sometimes built on this knowledge by deliberately creating these emotions at work; by 'creating the burning platform for change' to create urgency about the need for change.

Such tactics may well produce energy for change, however there are some drawbacks.

- The energy may not be accompanied by much creativity: the aim is to avoid, not to create.
- The energy may not be very sustainable: once the threat is seen to have receded the escape behaviour ceases and old patterns reassert themselves.
- It tends to produce more compliant behaviour than active commitment.
- It can create a very unhealthy and unhappy working atmosphere.

I thought the HR director asked a great question: how to create an urgency about positive change? In other words, how to create an awareness of an urgent need for change without creating a burning platform for change?

Interestingly, only this week I did just this. I was due to attend an initial meeting with an organization I had been invited into by a concerned senior

---

34 These days we tend to refer to such emotions by other terms such as 'unpleasant' or 'less pleasant' in recognition that these emotions serve a useful purpose and so to label them as 'negative' is unhelpful.

manager. He reported the CEO didn't see the need for change and probably wouldn't even come to the meeting. In the event he was present.

During the meeting with the senior manager and the CEO, I worked to positively 'reframe' some of the account I was being given, by:

- Highlighting the strengths of the individuals and the organization present in the predominant stories of doom, gloom and inadequacy.

- Affirming some of the CEO's key decisions and actions.

- Affirming his positive motivations – feeling of responsibility, desire to improve, commitment to ensuring a future.

- Turning 'don't wants' into 'do wants'.

- Creating a picture of how things could be if the organization was working 'at its best'.

- Telling stories of other situations where things had changed successfully.

- Creating attractive images of how things could be different for him in his role if he shared the burden of saving the company with everyone else who had a stake in it (you are not alone).

- Creating stories of possibility – of both outcomes and process.

In short, by helping him feel good about himself (so more able to take action), creating hope and optimism about the possibilities of change, and creating potential pathways.

At the end of the meeting all was urgency. How quickly could we start? From a beginning of little perceived need and anyway, 'no money or time', we had moved to a desire for urgent action. We had created Rowland and Higgs'[35] 'magnetic pull' towards the future, which they found in their research to be a key feature of effective leadership during change.

Create a magnetic pull towards the future

Positive and appreciative approaches to change have a strong emphasis on creating hope, optimism, group cohesion, strong visions of attractive possible future states, desire and ambition. They strengthen relationships, build social capital, create interdependencies and identify shared goals or aspirations. They build trust, illuminate shared values, and have a positive effect on motivation and morale.

---

35 Rowland, R. and Higgs, M. (2008) *Sustaining change: leadership that works*. West Sussex: Jossey-Bass.

In short, they create a 'together we can' understanding of their collective abilities to influence outcomes. This, combined with co-created aspirations for, and visions of, future states, forms the basis of the energy for change.

A desire for change created from these more positive emotional states may take a little longer to release, discover, create or build, but it is likely to be more sustainable as a force for change. Working with groups you can see when a particular idea about, or vision for, the future really starts to take hold. It won't go away. It exerts a continuing fascination, an attraction. This creates its own urgency: a desire to engage others with this powerful aspiration. It acts as a powerful light in the hazy vision of the emerging future, allowing for constant re-orientation. It is a pull towards the future and as such tends to create a much more sustainable energy over time than the push energy created by an awareness of the need to avoid present danger.

An awareness of present danger can make us jump fast and without thought. An aspiration to achieve a desirable future state can draw us ever onwards.

19: Organizational energy and Appreciative Inquiry: the relationship

This chapter explores the importance of organizational energy to engagement and performance, positioning it as an emergent phenomenon that can be created and released by Appreciative Inquiry practice.

I have recently come across a great paper about human energy.[36] It set me thinking about what it was saying in relation to Appreciative Inquiry. These are my thoughts.

Energy as transforming

Energy can be a transforming resource. When people become 'energized' they are transformed before our eyes. We talk about how people become 'fired up' or are 'on fire'. We see increased animation, people seem more dynamic; quiet wallflowers are suddenly able to hold a room's attention because they are talking about something that really matters to them. The generation of this energy transforms potential futures, as while un-energized people are disinclined to 'spend' any energy or to exert any energy to get something done, energized people are a force for movement.

What is this energy?

We know from earlier theorists that we can conceptualize energy as non-activated, that is, latent, and, as activated, that is, 'in motion'. We understand human energy to be made up of different elements e.g. to have affective, cognitive and behavioural dimensions. Human energy can be characterized as being positive or negative in intent or direction.

Understanding organizational energy

Organizational energy, while clearly related to individual energy, can also be thought of separately as a resource of a collective unit. Four different collective or organizational energy states have been identified: productive energy, comfortable energy, resigned inertia, and corrosive energy. These

---

36 Vogel, B. (2017) Experiencing human energy as a catalyst for developing leadership capacity. In: Vogel, B., Koonce, R., and Robinson, P. *Developing leaders for positive organizing: a 21st century repertoire for leading in extraordinary times*. Bingley, UK; Emerald Publishing Ltd.

names have great face validity with me: armed with this language I can see I am in the business, frequently, of transforming resigned inertia or corrosive organizational energy into productive organizational energy that is going to work to move things forward.

These four states can be seen as lying across two dimensions: intensity and quality. Intensity as a dimension ranges from high (activated energy) to low (non-activated energy). While quality ranges from positive to negative reflecting how the energy is constructive or destructive of the organization's goals.

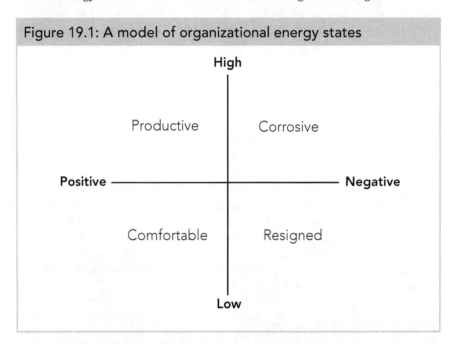

Figure 19.1: A model of organizational energy states

How is productive energy created in an organization?

Productive (high positive) organizational energy can be characterized as a collective temporary emergent state. Temporary of course means not permanent, collective means involving everyone. The idea of an 'emergent' phenomena comes from the theory of complex adaptive systems and suggests that the phenomena of productive (high positive) organizational energy 'emerges' from the behaviour of individual actors in the system. The behaviour of these individual actors works to create collective high positive organizational energy. Individual interactions in settings of mutual dependence can facilitate the creation of shared interpretations of shared events; and the generation of shared emotional or cognitive states e.g. shared states of high, positive energy. Or indeed shared states of any of the forms of energy.

It was at this point of my reading that I sat up and took notice. This is exactly the area in which Appreciative Inquiry and other dialogic, co-creative change methodologies create their magic. It is precisely by actively working with the interactions of people in situations of mutual dependency (a whole system), by creating shared interpretations of shared experiences (the process we take people through to create 'account' of past, present and future) and by the deliberate generation and expansion of positive emotions (Appreciative Inquiry particularly) that we are able to have a positive effect on the energy of a group or an organization and so the potential for action and change. I find this articulation of the phenomena of organizational energy and how it relates to the processes of Appreciative Inquiry very exciting.

How does this relate to Appreciative Inquiry?

In this paper energy is described as a resource that allows actors to generate new cognitive frameworks to organize their understanding of a situation. In other words, as we have different experiences together, so we see things differently together, and therefore we can act differently, together. As the paper explains, once a group starts to experience a shared enthusiasm, shared cognitive activation (brain or thought activity) and shared sense of working for joint goals, so the situation begins to feel more one of mutuality and less one of antagonisms. As the sense of mutuality (we're all in this together) grows, so people are more likely to get involved, helping to create meaning, direction setting, deciding, motivating others and in general taking on such leadership tasks in some area or other. The leadership capacity of the system expands. Leadership capacity and leadership enactment becomes less a property of a job title and more a property of the social system. It is this shift in the leadership capacity and pattern in the group, as well as the emergent productive energy, that allows change to happen. Again, this describes exactly what, as a practitioner, I see as the Appreciative Inquiry process unfolds.

And so I suggest that as we look to help organizations adapt and grow in changing conditions we need to attend to the phenomena of organizational energy. Thanks to researchers and theorists we have a language in which to describe what we see in organizations and to help us understand what underlies the effectiveness of these 'positive energy, whole system, dialogic' change methodologies such as Appreciative Inquiry. By giving us words and a framework they help people articulate something they instinctively know, i.e. the difference between the energy of resigned inertia and productive energy. They make it possible to explain what Appreciative Inquiry does and how: namely that it transforms the energy of resigned inertia or corrosive energy into productive energy by working with the collective phenomena from which the temporary phenomena of productive energy emerges. By so doing it creates a shift in energy state and an increase in leadership capacity allowing for effective organizational action.

20: The economic value of social capital to organizations

This chapter introduces the topic of social capital, addressing it from an economist's perspective and relating it to organizational development.

What is social capital?

Elsewhere in this book we talk about social capital as a group or social phenomena that adds value by increasing trust and information flow around an organization, however it can also be understood from an economic perspective.

From this perspective it can be defined as a combination of the number of relationships someone has, the economic usefulness to them of those relationships, and the quality of them. Effectively, how well known someone is, in what circles and with what degree of affection. It is the social capital in an organization that means that we care about the effect our work will have on the next part of the production chain, rather than slinging substandard work over the functional line saying, 'done my bit, their problem now'.

Why is it important in organizations?

It is the social capital of an organization that influences the return gained on the value of the financial and intellectual assets. It is what makes the whole greater than the sum of the parts. It is social capital that releases organizational good citizen behaviour, high-level motivation and that 'good feeling' about work. Social capital is the antidote to the ubiquitous silo mentality that permeates most larger organizations: the tribal mentality that can act against the fullest realization of the potential value of the organizational assets.

An organization can purposefully invest in this valuable source of capital like any other. And as with any other investment, it is possible to identify the areas of investment likely to create the greatest return, and therefore carefully target investment activity. For instance, it is probably not going to boost an organization's social capital if it invests in helping the canteen staff to get to know the board as much as it would to invest in building social capital within the board (which isn't to say that the first option doesn't have some value, and in some situations might have the greater value).

Why don't organizations invest more in social capital?

Often leaders can intuitively see the value of social capital, however an inability to quantify this capital, and the return on their investment, prevents them from taking the risk of investing in it. Interestingly intellectual capital, a similarly non-physical form of capital, does show financial returns that can be directly attributed to it on the balance sheet e.g. licensing revenue and royalties. These returns can be used by leaders to justify the initial investment they made in developing intellectual capital. At present no such mechanism exists for capturing and measuring the return on social capital investment.

Measuring the economic value of social capital

It is tempting to conclude from this that social capital can never exist in the financial sense in the way that machines, buildings and patents do; that it is not worth leaders making the additional effort to try and identify its effect on the balance sheet. Recent developments in economics suggests such thinking can be challenged. Social capital not only exists as a factor in economics, but exists to such a real and definable extent that it is now used by banks as collateral for loans, particularly micro-loans.

The micro-finance story

Billions of dollars have been lent to (and repaid by) tens of millions of people in areas of the world where social capital is the only form of capital available, and not just in the third world. If you're reading this in London, Manchester, Birmingham or Glasgow, to name but a few places, this is probably happening within a few miles of you.

Social capital is the basis of micro-finance, the practice of lending very small amounts of money to the very poor. It has already revolutionized development policy across the world. The problem, identified by Muhammad Yunus in Bangladesh in the 1970s, was that the poor were unable to secure loans from commercial sources not because they *couldn't* pay it back but because that it seemed they had *no incentive* to do so. This was because they had no collateral that could be repossessed if they defaulted. As a consequence no private lenders were prepared to lend them money. Yunus's experience with the Grameen bank, and that of other micro-finance institutions, is that the poor, properly incentivized, have the highest repayment rates in the world when lent small amounts, almost 97%.

Yunus incentivized individuals by making possible future loans to others in the village conditional on the repayment of the loan by each borrower. In other words, he secured the loan against each villager's social capital. If she defaulted, none of her friends or neighbours would get loans and she (the vast majority of micro-finance customers are women) would be persona non grata in the village. This suggests that for a particular individual her stock of social capital must be worth more to her than the value of the loan or she would not repay it. A Bangladeshi villager making the decision to repay a $20 loan is making a sophisticated calculation about the value of an intangible asset: her social capital. This clear behavioural indicator of choice suggests that a financial value can be put on an individual's social capital.

Can social capital be measured in organizations?

The micro-finance experience suggests that social capital can be measured. The question is how can organizational leaders find a way of making such calculations for the stock of social capital in their organizations?

There is not a yet a clear answer on this. We can begin to recognize the social capital in organizations by reflecting it in our ways of talking about our organization. For example, referring to the member of staff who takes the time to contact colleagues to check out their needs and expectations, or who takes the time to let others know something has changed so they don't waste their time, as *invaluable*, doesn't help us recognize the value she adds. On the other hand saying she, and her actions, are *valuable*, starts to lead us to ask the right questions about 'how valuable?', and 'how can we measure that?' and 'how much value does that behaviour add?'

How can we build social capital in organizations?

We may not yet know how to measure social capital in organizations with any financial precision, but we do know how to invest in it and build it. Organizational development activities developed over the last few years, based on an understanding of the organization as a living human system, act to increase social capital.

I was assisted in this chapter by Jem Smith.

21: How to cultivate a positive organizational culture

This chapter asks how we can recognize a positive culture and how we can create it.

What is a positive culture?

Cameron's[37] research has revealed three key distinguishing features that define a positive organizational culture. Essentially these are: an interest in learning from success to exceed standard performance; the cultivation of graceful behaviours such as helpfulness, patience, humility, forgiveness; and a bias towards spotting and affirming the good in people and situations.

The nature of culture

Organizational culture is fascinating. It is complex and paradoxical, slippery and intangible and yet highly impactful on organizational behaviour. It acts as a constraint on the possible for organizations. This becomes particularly pertinent when an organization decides it needs to change itself in some way. Organizational culture has a big impact on attempts at change while being highly resistant to change itself.

Changing cultures

Culture is as culture does. It is hard for organizations to step outside their existing culture, to act 'as if' they weren't in their existing world. Attempts to 'bring in' or in any other way impose a new culture by diktat, plan or rhetoric is pretty much doomed to failure. New cultures need to be cultivated; they need to be grown from within the organization, which means exploring the variance that already exists within the organization to find that which already exists and is emblematic of the desired new culture. In addition, we can create variance.

Growing cultures

When considering this, it is helpful to think of the organization as a complex adaptive system, that is, a living human system. From this perspective the organization is both created by, and constrains, the small daily habitual

---

37 Cameron, K. (2008) *Positive leadership: strategies for extraordinary performance.* Oakland, CA: Berrett-Koehler Publishers.

patterns of interaction and communication of everyone in the organization. These patterns are at the root of consistency (replication) and change (variation). Change these and you change the organization.

The patterns of behaviour are both products, and reinforcers, of our patterns of mind, that is, our habitual way of understanding the world. As we understand the world, so we act. Change our mental models or underlying beliefs about the world and you change the action potential. Powerful experiences that can't be accommodated by our existing world views are the things that change our mental models. Such experiences can be located in either action or thought mode.

Exposing someone to different experiences can work to shift their views, for example sending the production manager out with a salesman to experience customer behaviour and need first hand. In a similar way, creating events where people experience each other differently can shift their beliefs about each other as they discover aspects of, and qualities in, the person to which they had not previously been exposed.

Alternatively, the powerful experience can be an internal one, for instance when we are asked a powerful question that causes us to have thoughts, make connections, see things that we haven't up to now. The experience of being asked a really powerful question is akin to having the world shake on its axis as many neurons unexpectedly fire off at once in response to the pinpoint accurate stimulus of a good question. Thought and action are interactive and iterative. To affect one is to affect the other. We often talk about the need for behaviour change in organizational change. Then we think in terms of training courses and job descriptions. Both of these are possibly useful. The smallest point of leverage though is to affect people's understanding of the situation they are in by getting them to think differently by asking them different questions.

Why is culture change so hard to achieve in organizations?

Essentially because it is about social dynamics not formal structures, processes and procedures; these are surface phenomena and as such easy to change. To affect the social dynamics of an organization we need to work at the deeper level of recurring patterns of interaction, relationship and communication. Whole system change methodologies such as Appreciative Inquiry do exactly this.

So, how do we cultivate culture?

- Recognize it as a moral act, a judgement call on what is 'good' and involve others in making these judgements.

- Focus on patterns of interaction as much if not more than on individuals.

- Ask world-shift questions of people, groups, the organization.

- Identify and build on the positive core of values, strengths, resources, abilities and positive organizational experiences.

- Use a methodology like Appreciative Inquiry to grow it not order it.

Our colourful pack of 'Positive Organizational Development Cards'[38] contains sixty questions to help stimulate conversations about positive organizational development, sixty action ideas to kickstart change.

---

38 https://www.acukltd.com/store/positive-organizational-development-cards

22: Using psychology to encourage green behaviour at work

Positive psychology has to include an interest in sustainability. Indeed, the Businesses as Agents of World Benefit project[39] is specifically targeted at noticing and amplifying this aspect of positive psychology at work. This chapter aims to apply behavioural psychology to this particular challenge.

There is a ground swell of interest amongst organizations in 'going green'. The challenge for leaders is how to change habitual behaviour: their own and other people's. While the arguments for going green may be compelling, they are not always sufficient to change behaviour. Without behaviour change, organizations are in danger of creating a swath of 'greenwash' policies and little genuine green-minded behaviour. Leaders are more likely to be successful in achieving real change if they apply psychology, as well as issue directives.

Encouraged by regulations such as The Waste Electrical and Electronic Equipment Directive and the Carbon Reduction Commitment, and recognising some of the business benefits, more and more organizations are interested in 'going green'.

However, they are finding that doing so isn't always as easy as it sounds, because it's not always easy to get people to do things differently. Whether it's encouraging employees to put the right waste in the right bin, or to give up cars and foreign travel for public transport and video conferencing, the heart of the challenge is the same: how do you get people to change their behaviour?

Fortunately, there are some principles drawn from organizational psychology that can be easily applied to produce, encourage and maintain greener behaviour:

- Do the 'quick wins' that don't take any effort from individuals e.g. timed lights and taps – and publicize the difference they make.
- Do the easy things first: energy saving light bulbs, recycled paper. Publicize what you are doing, and why, and the difference it makes.
- Educate and motivate people about the initiative. Run fun workshops.
- Avoid using guilt as a motivator.

---

39 https://weatherhead.case.edu/centers/fowler/

- Tell people about the good they can do, not the harm they are doing.

- Recognize what people are doing already that points in the right direction: cycling to work, being vegetarian, switching their computers off at night.

- Capitalize on the existing interest and enthusiasm in the workforce for these initiatives. Find the staff members who know more about this than you do and involve them.

- Set up research groups, give people a specific challenge, set the parameters, and give them the time and resources to investigate it. Only do this if you are prepared to take note of what they come up with.

- Be clear about exactly what behaviour you want. 'Being greener' is not sufficient, be specific.

- Measure the level of that behaviour that already exists and set reasonable, feasible targets for change.

- Break big challenges down into smaller achievable steps. So, don't go from everyone has cars to no one has cars. Work out steps, such as reducing mileage, replacing with greener cars as the opportunity arises.

- Create longer-term strategic plans to tackle the bigger changes: instigating supplier standards, reducing international travel, and publicize them.

- Recognize that change takes energy, time and attention, and allow for this. Accept that when people learn to do things differently or do different things, for instance video conferencing, initially it will seem harder than things they can do habitually, such as driving on autopilot to the regular meeting place.

- Acknowledge that some things will be harder than others and will incur a cost of convenience, time, privacy, enjoyment etc.

- Find compensatory rewarding activities for losses, for example, make sure they get back some of the time saved by video-conferencing. Use some of the money saved on 'jollies' abroad on fun/unusual/educational activities closer to home. Divert money saved into 'adopt an endangered animal' scheme and pin-up the newsletters.

- Recognize that different people will find different changes difficult or hard to make.

- Make it easy for people to make the changes: find a place to padlock bikes, label the bins clearly, label which printers are for best (and set for double sided), and which for draft (recycle used paper). Make sure this difference shows on their computer screen (in the printer name) so they can easily select the correct printer for their task.

- Show them what they need to do e. g. how to get between sites on public transport.

- Notice and reward early efforts frequently and generously – yours and theirs. Continue to acknowledge and reward the behaviour you want.

- Measure what isn't happening (due to their changed habits) as well as what is e.g. miles not driven, paper not used, energy not consumed – and publicize the difference that makes to the planet.

- Pilot initiatives, measure effectiveness and learn what helped them be effective or ineffective.

- Publicize your achievements to the wider world: attract strategic, future minded recruits, go for awards, create pride.

- Use visual feedback – graphs, pictures, videos to show the difference people's efforts are making.

- Create some memorable statements of intent (with your people). We choose the greener path. Leaving the world a better place. A heavier boot, a lighter footprint.

- Most importantly, as leader, you have to change your own behaviour:

  - Do what you are asking others to do.
  - Bring 'green' considerations to the heart of all discussions.
  - Develop some standard questions for business decisions 'Is there a greener way to do this?' 'What will be the consequences in environmental terms of doing it this way – good and bad?'
  - Put some money where your mouth is: set up a shuttle bus to and from the station, maybe just one day a fortnight and reward people for trying it out.
  - Think both/and, e.g. how can we do profitable business and be green?

By thinking constructively about how to encourage behaviour change and by applying these sound psychological principles, leaders and organizations have an opportunity to avoid the dangers of policy driven 'green wash', and instead to create activity driven green-mindedness.

By being creative in publicizing the difference the organization's efforts are making to the long-term future of the planet, leaders can create a positive cycle of effort, reward, motivation, awareness.

23: Many hands make light work: crowd-sourcing organizational change using Appreciative Inquiry

This chapter offers another way to understand how Appreciative Inquiry works.

Barack Obama famously crowd-sourced the finance for his election campaign, a powerful example of the ability of new technology to create a great aggregate result out of lots of small voluntary actions. But this process is not as new as it seems: Sir James Murray used a similar approach to create the Oxford English Dictionary back in 1897.

So, while crowd-sourcing seems like a new and sexy concept, it really refers to the age-old process of recruiting groups to complete tasks that it would be difficult, if not impossible, for one person to complete alone.

Wikipedia defines it thus: *'Crowd-sourcing is a process that involves outsourcing tasks to a distributed group of people. This process can occur both online and offline. The difference between crowd-sourcing and ordinary outsourcing is that a task or problem is outsourced to an undefined public rather than a specific body, such as paid employees'*. But it also says *'Crowd-sourcing is a distributed problem-solving and production model'*.

It seems to me that the distinction is the voluntary nature of the participation rather than necessarily the paid/unpaid divide. In other words, can crowd-sourcing be said to occur when people are not compelled to do the tasks by a job contract, but volunteer to be part of an organizational project? It is this volunteer element that makes me think Appreciative Inquiry can be seen as a form of in-house crowd-sourcing.

Appreciative Inquiry is an approach to organizational development that originated when David Cooperrider[40] noticed how organizational growth and development can stem from understanding and building on past successes as well as on understanding and solving problems. As he and others experimented with focusing on learning from success and growing more

---

40 Cooperrider, D. and Whitney, D. (2001) A positive revolution in change: appreciative inquiry. In: Cooperrider, D.L., Sorenson P.F.Jnr., Yaegar, T.F. and Whitney, D. (eds) *Appreciative Inquiry: an emerging direction for organizational development*. Champaign, IL: Stipes Publishing.

of what you want in an organization, rather than concentrating solely on eliminating what you don't want, they evolved a methodology based on clear principles of organizational life. One of these is the principle of positivity, which basically suggests that change takes energy, and that positive energy (feeling good) is a more sustainable source of energy for change than negative energy (feeling bad). When the field of positive psychology emerged at the end of the 1990s it fitted perfectly with Appreciative Inquiry's emphasis on achieving excellence through focusing on what works.

I was fortunately enough to stumble upon Appreciative Inquiry as an approach to organizational change and development in the 1990s and have been incorporating it into my work ever since. And the more I work with Appreciative Inquiry, the clearer it becomes to me that the volunteer aspect of the model is crucial to its success. In this way I see a connection between crowd-sourcing and Appreciative Inquiry. The power of Appreciative Inquiry is based on the power of the volunteer model in the following ways.

1. Voluntary attendance

Ideally people are invited to attend the Appreciative Inquiry event. The event topic, the nature of the event, and the invitation have to be sufficiently compelling that people prioritize being there of their own volition. When people make an active choice to invest their time in the event, they are keen to get a good return on that. When they are compelled to be there by management diktat, it can be a recipe for frustration and even sabotage of the process.

2. Voluntary participation

The voluntarism principle needs to extend to participation in any and every particular activity or discussion that is planned for the day. We never know what may be going on in people's lives to make some topics of discussion unbearable. They may need, during the day, to prioritize their own need for some quiet time, or to make a timely phone call. It is my experience that when people are treated as adults constantly juggling competing priorities, trying to make good moment-to-moment decisions in complex contexts, they manage it very well, and with minimum disruption to the process.

3. Voluntary contribution

One form of crowd-sourcing is the wisdom of the crowd. Again I quote from Wikipedia: '*Wisdom of the crowd is another type of crowd-sourcing that collects large amounts of information and aggregates it to gain a complete and accurate picture of a topic, based on the idea that a group of people is often more intelligent than an individual*'. Calling on collective intelligence is a key feature of large group processes. However, people are free to choose whether and what to contribute; so, the event needs to create an atmosphere where people feel safe and trusting and therefore want to share information and dreams and to build connection and intimacy. And, of course, the general principle doesn't hold in every case, sometimes expert knowledge is more valuable and accurate than 'the general view'.

4. Voluntary further action

With most Appreciative Inquiry based events, at some point there is a shift of focus from the process of the day to actions in the future. Often this involves forming project or work groups to progress activity. And the groups need members. Again, group membership needs to be voluntary. The desire to contribute to changing things for the future needs to stem from the motivation and community built during the day. Forcing everyone to sign up to a post-event group activity, regardless of their energy, time or passion for the topic or project, just creates drag, and sometimes derails the whole process.

There are some of the ways in which I think Appreciative Inquiry can be seen as a form of in-house crowd-sourcing around the challenges of organizational change or adaptation. The ideal outcome of an Appreciative Inquiry event is that everyone is so affected by the event process, discussions and aspirations, that they are motivated to make small changes in their own behaviour on a day-to-day basis that will aggregate to a bigger shift, and even transformation within the organization as a whole. In addition, they may volunteer to be part of specific groups working on specific projects. By definition these personal shifts in behaviour and the group project activity are above and beyond their job description: it is voluntary, discretionary behaviour. In this way, the voluntary basis of the Appreciative Inquiry approach qualifies it to be seen as a form of crowd-sourcing even though it is activity undertaken by paid members of an organization.

If you are interested in, or a convert to, the power of crowd-sourcing to get big things to happen with a small amount of effort from many people, then Appreciative Inquiry might be a way of bringing it into your organization.

24: Bringing the appreciative approach to projects

A more nuanced understanding of project work makes clear the potential of Appreciative Inquiry to improve the performance of project teams.

Projects can sometimes appear as the archetypal bureaucratic approach to change, with their emphasis on tracking and monitoring progress against milestones and targets. However, Charles Smith,[41] an experienced project manager turned organizational psychologist, has performed a fantastic analysis of how successful project managers actually do project management compared to how they tell us they do it. Not surprisingly the best take a very psychological approach. In the process he has discovered some very useful ways of thinking about projects and the role they perform in organizational life. In particular he notes that successful project managers have an unrecognized project-craft that they call on to aid the delivery of the 'formal plan'. Below I explain some of his findings, and consider how they can be viewed from an Appreciative Inquiry perspective.

1. Project managers need to help the organization develop a local language for talking about change, above and beyond Prince2 language – talk of swim-lanes and stop/go gates doesn't cut it. Change needs to be contextualized. Appreciative Inquiry helps the organization to grow its own metaphors of change and to develop dreams of the future the change can deliver.

2. Projects are about managing uncertainty and complexity; they create stories of order to help keep chaos at bay. While this is an important function, leaders at least need to be able to remember that all is conditional, and that as the situation develops different possibilities and ways forward may emerge.

3. The project is not real; it is a social construction. This means the project needs to be in service of the social world, not vice versa. Appreciative Inquiry is predicated on a social constructionist view of the world, and so can help negotiation between the project reality and the organizational reality.

4. It is useful to think of negotiating amongst tribal loyalties rather than the blander 'stakeholder management'. This highlights the morass of divergent agendas, cultures, identities, priorities, power-plays and affiliations among which project managers are trying to form commitment and conjoint action.

---

41 Smith, C. (2007) *Making sense of project realities: theory, practice and the pursuit of performance.* Hampshire UK: Gower.

Recognition of the many organizational voices is key to Appreciative Inquiry, as is the negotiation of many different organizational realities.

5. Tribal identities are strong and permanent; project identities are weak and temporary. Projects are political alliances.

6. Project action and talk is all about sense-making. As are Appreciative Inquiry and the other dialogue-based interventions such as Open Space and World Café. Again, we are reminded that unless people's sense of the world shifts, nothing much will change regardless of how many plans are produced.

7. Project artefacts – diagrams, maps, risk registers – are physical enactments of sense-making and are important for this purpose. In other words, they are records of changed thinking, understanding and ambition, rather than drivers of the same. Sense-making first, record-making second.

8. Sense is driven by identity, therefore the project manager needs to know people affected by, or involved in, the project in a meaningful way to be able to influence or negotiate with them.

9. The risk register is a political document reflecting power and choice, not a neutral record of fact. Again, we are reminded that all is socially constructed.

10. A project is a social process. Appreciative Inquiry is a social change methodology. So, despite their seeming location in different worlds, it would seem that project thinking and Appreciative Inquiry can be brought fruitfully together.

25: Five ways to increase efficacy and resilience during change

This chapter applies Appreciative Inquiry principles and positive psychology process to the specific challenge of helping people during change.

It is very easy for people to become demoralized or demotivated during change, as work becomes harder (less familiar) and possibly less rewarding (we're not yet skilled at it). There is often a sense of loss of past habits or pleasurable activities, and a disruption to rewarding relationships. At the same time the manager can be so distracted and pressurized with all the meetings and decisions to do with the change programme that they are less relaxed and more critical than usual. They may also be around less, removing a valuable source of positive feedback for people.

To counteract this and to ensure that people maintain good morale, are motivated, effective and resilient, we need to concentrate on helping people maintain a positive emotional state and a belief in their ability to influence things happening in their world.

1. Create hopefulness

Hope is a future-oriented motivating emotion that can be an early casualty of imposed change. People lose hope when they no longer believe that they can influence what is happening around them, or the future that is unfolding. By helping them focus on what they *can* influence rather than what they *can't*, you can plant or re-activate the seeds of hope. You can build on this by helping them realize how by being pro-active, they can influence more than they thought. In this way you encourage hopefulness to grow. Hope makes us more resilient when we are buffeted off track, and it increases our efficacy through its empowering nature. Hopefulness is further enhanced when people have a vision of a better future that they are moving towards.

2. Create dreams of positive future states

Often during change the focus is on what is pushing the change rather than what is pulling the change forward. Push change factors are not always highly motivating beyond achieving compliance with something or escape from something. To generate real commitment to the future, and to activate the energy and motivation that goes with that, people need to feel they are moving towards something desirable. Help people work out how they can create attractive futures in the change process.

3. Redefine success

Another frequent early causality of change is a sense of achievement. The existing patterns of effort and success are broken or no longer relevant. The new patterns are not yet established. During the disruption and transition of change it is often helpful ask 'In our changed circumstance, what does success look like?'

For example for a team that is to be disbanded, success criteria can shift towards factors such as 'Supporting each other to find new positions' or 'Creating a great celebration of the team's achievements before we close' or 'Ensuring we look after our clients until the last moment'. The creation of feasible, achievable targets in the midst of the general uncertainty helps people focus on things they can do in a motivating way, while lifting mood and enhancing resilience.

4. Amplify success

This is related to the point above. Successes and achievements can get trampled or overlooked in the frenzy of change activity. To help boost or maintain motivation and morale it's a good idea to make extra effort to highlight and amplify the good work that is still being done, even as everyone's attention is focused on the change. Internally this can be done in one-to-one conversations or in team meetings. Publicizing continuing good work externally, through newsletters, emails or in other meetings, can also help maintain high morale during difficult times.

5. Encourage savouring

Savouring is essentially the process of taking the time to enjoy or experience a good or pleasant thing. In our busy lives we pass through a lot of moments without really noticing them. When under pressure, we are particularly inclined to do this with good moments, as they don't demand our attention as vigorously as difficult moments. However, taking a moment to savour a tricky conversation well-navigated, a potential disaster adroitly averted, or the first bite of a juicy peach, is a way of creating little blips of good feeling for yourself throughout a difficult day. It is a way of redressing the balance of good to not-so-good moments: a balance that is key to our sense of well-being which is in turn related to our sense of efficacy and resilience. Redirect your attention to ensure you notice and savour good moments and encourage others to do the same.

26: When you have to let your people go, how to do it appreciatively

These next few chapters focus on using Appreciative Inquiry and positive psychology to help with the more difficult aspects of change.

Introduction

Unemployment figures are rising relentlessly despite talk of 'the green shoots of recovery'.[42] Many organizations continue to have to unexpectedly and rapidly 'let people go'. The organizational processes involved range from early retirement via voluntary redundancy to compulsory redundancy; and accordingly, the emotions involved may vary from joy at an unexpected windfall to shock, anger and fear. The strong emotional content can make leaders shy away from personal engagement; and the negative connotations of 'redundancy' can cast a cloud of shame over the whole process. It doesn't have to be like this: it is possible to let people go in an appreciative way.

How can an organization let people go appreciatively?

At first glance celebrating the departure of someone who had no intention of leaving, or retiring, right now, seems insensitive, and so the temptation is to play down the event and hope they go quietly.

However, research and experience suggest you will be doing them, and yourself, much more of a favour if you can find a way to help them celebrate their time at your organization.

By helping them to let go of the past, say their goodbyes, and express both their appreciation of times past and sorrow at present circumstances, you are putting them in a much better position to move forward to the next stage of their life. You will also be doing yourself a favour if you are able to acknowledge the pain and regret these financially necessary actions are causing you. To acknowledge that you are not an inhuman organizational machine, that you have the same feelings as those upon whom the axe has fallen, enhances rather than diminishes your leadership.

---

42 At least, they were at the time of writing!

What can you do?

Here are five ideas for how to show your appreciation of people you are having to let go:

1. In a public place create a talking wall of the achievements of those who are leaving. The technology can range from video clips or interviews with colleagues, to flip-chart paper and Post-it notes. Depending on your industry and their specialism you might include accounts won, innovations developed, sporting teams led, social relationships fostered, talent nurtured and so on. Invite people to add their own messages of shared peak moments of fun or achievement, sorrow at parting, support, and reminiscence.

2. Be sure to honour their leaving with an event, a ceremony with some ritual. Think of an appropriate model: this is your life, a degree ceremony, a passing-out parade, a party, an apprenticeship completion. Make sure friends and colleagues can be there, maybe invite family.

3. At the ceremony be sure to have someone honour each departing individual. Someone who can speak with genuine appreciation of what they have brought to the organization. This might well be a work-mate rather than senior management. Someone who can say from a state of knowledge how sorry they are to see this person go.

4. Organize practical support, whether it's 'how to adjust to retirement', to 'how to work your network'. Find out what help people need to start the next phase of their life and make it easy for them to access that help. Include other family members if it's wanted.

5. Negotiate individual leaving packages that meet their needs e.g. some might want to keep the company car for a month to help with appearances and confidence at interviews, while others, keen to launch their business idea or take up their hobby might want everything converted to cash.

And for yourself?

- Be crystal clear why the organization has to let people go.

- Remember that just because you have to do something someone might be experiencing as a bad thing doesn't make you a bad person. You are not the sole architect of their fate.

- Don't avoid people; seek them out so you can tell them personally how sorry you are that it has come to this.

- If appropriate let them know that you personally are happy to write them letters of recommendation and that when things pick up you would be very happy to offer them employment if they are still around, but sadly, for now, to ensure the company's future, you have had to make some very hard decisions.

27: How to do redundancy well

This chapter continues to explore the theme of how to do redundancy well.

Why do organizations make people redundant?

Organizations make redundancies during a downturn either because they have to avoid bankruptcy or because they want to reduce numbers and see an opportunity to do so. However, Kim Cameron found that as well as causing quality and customer service problems, downsizing often causes productivity and financial performance, after a brief improvement, to deteriorate over the long term. This can happen even when the redundancy programme is well designed in a technical sense, releasing the right people and conforming to labour regulations, because of the negative effect it can have on the morale, loyalty and productivity of those staff who remain.

Eight long-term negative consequences of downsizing if done badly

1. Greater isolation

Employees who remain can be deprived of colleagues they rely on for emotional support, advice and to get things done outside of official channels. If they were made to compete to keep their jobs, they can become cautious and suspicious of each other and management, reducing teamwork, communication, willingness to experiment and use of initiative.

2. Decrease in loyalty

People not consulted by management over the process of managing the redundancy may feel less loyal to those who appear arrogant to them. Criticism, scapegoating and complaints about management all increase.

3. Disempowerment

Even employees not actually in danger of being cut will suffer from anxiety if the redundancy strategy is not clearly communicated. They may learn to become more risk-averse and push decisions up the line just to be safe, and generally put more effort into 'playing politics'.

4. Morale declines

Remaining staff may suffer from 'survivors' guilt', especially if the criteria by which people were let go seems arbitrary to them. As well as being a general problem this may make it seem disloyal for them to embrace or engage with the changes made during the redundancies.

5. Resistance to change increases

Especially if management used the crisis to force through changes to employees' hours or working conditions, as they may feel exploited and betrayed.

6. Short-termism becomes more prevalent

This may happen if employees and managers feel they need to deliver immediate evidence of their value, especially if they were made to compete with colleagues to keep their jobs during the crisis.

7. Conflict escalates

An obvious consequence of the increase in competition for scarce resources, as well as the heightened stress of having redundancies hanging over people, can lead to people becoming more prone to conflict with their colleagues.

8. Cross-function problems increase

People can become less willing to communicate openly and share information, as people become more inward looking, try to consolidate their power bases and become more distrustful of those outside it.

Result: the good people leave anyway

Charlie Trevor and Anthony Nyberg of the Wisconsin School of Business[43] found that this collapse in morale amongst those staff who are retained not only affects productivity directly, but often means there is an exodus amongst the remaining staff, particularly the most talented, even if the redundancy programme had been carefully designed to avoid that.

How can these negative effects be avoided?

There are two key factors that make a difference:

1. Consult, involve, innovate

Firstly, during the whole period redundancies are being considered managers must make active efforts to counter the eight points listed previously, i.e. they should:

---

43 Nyberg, A.J. and Trevor, C.O. (2009) After layoffs, help survivors be more effective. *Harvard Business Review* **87**(6) 15.

a. Keep staff informed throughout.

b. Consult widely and listen to and take action on the best of their staff's opinions and ideas about how to do redundancies fairly.

c. Make clear to all the basis on which the final decision was made regarding who goes and who stays.

d. Don't panic: plan redundancies carefully so that it only needs to happen once; that way the survivors can draw a line under what happened and feel secure in their jobs and able to take risks again.

e. Do everything out in the open, without humiliating those who leave. Colleagues seemingly disappearing all around you without any announcement can easily create a somewhat chilling nobody-is-safe effect in an office. Much better to honour those leaving and celebrate their achievements, successes and contributions to the organization.

f. Don't use the threat of redundancy to bully staff into changing their contracts or into explicitly competing with each other.

2. Build resilience and relational reserves

Secondly the leader's ability to do all the above will depend to a great extent not only on their actions during the crisis, but the social capital the organization has built up over previous years, particularly in terms of trust between workers and management. Organizations which already have good communication, high levels of trust, good internal relationships, good information flow, empowered decision making, a positive working culture and so forth, have greater organizational resilience and will find keeping their employees onboard during the redundancy process, and bouncing back after the sad goodbyes, much easier.

What helps?

Active organizational interventions to rebuild purpose, connectivity, morale, motivation and energy all help an organization to rebuild depleted relational reserves and social capital and encourage a swifter return to high performance levels. The emerging collaborative methodologies such as Appreciative Inquiry have a particular strength in this context.

28: How can I create a positive work environment during cutbacks?

This chapter offers further ideas on how to counteract the effects of redundancy of both those staying and going.

There are a number of things human resources managers or departments can do to help create positive work environments during cutbacks.

1. Develop a success and achievement strategy

It is very easy during difficult times to lose sight of achievements and successes. All too quickly it begins to feel as if there is no good news only more bad news. Motivation and morale can fall off as people become demoralized, followed quickly by a drop in performance. In the worst cases a vicious downward cycle of negativity and often conflict develops. One way to counteract this is to develop a strategy for recognizing, capturing and broadcasting the great things people and teams are still managing to achieve, despite a difficult context. In a redundancy situation this can extend to capturing any good news about people's job search efforts and outcomes. Help people focus their attention on the good news amongst the gloom by asking positive questions such as 'What has been your proudest moment at work in the last month?' or 'Tell me about a recent success at work'.

2. Include positivity in your leadership development and equip leaders with practical skills to encourage positivity

For example, educate leaders about the work of Losada and Heaphy[44] and the magic ratio of 3:1 positive to negative experiences necessary to enter the zone of creative problem solving. Explain how spending time creating good emotional states helps people work well together on the difficult decisions that often need to be made in times of cutbacks. Equip them with techniques like appreciative questions and effective positive feedback skills.

---

44 Losada, M. and Heaphy, E. (2004) The role of positivity and connectivity in the performance of business teams: a nonlinear model. *American Behavioral Scientist* **47**(6) 740-765.

3. Develop a 'hotspot' team

Have a human resources or organizational development hotspot team that can work with any team area or division where early warning signs surface such as a fall-off in performance, conflict-based relationships, decisions being pushed up the line, increased complaints against management and so on. Using team-building and organizational development techniques, they can help re-build trust and goodwill amongst group members before the problems become intractable.

4. Actively engage with the emotional challenge of redundancies for all staff

A round of redundancies produces all sorts of emotions for people, both those going and staying. The more people are able to influence the process of seeing the redundancies through the better. It is possible to help people support each other through leaving and staying in a way which enhances the experience of both and allows for the expression of positive emotions and hopes for the future, without people feeling they are betraying their colleagues. But it doesn't often happen without positive help.

5. Help leaders and managers understand that the focus of their leadership must shift to people

Sometimes leaders and managers perceive dealing with 'people problems' as an interruption to their real work, of planning, managing budgets, making things and so on. It is really important during difficult times that managers and leaders appreciate that the context has shifted, and so have the priorities of their role. Maintaining morale and motivation isn't a 'nice to have', it is a business necessity. Feeling good is key to keeping up performance and making it possible for people to rise to the challenge of 'doing more with less' or 'working smarter not harder'. In these times, more than ever, the people are the work not the interruption to the work.

6. Create an attractive pull to the future

Many factors may be present as the push for change. It really helps to have an attractive pull towards change. The more you can help people see bright spots ahead, that they are invested in creating and want to achieve, the greater the chance of them being energized to make changes. Appreciative Inquiry is a particularly powerful approach in this regard.

7. Hard facts and safe spaces

Part of the human resources role, along with senior leadership, is keeping the hard facts of the case in the conversation. 'Sales have dropped by 70%' or whatever the underlying reality is that is driving the cutbacks. At the same time there need to be safe spaces where people can engage with these hard facts in a creative way, where it is possible to ask the un-askable, question the unquestionable, and be irreverent about sacred cows. In other words where the usual conversational rules are suspended so that new ideas and possibilities can emerge. Having a space to grapple with the meaning of the imposed changes and to be freely creative in finding ways forward can be highly motivating. Human resources and unit leaders can have a role in creating these conversational spaces.

Section Three:

Positive and Appreciative Leadership

This section starts by addressing the challenge of leading through turbulent times. The chapters reflect a line of thought initially developed following the challenges created by the downturn in 2009 and continuing through the identification of the emerging present as a VUCA environment, that is, one characterized by volatility, uncertainty, complexity and ambiguity. We then move on to look at leadership from the perspective of positive and appreciative practice, including drawing on lessons from economists and from the military. We consider some key questions any business can ask itself to add value to the bottom line, and we end with an optimistic list of ten tips for creating positive and appreciative organizations.

29: Ten top tips for weathering the storm with strengths-enhancing appreciative leadership

This chapter suggests ways to adapt to difficult times without reaching for the first, easy solution.

When disaster strikes, under the intense pressure to do something fast, it is very easy for leaders to make quick, isolated, obvious decisions i.e. to have a round of redundancies. Very few people like to have to do this, but often feel they have no alternative. However, alternatives are available, what they demand is a willingness to go beyond simple and obvious solutions and to call upon the wisdom and goodwill of the workforce. A leader who is willing to work appreciatively with his or her workforce in finding ways to survive and thrive in these challenging trading times will reap the benefit now and later.

Here are ten top tips for showing appreciative leadership to weather the storm

1. Stay creative

Don't get drawn into 'there is no alternative' solutions or decisions. There are always alternatives; sometimes they are harder to see than the obvious solutions.

2. Work with choice over compulsion

If you need to cut the wages bill consider ways other than compulsory redundancies. Clearly voluntary redundancy and early retirement are good first places to go. Ask if anyone is interested in unpaid leave or working part-time for a while. Then spread the pain and include yourself. For instance you could reduce everyone's working week and pay by 20%, including your own. Fix a date for review. Yes this is likely to introduce a scheduling challenge. What are your managers for? Make it clear that people have choices to work with you or to choose to leave if they think they can do better elsewhere.

3. Don't cancel Christmas!

Just do it differently. For many people it's a huge job perk. And it's effectively a reward for their work and loyalty over the year. Cancelling the Christmas party will be experienced as a punishment (the withdrawal of something nice in the environment) by many people. Instead get creative. How can you still provide a party for your staff on a less extravagant scale? Involve them in this question. Make it clear you still want to create the opportunity for an organizational celebratory gathering but the budget has, understandably, contracted. What ideas do they have for creating a cheap, fun event? Call on your people's strengths, who is the natural party animal, who will be motivated to find a way to make it happen? Delegate and empower, you have other things to worry about.

4. Create and spread messages of hope not doom and gloom

Such messages might be around the themes that you have faith in your people, that this too will pass, that this slack time creates opportunities for investing in refining and improving processes, that the organization can emerge stronger and so on.

5. Use the intelligence, creativity, and resourcefulness of the whole organization

Don't feel that because you are the well-paid leader you have to do it all yourself. People will be as keen as you that the organization survive. They won't be as aware as you of the immediate dangers because they don't have access to, nor do they focus on, the forecast figures. So, you will need to create and provide structures and processes to allow people collectively to understand, contribute and influence. Sending out a memo asking for ideas is unlikely to be sufficient. There are many existing methodologies that can help with this: Appreciative Inquiry, Open Space Technology, Workout and other large group techniques.

6. Welcome volunteerism

You may only be able to pay for four working days but in the interests of the organization's survival some people may be willing to work more. Welcome, appreciate and put to good use such offers, don't assume or take such support for granted. Don't penalize those who, for whatever reason, can't do more. Ask and appreciate, don't demand and expect.

7. Welcome flexibility

Put your people on the most important task. This may not be their usual task. 'All hands to the pumps' is a call people recognize and understand.

Play to their strengths. If the most important task is talking to existing and potential customers then maybe some of your people could team up with a sales person to do their admin so they can spend more time actually talking to customers. Who has 'informal' relationships with your customers and could be called into play? Identify natural strengths, train in anything else needed.

8. Talk to your people

Share your knowledge in a carefully framed way. This is a time for inspirational leadership. It is also a time for humbleness and honesty. You need to combine an awareness of the scale of the challenge and of the hopefulness of success. You can't make all the changes necessary to adapt quickly to new circumstances on your own or by diktat. To coin a phrase, it really helps if people want to change. Work to motivate them through hope and a belief in the future, not fear and despair about the present.

9. Be visible

Spread faith and confidence by your presence. Talk to people; be available for people to talk to. Resist the temptation to lock yourself away solving the problem. Ensure that your management team is out getting the best from their people, not locked away obsessing over spreadsheets.

10. Above all don't panic

Don't allow others to panic, and don't be panicked by the anxiety of others. People in a panic are rarely able to think creatively or flexibly, or to create confidence in others. Stay calm, create choice, involve others, offer affirming and appreciative leadership and find some support for yourself to enable you to do this.

To behave like this when all around you are going for the quick win of shedding longstanding and loyal staff is not easy. This is the time to recognize your organization as a collection of people of whom you have the privilege to lead. Recognize them as honoured followers, call out the best in them. Make it everyone's challenge and not just yours to find ways to survive and thrive that are as good for the people, the organization, the present and the future as they can be.

You can learn more about this from our Udemy for Business training video called 'Successfully Leading through Change and Uncertainty' produced in partnership with Skill Boosters.[45]

---

45 https://www.udemy.com/leading-through-change/learn/v4/overview.

30: Leading through uncertainty: seven principles for practice

The next few chapters look at the challenges posed for leadership by the VUCA environment. This chapter starts by offering straightforward guidance for leading through uncertainty derived from a work project.

Many leaders are currently facing the challenge of leading in conditions of great uncertainty in an unpredictable environment. Yet much leadership and change guidance is predicated on the assumption of a relatively stable or foreseeable future – for which plans can be made. Here are some principles to help leaders continue to offer leadership even when firm predictions are hard to come by and plans are difficult to make.

1. Keep leading

When researching his book *The Checklist Manifesto*[46] Atul Gawande turned to the airline industry for case studies on how to prepare emergency checklists. He discovered that these pioneers in the creation of a checklist for every scenario had quickly learnt that the first instruction on every list had to be 'keep flying the plane'. Similarly, all may be in turmoil about you, but 'keep offering leadership' has to be at the top of your checklist.

2. People first

When things are running smoothly people issues can seem to be looking after themselves, and leaders often devote their energies to more of the task aspects of the role. Once uncertainty and unpredictability become a key part of the picture – are we being sold? Will there be redundancies? Is our line/factory/project being discontinued? – all this changes, and working with your people must become the main focus of the leadership role. Essentially all managers have to become leaders, able to inspire loyalty, trust and courage. This may not come easy to those promoted on their technical skills. They need support to understand that spending time with people to help them remain motivated, optimistic and performing is now the key aspect of their job.

---

46 Gawande, A. (2011) *The checklist manifesto: how to get things right*. London: Profile Books.

3. Engender hope and optimism

One of the first causalities when uncertainty looms large is hope. People can't see the future clearly; they don't understand how they can influence it. They feel hopeless in the face of bigger circumstances. A collapse in motivation and morale can quickly follow. Creating a sense of hope and optimism is a key factor in restoring motivation and therefore levels of productivity. Appreciative Inquiry as a change methodology is particularly effective at this. The general principle is to help people who are in the midst of gloom and despair to focus on what is good, is still working, is worthwhile, and on what they can influence. Help them be proactive in dealing with, coping with, responding to or interacting with the situation. These things engender hopefulness.

4. Learn to love emergence and discovery

Many change approaches rely on analysis and implementation through planning. This approach is too slow, too inaccurate and too prone to be rendered obsolete by a sudden shift in the wind in conditions of great uncertainty. Instead we have to become experts at sensing small shifts, capturing emerging trends, discovering ways forward by trying things out and seeing what happens. We have to engage pro-actively with an emerging future. Working this way can initially feel messy, inefficient, and worryingly uncontrollable. By the same token it is timely, fast, flexible, engaging and involving and can lead to surprising discoveries about the possible. Appreciative Inquiry and the other collaborative transformational approaches such as Open Space and World Café are good approaches for emergent situations.

5. Call on the collective intelligence of your unit

When things are changing fast and new information is constantly emerging it is impossible for one person, or even a small group of senior people, to keep on top of it all, never mind sorting it, sifting it and creating new possibilities for action. The collaborative transformational technologies allow the collective intelligence of the whole unit to work together in an effective way. Involving others adds value and effectiveness to the process. It greatly increases the likelihood of creative, collectively endorsed ways forward emerging. Involve your people in the challenge. Recognize them as intelligent adults and reap the rewards of a huge increase in brain power on the task. Make finding ways forward and staying proactive everyone's challenge.

6. Have many review and reflection points

As situations constantly change so must our plans. Learning from fire-fighters, Weick and Sutcliffe[47] suggest a shift is necessary in highly

---

47 Weick, K. and Sutcliffe, K. (2007) *Managing the unexpected: resilient performance in an age of uncertainty*. San Francisco: Jossey Bass.

uncertain situations from decision-making to sense-making. Leadership behaviour in these highly changeable situations is characterized by ambivalence, an ability to move quickly between seemingly contrasting states – such as taking risks and being cautious, using repetition and improvisation, or working with intuition and deliberation. In addition, proceeding by trial and error, they assess and reassess the appropriateness of their actions frequently, involving others as well to 'calibrate' their sense of the situation and the appropriate action against the insight of others. Constant adaptation of plans is adaptive in these situations.

7. Reveal your authenticity and integrity

In unpredictable and uncertain situations it is easy to be blown off course by the temporary prevailing wind. Good people can find themselves doing bad things when they lose their bearings. Research by Avolio and colleagues[48] identified four key features of authentic leadership, one of which is having a strong internal moral compass. Make sure you consult yours often. Another is what they term 'relational transparency', by which they mean allowing people to know you, the real and true you. This may mean sometimes letting people know that you too are only human and sometimes falter or feel vulnerable, as well as sometimes feeling strong and certain. This is not licence to collapse all over your team in a heap – get a coach for that – but rather, as Goffee and Jones[49] put it, be your (best) self, more, with skill. Over time it builds trust and increases group capability as others step up to the mark to help.

Offering leadership during times of uncertainty is no easy task. It requires a different understanding of leadership and different leadership behaviours. Finding ways forward in a rapidly changing environment that will enable the organization to continue to flourish is too big a demand on any one individual. There is too much information, too many variables. However Open Space, World Café and Appreciative Inquiry all offer ways to call on the collective intelligence of the unit while still adding value from the unique position of 'leader'.

You can learn more about this from our Udemy for Business training video, 'Successfully Leading through Change and Uncertainty',[50] produced in partnership with Skill Boosters.

---

48 Avolio, B., Griffith, J., Wernsing, T. S. and Walumbwa, F. O. (2010) What is authentic leadership development? In: Linley, P., Harrington, A.S. and Garcea, N. (eds.) *Oxford handbook of positive psychology and work*. Oxford: Oxford University Press.

49 Goffee, R. and Jones, G. (2000) "Why should anyone be led by you?". *Harvard Business Review* **63**.

50 https://www.udemy.com/leading-through-change/learn/v4/overview

31: The credit crunch and the leadership challenge

This chapter identifies the challenge of the unpredictable, from Nassim Nicholas Taleb's[51] work in this area.

With the benefit of hindsight there may have been signs of possible economic meltdown but few people saw it coming, and even fewer prepared for it. Leaders, who expect to be able to shape the world to their purpose, can become paralyzed when suddenly dealing with a big unpredicted event. Fortunately there are things leaders can do to reduce their vulnerability to unexpected events and to increase their ability to respond when they happen.

The basic problem of predictability

There are things we do know and things we don't know.
There are things we can know and things we can't know.

The balance of predictability in the world is shifting, argues Taleb, from a preponderance of things we can know (there is some possibility of prediction e.g. the housing market bubble will eventually burst) to preponderance of things we can't know (there is no possibility of prediction e.g. the whole financial system will unravel in days).

In others words the problem of being caught by surprise is only going to get worse.

The basic challenge with unpredictable events is:

■ The past is not a reliable predictor of the future.

■ We don't know what we don't know.

■ What we don't know is likely to be more important and impactful than what we do know.

■ Studying what we do know more won't tell us what we don't know.

■ We think we know more than we do, and we don't know how much we don't know.

51 Taleb, N.N. (2008) *The black swan: the impact of the highly improbable*. London: Penguin.

The problem for leaders and the essential forecasting conundrum

Organizations rely on the tools, planning, forecasting and experts that can only predict the predictable. Our focus on the predictable prevents us seeing the infinite unpredictable possibilities. It is the unpredictable that will have impact and that should be important to us. 'Our world is dominated by the extreme, the unknown and the very improbable, while we spend our time focusing on the known and repeatable.'[52]

What can leaders do?

1. Embrace the power of the not knowing and the wisdom of un-knowledge

- Accept that you can't know the future.
- Appreciate that you can't assess 'total risk'.
- Recognize that what you don't know is more important than what you do know.
- Reduce stress by letting go of the illusion of knowledge and control.

2. Invest in preparedness rather than prediction

- You can't plan for the improbable, unthinkable, highly impactful event. You can only be ready to respond to it.
- There will always be unpredicted consequences to actions: they may even be an opportunity.
- Beware of precise plans.
- Don't ford a river 'on average' four feet deep (you may drown in the deep bits!).

3. Dance with the unknown

- Use imagination as a resource. Imagined things become possible things.
- The rational brain only knows what it knows, to get to what you don't know you need to work with image, metaphor and music.
- Aggregating knowledge dilutes it (thinking of our river as 'on average only' four feet deep we lose the information about the range of depth, which is actually more important). So work with the whole system in its messiness.
- Explore consequences, 'what if?', rather than probabilities, 'how likely?'

---

52 Taleb, N.N. (2008) *The black swan: the impact of the highly improbable*. London: Penguin.

4. Get lucky

- Tinker about with your organization; it creates opportunity and learning.
- Invest in trial and error, recognizing that it means trying a lot and tolerating a series of small failures.
- Learn to recognize opportunities and seize them; they come disguised as mistakes, interruptions, distractions and failures.
- Look out for positive accidents.

5. Do change differently

Appreciative Inquiry, Future Search, Open Space technology, World Café and other new approaches to change all work with an awareness of the power of the system, imagination, emotion, not knowingness and 'doing things'. They can be used to help with preparedness or as a rapid response to the unexpected.

32: Black swan leadership for the VUCA world

This chapter relates Nassim Nicholas Taleb's work on the black swan phenomena to the challenge of leading in volatile situations.

A new phrase has entered the leadership lexicon: 'VUCA', standing for volatile, uncertain, complex and ambiguous. It's used to describe the context in which many leaders are trying to offer effective leadership. Uncertainty creates new challenges and demands a new understanding of leadership.

The challenges of leading through uncertainty are many

- How to keep up morale and motivation in an atmosphere of increasing despondency?

- How to maintain a sense of moving forward when the future is uncertain?

- How to create hope and optimism in a general atmosphere of pessimism?

- How to remain pro-active while reacting to events you can't control?

- How to keep your best people while they wonder how safe the ship is?

- How to stay closely attuned to changes in the business environment while focusing on getting the best from your organization?

- How to be flexible enough to respond to changing situations while still making plans and doing things?

- How to continue to get the best from people while they are distracted by concerns for their own future?

While some of these challenges are about business acumen, most are about knowing how to lead and manage people when you can't give them what you think they want: a rosy picture of the organization's and their future.

Many leaders become paralysed by their inability to give clear, far reaching answers about the future and so try to avoid such conversations altogether. Alternatively, they offer false hope and promises, which are rapidly spotted as such by those they seek to reassure.

So what can you do instead?

Become a black swan leader, able to hold contradictory ideas in mind at the same time, such as being prepared and being flexible

- Be honest with people that you don't know for sure what the future holds. At the same time, be optimistic about possibilities.

- Engage and involve people as much as possible in making the decisions that CAN be made.

- Develop the ability to act 'as if' you knew what to do for the best, while at the same time being flexible enough to change tack when new information comes in.

- Recognize that everything you say and do as a leader has meaning for your followers, there is no such thing as a neutral transmission of information or 'doing nothing'. So make sure you manage the meaning you create by how you communicate and by what you focus on.

- Help your people make the most productive and useful sense of what is happening.

- Act 'as if' they have a future both inside the company and out. For example, ensure that they realize that the projects they are doing will increase the likelihood of the company surviving, and, increase their market worth.

- Don't make promises you can't keep.

- Find someone outside the organization (a coach for instance) with whom you can have the 'dark night of the soul' conversations, don't burden or scare your staff with these. Yet at times, be prepared to be honest that you too have doubts and uncertainties about the future, your future even.

- Be prepared to listen to people's concerns about the future and offer what you can to help them feel better.

- Try to ensure that people continue to feel that they have choices about what they can do.

- Find ways that people can be proactive in dealing with the needs of the business and their concerns.

- Recognize that you have a wealth of expertise, intelligence, skill and resources, in your organization to help meet the challenges ahead.

- Don't feel because you are the leader you must have all the answers.

- Be your best authentic self.

■ Recognize and encourage the value of positive emotions: laughter, playfulness, and passion.

■ Create stories of hope, possibility and good futures that are accepting of current realities.

People know you can't fortune tell. What they want is that you acknowledge how they feel and work to help them feel better about things so that they can pro-actively do things to help make a good future more likely.

33: How to do management while killing leadership

This chapter looks at how managers can accidentally squash leadership and creativity in organizations.

When people first enter management, rarely are they offered effective management development, instead they are left to get on with it as best they can. Many of the behaviours they call upon have the unintended side effect of stifling creativity and of killing off nascent leadership qualities in their staff. This creates staff retention, talent development and succession problems for the organization as well as causing problems for the individuals.

Some of the things they do are:

- Kill enthusiasm through micromanagement, coercion and disrespect.

- Kill excellence by focusing on weaknesses.

- Kill initiative by having all the answers.

- Kill good cheer through aggressiveness, lack of emotional intelligence, lack of empathy.

- Kill understanding by using partial, inconsistent communication.

- Kill commitment by setting individuals' goals for them.

- Kill creativity by punishing all and any mistakes.

- Kill hope by offering no vision of a better future.

- Kill optimism by problem-focused appraisals.

- Kill engagement by setting individual objectives that don't align with group goals.

- Kill performance by rewarding the wrong things and offering the wrong rewards.

- Kill trust through unfair recruitment or reward decisions.

- Kill growth in capacity and capability by working with the role definitions, not the people here present.

- Kill generative communication by using only the written word.

- Kill working relationships by addressing relationship issues with only one individual.

- Kill willingness by blaming their staff for difficulties and problems.

- Kill leadership by desiring and rewarding only unquestioning compliance.

Managers unintentionally cause problems amongst their staff because they don't understand how their behaviour contributes to their staff's poor performance.

Many managers believe that always knowing the answer is the expected justification for their salary. They don't understand the many unhelpful consequences that follow from this e.g.:

- Stress for themselves.

- A fear of being found out as a fraud.

- Staff who stop thinking (why should I try to solve the problem if you are going to do it your way anyway).

- Ineffective problem solving (the person who does the job is likely to have a very good idea about the answer).

- A loss of creativity, and the replacement of commitment from staff to actively engage with making things better with a passive compliance of 'doing what the boss says (even though I know it won't work)'.

Similarly managers often believe that the way to improve the performance of themselves and others is to concentrate on their 'weak areas'. Inadvertently all feedback becomes about people's 'weak areas'. The unintentional effects of this are many.

- First we need to recognize that there is a limited amount we can do about weaknesses by the time we are 25 years old+.

- The investment of a lot of effort and energy can result in remarkably little visible effect.

- It is demoralizing, confidence sapping and unpleasant to be constantly focusing on what you can't do.

- People come to feel that they are under constant criticism, unappreciated, unvalued and unsure of themselves, and all because their manager is trying hard to help them.

In this situation people shrink into themselves and try not to get noticed, they stop volunteering to try new things. Sometimes they leave, and it is too late at that point to try to convince them that they are a valued member of the team.

Our Udemy for Business video, 'Seven Tips for New Leaders – Avoiding Common Mistakes',[53] made in partnership with Skill Boosters, may help new managers or leaders to avoid some of these unintended consequences of well-intentioned actions.

---

53 https://www.udemy.com/seven-tips-for-new-leaders/learn/v4/overview

34: The sweet spot of leadership: seven strategies for achieving it

This chapter outlines Lisa Kimball's[54] identification of the key behaviours exhibited by successful leaders during change.

These strategies allow leaders to focus on creating space for maximum engagement while also maximising the positive power of leadership energy. This is in the context of a co-created change initiative.

1. Show up

Demonstrate that you value and respect what people are doing simply by being there. In other words don't come in and run, instead stay for the day. People will be thrilled that you have invested the time in staying with them, interested and listening. And it gives you the opportunity to build relationships, understand your people, correct misapprehensions and encourage and motivate at an individual level.

2. Say yes

Try really hard to say yes to staff-generated initiatives, especially early in the initiative. The quicker you can demonstrate that there is purpose, will, budget and energy behind this co-creation approach by approving and implementing staff-generated ideas, the quicker engagement and the flow of ideas will build, as people come to believe that it is worth the effort to create suggestions as leaders are ready to take action.

3. Spend your social capital

You have the connections and the influence to smooth the path for those less powerful or more isolated. People working from the grassroots can very easily get blocked and then discouraged when they can't get what they need from another department or institution. In a word, they don't have the clout to get noticed or heard. You do. Use it, ask favours, bend ears or persuade to help ease the path for others.

---

54 Kimball, L. (2011) The leadership 'sweet spot'. *AI Practitioner* **13**(1).

4. Share stories

Develop your appreciative ears. Learn to hear the early signs of a change in culture, attitude or behaviour. Take these examples and repeat them elsewhere in the organization. By doing this you are showing people 'what good looks like' in the new world, you endorse it by your attention to it, and you are creating positive mood. It's an easy and effective way of 'growing' the change. It can be a grandstanding event or a micro-moment conversation.

5. Synch-up scattered programs

While you may have an overview that connects all the parts of the change program, your front-line colleagues often have a rather more disjointed experience. Help people link the parts up. Move them across silo lines, bring them together to make connections, or ask questions that encourage them to make the links.

6. Sweat the small stuff

Big change is made up of many small actions. Noticing, appreciating, thanking or in other ways, expressing gratitude, goes a long way. Begin to do things differently yourself. Start with a question not an answer. Begin meetings with positive accounts before getting to today's challenge. It's what you are doing between the big announcements and how you are doing it that makes the real difference.

7. Suspend judgement

This can be very hard for leaders. However, if people come up with an idea that has real energy behind it, and they are convinced it will offer a way forward, then you would be wise to let them explore it further even if your experience suggests it won't work. Why? Because either you will be pleasantly surprised as new thinking emerges, or, they will learn why this solution won't work *without losing energy for finding a solution*. This is a very different experience and outcome to being told your idea is no good.

35: Ten tips for effective strategic development

This chapter offers an alternative approach to strategy development.

Strategy is often thought of in organizations as a plan for achieving a specific future. The plan is created by a small group of people who then inform others of the vision of the future and the plan to get there.

This process can result in the production of a strategic document that appears opaque, if not irrelevant, to the rest of the organization. I have sat with many a group attempting to 'decode' the strategic document just handed down from on high into something that is meaningful, useful or compelling in their local context. Generally, the connection, the relevance, is more created than uncovered.

Strategy is the lodestar of organization: it creates direction and holds things together. Without a sense of the over-arching purpose, direction and values of the organization, it is difficult for people to prioritize amongst the many competing demands on their time and energy. A good strategy acts like an internal compass for all employees, enabling them to prioritize their activities against a common understanding of 'the most important things', even when working in isolation.

It is possible to create strategy in a way that understands it, not as a plan handed down by omniscient others, but as a co-created organizational story of future direction and intent. Here are some tips for working with strategy in this way.

1. Invert the usual process

The usual pattern for strategic development is that a small group of people design 'the strategy', which they then attempt to get the rest of the organization, the large group, to adopt. It is quite possible to invert this process by involving a large group of stakeholders in initial strategic conversations, which a small group then write up as the strategic document. This approach allows data analysis, theme identification, creation of new initiatives, commitment to outcomes, common vision, motivation and energy for change to be created simultaneously, rather than in staged sequences. Given this, change is likely to happen much more quickly.

2. Create positive energy for change

Large group co-creative approaches such as Appreciative Inquiry or SOAR,[55] create energy for the change right from the start. However, if the organization is doing strategy more traditionally, all is not lost. We know that inducing positive mood states and helping people identify their strengths helps people engage with change, even if it is imposed rather than self-generated. So, create opportunities for groups to identify what they are doing that points in the new direction, the successes they are achieving, the changes they are making, the resilience they are demonstrating, as well as the endless opportunities for identifying shortfalls, delays etc. Spend time helping people identify their strengths and working out how to apply them every day.

3. Recognize that strategy is what people do

Strategy becomes a 'lived' process as people make different decisions, moment-by-moment, to those they made in the past. While big 'strategic' events are important for various reasons, it's micro-moment differences and decisions that add up to change. Every conversation, every decision, every action, is either pointing towards the desired future direction or away from it. However, habitual behaviour, aligned to past strategy, is strong. Therefore, attention has to be paid at the granular level to the language used, and the way things are talked about, as well as to what is done to create new patterns.

4. Use 'word and deed' to create new organizational fields

Drawing on quantum physics, Margaret Wheatley[56] identified that effective leaders implement new strategy by their words and deeds. They choose words and deeds that fill the conversational, meaning, social space with clear and consistent ideas about the new strategy, for example 'how the customers are to be served'. This kind of behaviour creates a new system 'field'; one strong in congruence, influencing behaviour in only one direction. In effect they create a field of influence that make certain behaviours more likely.

5. Help people understand what 'strategically aligned behaviour' looks like

People often have difficulty translating the words on the page of a strategic document into 'what it means for us'. One way to help people create a stronger vision and sense of what the new strategy looks like is to seek

55 Stavros, J. and Hinrichs, G. (2009) *The thin book of SOAR: building strengths-based strategy.* Bend, OR: Thin Book Publishing.

56 Wheatley, M. (1999) *Leadership and the new science-discovering order in a chaotic world.* Oakland, CA: Berrett-Koehler Publishers.

out early examples of behaviour that is 'pointing in the right direction' and to pro-actively amplify and broadcast these stories. These are stories that exemplify 'yes, this is what we want, this is what we mean'. It's hard for people to imagine things they have never experienced. Sharing stories that act as models of what is required helps people to 'get it'.

6. Recognize strategy as an emergent process

Strategy becomes a lived reality in an organization through an emergent process. People have to feel their way into 'doing' the new strategy. Sometimes organizations act as if strategy can be dictated and people can start working in this new and different way with never a false step being made. This expectation both hampers progress, as people are afraid they will make a mistake, whilst also quickly creating the sense of things going wrong. Recognizing the enactment of strategy as a discovery process, with false starts, blind alleys and as a generally iterative 'two steps forward, one step back' process, helps greatly in creating and sustaining momentum for change.

7. Retell the story of strategy around the organization

The strategic 'story' needs to be shared in many different ways in many different contexts with many different groups. We work out what we mean by what we say through this process of telling and retelling. The creation of strategy is not a unidirectional communication process, it is a collaborative co-creating dialogue process. Organizational understanding of what the words on the paper mean in practice emerges through shared dialogue.

8. Create a strategy that is both familiar and different

We can conceptualize strategy as a fiction. It is a fictional account of a possible future. Ideally it is a co-authored story (see point 1) but often it is a story created by some that they need others to believe. To grasp and hold our interest, stories need to be both credible and unfamiliar. Appreciative Inquiry is perfect for this. The articulation of the best of past in which we recognize ourselves offers the 'credible' part of the story, while the following three stages: dream, design and destiny, offer the generative part of the story. During these phases, the organization creates a picture of itself that is built on the familiar, yet is importantly different, new.

9. Make the strategy tangible

The way this is usually done is to produce a report. The printed word is more tangible and carries more weight than just words. When we hold the document in our hands we can see that we have done something, much more so than when we emerge from a dialogue event with 'just' different ideas in our heads. The challenge is to go beyond just a document. How else can the organization make the new strategy tangible? Pictures, logos, diagrams are all part of this process. Encouraging people and groups to physically model (with Lego or plasticine for example) the past and the future, and then talking about the difference, can help with this.

10. Strategy is a verbal activity

Finally, as a summary of most of the above, it is important to recognize that strategy is a verbal activity. How we talk is different to how we write. The written strategy document is unlikely to be a direct source for effective verbal explanations. Different groups and different people need different approaches if they are to 'get it'. Ideally the talking comes before the writing, so people can see their words in the document. But it is quite possible to reverse the process, helping groups create a verbal account of the handed down written word. Which I believe brings me back to where I started.

36: Making your own mission: lessons from the military

This chapter gives an example of a leader taking a vague ambition and creating their own clear objectives, in a way that made a real difference to action. WARNING: this chapter refers to conflict and war casualties in Bosnia that may be distressing to some readers.

What difference do clear objectives make to performance?

In this short chapter we outline a military case study that helps us understand the importance of ensuring we are working to clear directives and not vague expressions of desire such as, 'increase employee engagement' or 'heighten brand awareness'. Fuzzy directives like these can lead to negative outcomes such as:

■ Lack of focus and motivation in individuals.

■ Deterioration in office culture.

■ Low morale.

■ Uncoordinated or unproductive actions.

■ Teams working for mutually exclusive goals.

■ Loss of confidence in leadership.

■ Loss of ambitious staff.

One leader who found himself in this situation is Colonel Richard Westley, OBE, MC, who was sent with his men to Gorazde, Bosnia in 1995 during the genocidal war there. Their orders were twofold:

■ To serve as the eyes and ears of future NATO/UN action.

■ To protect the civilian populations of the designated safe areas against armed attacks and other hostile acts, through the presence of its troops, and if necessary, through the application of air power, in accordance with agreed procedure.

No guidance was given as to what this meant in practice. However, he and his immediate superior knew the risks of not having a clear mission and decided on a simple solution: to make their own, e.g.:

■ To prevent any Serbian encroachments into any part of the safe zone of Gorazde, with force if necessary.

■ To prevent any Bosnian forays out of the safe zone.

■ To establish a strong psychological presence by operating on both sides on the exclusion line, establishing freedom of action and showing they wouldn't be bullied.

■ To prevent civilian casualties if possible.

■ To neutrally liaise between the two sides when possible.

■ To update UN command to any developments in and around the safe zone.

In practice this was a decision to change from peace keepers to peace enforcers. Shortly after, the Serbs attempted to capture Gorazde and then Srebrenica. At Gorazde the British opened fire giving the Bosnian soldiers time to move up to the ridges, relieve the British and protect the town themselves. Colonel Westley called on Bosnian forces as soon as fighting began in order prevent a massacre. This was against UN procedure, but in line with their redefined interpretation of their orders.

In contrast another European force at nearby Srebrenica did not try to make their own mission, which sadly meant that when the Serbs chose to seize the town and murder all the males, the peacekeeping force were in no position to resist and had lost the will to do so. At each stage they were attempting to follow their vague orders while not overstepping them, and were being constrained by standard UN procedure.

Colonel Westley pursued a smaller but more defined mission while giving himself more freedom of action, and was thus able to focus on and prepare for the worst eventualities, in contrast to the other force who dissipated their effort on several contradictory aims, achieving none of them and losing their focus on the main goal of preventing ethnic cleansing.

Applicability to organizations

Individuals, teams, departments and companies all work better towards clear, defined and measurable goals. So, when you receive that next aspirational contradictory pie in the sky instruction from upper management, or indeed if you are in danger of issuing it, don't ignore it, but redefine it to be:

- Concise.
- Easy to understand.
- Measurable.
- Achievable.

Doing a few things right is a lot better than doing many things wrong.

With thanks to Jordan Smith.

37: Moving from micro-management to using micro-moments

This chapter explains how micro-management adversely affects work relationships, and how to use micro-moments to enhance work relationships.

Recent research into high and low quality connections or relationship between people in organizations has shown the negative effects of micro-management. Low quality connections, that is interactions that people find of little value, most often occur when the interactions are highly prescribed. In such interactions little energy or motivation is generated, little new knowledge or information created. Low quality interactions are likely to occur when managers or supervisors are following prescribed processes and routines: working through standardized checklists or agendas at each meeting.

Why do we have routines?

Relying on prescribed routines of behaviour to ensure consistency of interaction is a well-established organizational process. Routines are devised to cover many interactions in organizational life. Seemingly time saving and efficient, they can lead to a mindless following of the routine, leading to insufficient attention being paid to the nuances of the interaction and the changing organizational context.

Prescribed processes and routines make no allowance for individual differences in knowledge or skill, approach or temperament, or for changes in context. Intentionally they restrict the autonomy of the supervisors or managers in order to produce consistency: they reduce negative deviance from a prescribed norm. Unintentionally they produce low quality connections: they can be demotivating, frustrating and can build resentment. In addition they reduce the likelihood of positive deviance.

The value of positive deviance

Positive deviance is the inconsistent behaviour in organizations that veers towards the exceptionally good rather than the exceptionally bad. Organizations can benefit from positive deviance in behaviour and performance. The opportunity to do so is unlikely to occur in highly prescribed, routine based interactions or organizations.

High quality connections

An alternative to low quality, routine based, manager-staff interactions exist. The experience of high-quality connections leaves people feeling energized, alive and motivated. There is a sense of personal recognition and affirmation. These micro-moments of connection can be a powerful leadership process for enhancing positively deviant performance, that is, excellent and excelling performance, while also creating the opportunity for course correction if behaviour is heading in a negatively deviant direction from the norm.

The importance of micro-moments

Adaptive, flexible leaders increasingly recognize the importance of the 'touch points' of micro-moments to important organizational phenomena such as culture, performance, motivation, morale, connection and communication. Effective management through micro-moments, rather than micro-management, requires managers who are alive to the dynamics of every interaction. Managers who recognize the power of what they say and how they say it in every situation they encounter every day. Such leaders and managers are mindful and heedful in their daily interactions: every micro-moment, every 'touch-point' can move the organization in a more or less helpful direction.

This research,[57] emerging from the field of positive psychology, suggests that to be effective, flexible and adaptive leaders and managers need to:

- Be aware of the quality of the connections they have with others.

- Be aware of the dangers of low-quality connections in their organization and their effect on morale, motivation and performance.

- Be alive to the power of the micro-moment for influence and creativity.

- Lessen their reliance on a 'one size fits all' approach to solving and re-solving the endless challenges of producing coherent organization amongst a group of diverse people.

The 'Choose Happiness at Work' game[58] features many micro-moments of life at work and many positive psychology-based ways of responding to them.

---

57 Dutton, J.E. and Spreitzer, G.M. (2014) *How to be a positive leader: small actions, big impact.* Oakland, CA: Berrett-Koehler Publishers.

58 https://www.acukltd.com/store/choose-happiness-at-work.

38: Decision making: I know, I just can't explain

This brief section introduces the idea of 'fast and frugal' processing, identifying the problems it poses for organizational decision-making.

Ever had that feeling that something didn't fit, wasn't right, was fishy, but been unable to explain why, or explain how you know? Then you may have been experiencing 'fast and frugal' processing.

Fast and frugal processing happens below the level of cognitive consciousness, in the blink of an eye. Malcolm Gladwell[59] has collected numerous examples of people who knew before they knew, that something wasn't right. The fireman who suddenly knew he had to get his people out of the burning building *right now*. The experts who knew the authenticated ancient statue wasn't genuine but couldn't explain why. The gamblers who behaved as if one pack of cards was the better bet, before they knew there was a difference and so on.

Organizations find this hard to deal with. If we are going to stop a big investment project it can't be because our finance director just doesn't feel right about it, or can it?

59 Gladwell, M. (2005) *Blink: the power of thinking without thinking*. London: Penguin.

39: Decision making: why we should make decisions in our organizations like brains not computers

This chapter applies our understanding of effective decision-making processes to the organizational challenges of decision-making, communication and goal-setting.

Proof that brains are more efficient than computers

Cognitive research illuminates how our brains make decisions, and how they are different from computers. Compared to computers our brains are slow, noisy and imprecise. And, paradoxically perhaps, this makes them much more efficient than computers, but only because brains have one big advantage over computers: they have goals.

The importance of goals to decision-making

Essentially life consists of billions of choice points. Choice is about value: what do we value over what? Having goals makes choice a lot easier: it makes it possible to assign values to options, as some have more value in terms of our goals than others. If I am trying to get to London and have come across a signpost labelled Dublin one way and London the other, one sign has much more value to me than the other. So, we make choices based on those values. Goals allow us to act efficiently and not waste energy in times of uncertainty. Brains are computational devices, as are computers, but brains compute in a different and more efficient way.

Brains as oddly efficient

Brains possess all the characteristics of highly efficient computational machines. Efficient computational devices, like brains, follow four principles:

- Drain batteries slowly.
- Save space.
- Save bandwidth.
- Have goals.

And it is the enactment of these principles that make them (relative to fast, quiet, precise yet goal-less and energy guzzling, wasteful computers) slow, noisy, imprecise and yet highly efficient.

How do these principles translate into organizations?

1. Drain batteries slowly

This means avoid high-energy spikes in decision-making by using slow and soft processes that use minimal energy. The implication for organizational life would be to aim for soft, slow decision-making (a pattern of small groups of people making small decisions frequently) rather than patterns of spiky decision-making (infrequent decisions involving everyone).

2. Save space

This dictum suggests that our computational device should have as few (message or information carrying) wires as possible, and those should be shorter rather than longer. This suggests understanding organizational communication as network rather than pyramid based. So communication (and decision-making) is based on short, local messages rather than lots of long 'wires' to get the same message from the top to the bottom of the organization and tight 'knots' where decisions get made.

3. Save bandwidth

The dictums here are: stay off the line, don't repeat yourself and be as noisy (as in random) as possible! This suggests to me that the centralized bombardment communication process of constant repetition of 'the message', broadcast across the organization, offering exact and precise instructions, at regular and predictable intervals, is highly inefficient. Instead information needs to be offered in local contexts in different ways, when appropriate.

4. Have goals

In efficiency terms this means: having a view of the destination but being imprecise about how to reach it; creating mental models; and making ongoing adjustments. In organizations this could mean creating rich mental models of the goals and using local guidance and expertise to achieve them, making ongoing adjustments. This describes an emergent change approach.

Message for leaders

- Create goals to act as a valuation system for decision-making.

- Create rich mental pictures of goals.

- Leave goal-achievement processes imprecise, work with local knowledge, adjusting plans as options emerge.

- Devolve decision making to the lowest level.

- Encourage frequent, small-scale local decision-making and innovation.

- Spread the message locally, contextually, and opportunistically; don't waste energy broadcasting to the nation.

- Use the emergent approach to manage, lead or ride change.

40: Why we should cultivate gratitude in our leaders; particularly in difficult times

This chapter explains why gratitude is an important emotion for leaders to cultivate.

One might have thought that the expression of gratitude was for the benefit of the recipient, to feel acknowledged and affirmed in their generous act, and possibly so. However, the experience of gratitude also brings great benefit to the donor, and some of those benefits can be seen to act as an inoculation against the dangerous seductions of privilege, power and position.

Gratitude is an acknowledgement that we have received something of benefit from others. The grateful person reacts to the goodness of others in a benevolent and receptive fashion. Classically it was considered to be the greatest of the virtues. However, like all virtues, it needs to be cultivated. Resentment at the good fortune of others and a sense of personal entitlement seem to come more easily to us. So why bother to cultivate a sense of gratitude? What are the benefits? And why might it be especially beneficial to leaders to experience gratitude?

1. Gratitude enhances resilience and coping abilities

Counting one's blessings in time of stress is a well-known coping mechanism. Such behaviour works by helping to facilitate a switch of attention from the negative and depressing in any situation to the positive and encouraging. It helps people switch into a more positive mental state, which in turn makes it more likely they will be able to adopt a proactive, adaptive coping mode following some set back.

Specifically, feeling gratitude makes it more likely that someone will be able to seek social support from others and that they will be able to positively reframe the situation (finding the silver linings). Gratitude has been found to be a key component of promoting post-traumatic growth rather than post-traumatic stress. And it plays a key part in determining transplant surgery post-operative quality of life.[60] Experiencing gratitude was a key component affecting resilience and post-trauma coping for American students in the aftermath of the shock and horror of 9/11.[61] All in all the evidence is fairly strong that the experience of gratitude promotes adaptive coping and personal growth following setbacks or trauma.

Leadership can be a stressful process: a degree of resilience is a requisite for the job these days. Cultivating a sense of gratitude for the good things going on and the benefits others bring will promote greater resilience, better coping, better mental and physical health and personal growth and renewal.

2. Gratitude builds and strengthens relationships

Feeling grateful encourages people to consider ways to reciprocate the goodness or kindness they have received. Such reciprocal behaviour builds social bonds, creating a mutually reinforcing positive cycle of expression and acknowledgement of interdependency. It enhances trust. In addition grateful people are attractive to others; being found to be extraverted, agreeable, empathic, emotionally stable, forgiving, trusting and generous. Gratitude is associated with empathy, forgiveness and a willingness to help others. These things inspire loyalty and commitment amongst other things. Gratitude is a vital interpersonal emotion, the absence of which undermines social harmony.

Leaders can't do it on their own, whatever the myth of hero leadership might suggest. Healthy relationships are key to organizational success. Leaders get things done through other people. Leaders need enthusiastic, committed, loyal and responsive team members and followers. Being grateful, recognizing other's benevolence, and reciprocating in kind help to build these essential social bonds and enhance organizational social capital.

3. Gratitude helps develop flourishing organizations

Cameron[62] discovered that an emphasis on, and prevalence of, virtuous behaviour is a defining feature of flourishing organizations and positive leadership. Gratitude acts to motivate virtuous behaviour, that is, action taken to benefit others. Gratitude acts as a benefit detector making it more likely that opportunities to express appreciation and gratefulness will be spotted. Expressing gratitude reinforces pro-social behaviour while

60 Emmons, R. and Mishra, A. (2011) Why gratitude enhances well-being: what we know, what we need to know'. In: Sheldon, K., Kashdan. T., Steger, M. (eds.) *Designing positive psychology: taking stock and moving forward*. Oxford: Oxford University Press.

61 Fredrickson, B.L., Tugade M.M., Waugh, C.E. and Larkin, G. (2003) What good are positive emotions in crises? A prospective study of resilience and emotions following the terrorist attacks on the United States of America September 11th 2001. *Journal of Personality and Social Psychology* 84 365-376.

62 Cameron, K.S. (2003) Organizational virtuousness and performance. In: Cameron, K.S., Dutton, J.E. and Quinn, R.E. (2003) *Positive organizational scholarship: foundations of a new discipline*. Oakland, CA: Berrett-Koehler Publishers.

feeling grateful motivates pro-social behaviour. In this way gratitude is a motivating and energizing emotion, not just a passive pleasant feeling. The benefits of gratitude can be far reaching. Acts of gratitude can stimulate virtuous circles of generous and grateful behaviour as the recipient of benefit is inclined to pass it on i.e. to do someone else a favour.

Leadership is all about cultivating and creating productive working environments. Virtuous circles of self-reinforcing beneficial behaviour that smooth organizational life and facilitate the effective transfer of skills and resources through acts of helping, the exercise of patience and forgiveness, and the expression of gratitude, all help to increase organizational capability without increasing hard cost.

4. Gratitude increases goal attainment

Interestingly, gratitude appears to enhance goal achievement. Often the assumption is that a state of gratitude might induce passivity and complacency. However, the limited research evidence available suggests that gratitude enhances effortful goal striving. One would imagine this is a product of the well-researched benefits of positive emotions in general: greater creativity, sociability, tenacity and so on.

Leadership is amongst other things about goal attainment. It seems that cultivating an attitude of gratitude in the process of goal striving, rather than giving into emotions of frustration and blame, aids goal achievement.

5. Gratitude increases personal well-being

Gratitude acts as a vaccination against envy. Envy is a negative emotional state characterized by resentment, a sense of inferiority, longing and frustration. It creates unhappiness and mental distress. Gratitude directs attention away from material goods and more towards social goods. Grateful people appreciate positive qualities in others and are able to feel happy about their good fortune. They are also less likely to compare themselves unfavourably with people of a higher status. By encouraging a focus on the positive and beneficial in the present moment, gratitude also seems to protect against the damaging effects of regret.

Grateful people are concerned with the well-being of others, both in particular and in general. This focus helps them fulfil the basic needs for personal growth i.e. relationships and community. They are less likely to define success in material terms. Materialism is damaging to subjective well-being and it is correlated with many things unhelpful to leadership such as less relatedness, less autonomy, and less competence.

Leaders often compete in a world where advancement and success are measured by the trappings of material possession: salary, office space, houses and cars. Given our straitened times and the shift in many sectors from a sense of abundance to one of scarcity – fewer promotions, fewer bonus payments, fewer corporate benefits – cultivating increased gratitude may help inoculate against the corrosive emotions of entitlement, resentment and envy.

Gratitude is the mindful awareness of the positives in one's life. It seems that counting one's blessings on a regular basis really does help with overcoming the vicissitudes of life and with maintaining optimal personal functioning. For those in leadership positions the benefits can expand to increase organizational functioning. Feeling gratitude doesn't come easily to many of us, but the evidence is mounting that the benefits it brings are worth the effort it takes to cultivate a grateful outlook on things.

41: Five questions that will add value to your bottom line

This chapter identifies five unusual questions as a route to increased profitability.

In the quest for ever great efficiencies, productivity and general cost saving, a few key questions can open up new avenues to improve performance and profitability.

1. How can we learn from our best performers?

An over-attachment to a view of organizations as a set of roles and role behaviours with expected minimum standards of performance, can blind us to the exceptional performance of our best staff. Focused on trying to prevent our worst performers from costing us money, we don't always focus on really examining how our best performers make or save us money. Research into these examples of positive deviance has demonstrated that there are distinctions between the best and the rest; and that these distinctions can frequently be small and replicable by others.

For example Atul Gawande,[63] a general surgeon, was interested to learn more about how the increase in life expectancy for people with cystic fibrosis had been achieved. The first hospital he visited had a good track record and an array of processes and procedures for treating and supporting those with cystic fibrosis. He was impressed. Then he visited the top performing hospital where the life expectation of people with cystic fibrosis under its care is almost double the average. What he found was that while they too provided excellent care in all areas, they had gone further by identifying one key feature, lung capacity, that made the key difference. It was the single-minded care and effort that went into supporting people to maintain or improve their lung capacity that seemed to be the distinguishing feature. This is not someone he could have learnt by studying the worst performing hospitals. Someone in your organization demonstrating double the sales figures, or twice the academic success rate? Be curious. Study and learn.

---

63 Gawande, A. (2014) *Being mortal: medicine and what matters in the end.* New York: Metropolitan Books.

2. How much is this saving costing us?

When people or organizations focus in on areas where savings might lie, and start to implement processes to realize those savings, they don't always account for the hidden costs of administering the process or achieving compliance. For example insisting that all requests for housing repairs are submitted to be assessed and approved by a manager might seem a good cost control idea. However, as some housing associations have realized, the hidden costs of bureaucracy and close scrutiny can be greater than the cost of many minor repairs. If the bureaucratic delay means that the situation then escalates into a formal complaint or dispute, then costs rise more and senior manager time starts to be eaten into. Some housing organizations have started to give front-line staff direct access to budgets to authorize payment for repairs. Not only has the overall repair budget not risen, but the benefits of engaged and committed staff who feel they can really make a timely difference and be helpful, and more satisfied clients, have been a real bonus to organizational culture and reputation.

In the same vein I recently read that the administration of the competitive tendering process in the NHS, that is the bureaucratic, managerial and legal costs, are conservatively estimated at £10 billion every year (and that's not counting the time spent by those hopeful of securing a contract submitting exhaustive tender applications for relatively small contracts.) So we know how much the 'saving' is costing the NHS, do we know how much it is saving in real terms?

3. What behaviour do we want and what behaviour are we rewarding?

Over time perverse incentives creep into organizational life. As people make changes, launch initiatives or develop projects, misalignments can occur between the desired behaviour and the behaviour rewarded by the contingences of the system. An example I have come across a few times concerns sales people. Rewarding sales people on their individual sales is a time honoured, effective motivational system for many sales staff. However, it is not uncommon for an organization to realize at some point that they are missing out on opportunities for cross-selling, either across products or between areas. They introduce a load of cross-product training and encourage people to try to sell other products, or introduce their colleagues to their clients. To spend time doing this, if the reward system hasn't changed, is perverse, since it lessens the time available for selling more of the thing you do get rewarded for. So there is a perverse incentive in the system not to spend time cross-selling.

4. How can we help people spend more time doing things they enjoy and less time doing things they don't?

The high cost of trying to get people to do things for which they have no aptitude and do not enjoy is not always apparent to leaders. First, when people have little aptitude for a part of their role, the return on investment of trying to train them in it can be invisible. In other words, hours of management time might be devoted to improving skills in this area to little avail. Second, even the most conscientious of people will be drawn towards putting off those parts of their job they dread, while the less driven find endless ways not to be in a position to do the hated deed. Somehow, we get focused on the short-term objective, getting this person to this, and lose sight of the bigger picture which is just that a particular outcome needs to be achieved; not necessarily in this way, not necessarily by this person. In other words, sometimes we would be better off to step back and ask, 'Who would be better suited to this task?' or 'How else can we achieve this objective?'

On the other hand we know that all other things being equal, people using their natural strengths are usually highly motivated, engaged and productive. Doing what we feel good doing is motivating, struggling with things about which we feel a hopeless inadequacy and dread (note this is different to being at the beginning of an eagerly anticipated learning curve) is demotivating. Demotivated people are a cost to your business.

5. How can we make our workplace a great place to be?

To some extent sickness absence is a discretionary behaviour. Clearly at one extreme we are too ill to rise from the bed, while at the other we are bursting with health and vitality. But between these extremes is the grey zone: tired, hungover, bit down, cold coming on, bit head-achy, it could be flu etc. Two factors affect whether that person decides to go into work or take a day off. The push or pull factors of the alternatives e.g. the pull of a sunny day or the push of all my mates are away and I've no money to spend; and, the push and pull factors of work. Push factors might include being fed up with the work they've got at the moment, problems with colleagues or feelings about their managers, while pull factors include loving the work, enjoying the company, feeling appreciated on a daily basis, believing your presence makes a real difference and feelings of mutuality and loyalty. Obviously, you don't want anyone coming in when they shouldn't and spreading infectious diseases, but beyond that a great place to work is likely to have a positive effect on attendance rates.

42: Ten top leadership tips for creating a positive and appreciative organization

This chapter pulls together some key ideas from positive psychology to suggest ways to create a better workplace. Think of it as New Year's resolution suggestions.

Difficult times loom ahead. Few of us feel at our brightest and most optimistic in the dark, cold days of January, February and March. How can we help maintain good cheer, hope and optimism amongst our staff, suppliers and customers? Here are some suggestions, maybe even a list of New Year's resolutions!

1. Start every meeting by sharing some recent successes

This is a good idea whether the meeting is going on to discuss good or difficult news. If it's a good news meeting, then sharing and celebrating successes only adds to the positive value of the meeting. If the meeting is going on to discuss difficult things, then the brain boost of positivity will help people to be creative, to think widely, and to avoid being drawn into the pit of despair.

2. Practice giving diamond feedback

Diamond feedback not only praises people, it lets them know what they did to earn the praise. Giving specific feedback on what the person did well helps both parties. Giving specific feedback feels more authentic than spraying 'well done everybody' around in a random manner, it's easier; and it allows people to learn what is valued about the way they work.

3. Acknowledge difficulties; grow hope and optimism

These are difficult times for many of us. There is no virtue in hiding your head in the sand. On the other hand, in the face of bad news, it doesn't take long for pessimism and hopelessness to take a grip. These emotional states are not conducive to dynamism, creativity and action. So, acknowledge difficult realities, and feelings, and move as quickly as respectfully possible into helping people identify sources of hope and optimism; because these states are conducive to energy, motivation and action.

4. Cherish the positive amongst you

We know some people are more naturally positive in their outlook and disposition than others. We also know that people generally like to be around or involved with these people: they make them feel good. Many find themselves at the centre of positive energy networks in organizations. These are highly valuable to organizations, especially when the general atmosphere is demoralized. Find them, cherish them, use them.

5. Develop an appreciative eye and ear

Positive emotional states need to be continually created and re-created if you want to reap the benefits of positivity in your organization. Develop an eye and ear that are constantly looking or listening out for excellence, exceptional performance, success, tenacity and other things you value at work so you can see it, say it, and celebrate it with those displaying it. Every time you express genuine and authentic appreciation you help grow positivity in your organization.

6. Be generous with your appreciation and mean with your criticisms

Many of us feel that to criticize is to help while too much praise may spoil. Criticism or correction is of course sometimes necessary and helpful. However, without a counterbalancing measure of appreciation, it can lead to a culture of constant criticism or that 'no feedback must mean I'm doing OK' uncertainty. Adding diamond feedback to the mix counteracts the negative effects of necessary criticism and creates certainty about what is wanted, as well as what is not.

7. Be the giver of good things to those around you

One of the hardest challenges of leadership is getting to hear the important things about the organization. You want people to feel they can tell you what you need to know to lead the organization well. The more you thank people for alerting you, telling you, bringing things to your attention the more they will be inclined to do so. The more you praise their bravery in saying something, their attention in noticing something, their dedication in correcting something, the more they will let you know about these things.

8. Cherish the bringers of problems

This of course is another way of saying 'don't shoot the messenger'. Remember that when someone alerts you to a problem, first they are often being brave, second they are creating an opportunity to change something, and third they are also saying they have a sense of how things could be (the dream). Consciously thank them for letting you know and ask them about how they think things could be and follow the conversation from there. Try to get the conversation future facing rather than backward facing into a blame-fest (finding root causes etc. can come later).

9. Learn to spot the strengths of others and to forgive them for not possessing your strengths

Most of us assume that the things we find easy to do are easy to do, so anyone should be able to do them. We also often assume that the way we do things is the right way and all other ways are wrong. Learn to let these two beliefs go and you will greatly increase your ability to get the best out of the people around you: find out the valuable things that they find easy to do and help them use those skills to achieve the outcomes needed.

10. Put yourself in situations that allow you to be your best self

Do more of what is valuable, you love doing, and are good at. Become even better at it. You will feel great and be better able to be kind, generous and supportive to those around you. Find other people who like doing and are good at the valuable things that you hate doing and are not good at. You will have two engaged and satisfied workers instead of two half content workers.

The 'Choose Happiness at Work' game[64] contains lots of positive micro workplace interventions, backed up by the research.

---

64 https://www.acukltd.com/store/choose-happiness-at-work.

Section Four:

Positive Performance Management

The chapters in this section outline how to get the best from the practice of performance management. We look at the challenges and paradoxical results of performance-related pay from an economist's perspective. The section introduces a number of useful approaches such as working with strengths, positive and appreciative coaching, nudging, positive deviance and diamond feedback. There are tips on how to have courageous conversations at work and information on the habits of highly creative people. We also take a look at the dangers of the functioning psychopath in the work place and the factors that predict executive derailment.

43: How to gain the benefits of effective performance management

This chapter outlines how to mitigate against the many dangers of performance reviews.

The good news is performance management works

'A *hospital that appraises around 20% more staff and trains about 20% more appraisers is likely to have 1,090 fewer deaths per 100,000 admissions.*'[65] Many other studies have also found this strong relationship between performance management, appraisals and organizational performance. How come then, it is a disliked process in so many organizations? Because it's hard to do well.

Performance management is hard to do well

Some common difficulties identified in research include:

- Poor quality performance discussions between managers and staff members.

- Standardized, jargon filled, prescriptive and overly detailed paperwork.

- Line managers lacking competence and commitment to the process.

- Employees having a poor understanding of the goals or point of the process.

- Rating and pay agendas dominating the discussion, driving out time for performance feedback and development planning.

- Lack of follow up or practical action between formal reviews.

Many of these problems arise because of a failure to recognize that it's a social process. Too often it is seen as a human resources owned and driven technical process. Understanding performance management as a social process helps us to realize that the important and key components are the quality of the relationship and the communication. From this perspective the paperwork trail becomes a supporting mechanism rather than the driving mechanism.

---

65 'Songs of Appraisal' by Michael West. Originally published in *Performance Magazine* I believe.

As one of the managers from the Institute for Employment Studies said, *'It's about having communications and good one-to-one conversations'.*

What does this mean for managers? What helps?

1. Recognize, and use, the power of positivity

Feeling good accesses many useful personal and organizational qualities – creativity, complex thinking, sociability, resilience and so on. Appraisal conversations are a good opportunity to create some positivity. To do this they need to contain a ratio of at least 3:1 positive to negative experiences for both parties. This means time should be spent genuinely seeking out and paying attention to things that have gone well, successes and achievements over the last time period. At the same time, it's an opportunity for employees to express their appreciation of their manager's support and guidance over the period.

2. Use positive psychology-based appraisal processes

Increasingly, practitioners are creating positive appraisal processes for the regular review meetings. For example, the enthusiasm story[66] that asks a manager prior to the meeting to think about when they are most enthusiastic about this employee, when they have seen them at their best. The best self-reflection exercise[67] encourages the appraisee to understand their strengths and attributes as seen by others. The feed-forward interview encourages the appraiser and the appraisee to focus on building forward from the best of the past.

3. Recognize performance appraisal as an ongoing activity

In addition, managers should be praising good work as it happens, not waiting until the formal 'appraisal event'. The diamond feedback process is effective here. In the same way, of course, they should be dealing with problems in performance as they arise. In this way the 'formal' appraisal becomes a punctuation point in an ongoing discussion that pulls everything together that has been happening over the last period, and links it to future activities. Formal appraisals really shouldn't contain any surprises.

4. Learn about success from studying success

One way to help develop a more positive feel to appraisal activity is to spend at least some time focusing on learning from success. There is a

66 Bouskila-Yam, O. and Kluger, A.N. (2011) Strength-based performance appraisal and goal setting. *Human Resource Management Review* **21**(2) 137-147.

67 Cameron, K. (2008) *Positive leadership: strategies for extraordinary performance.* Oakland, CA: Berrett-Koehler Publishers.

common misconception that one can only learn from mistakes and failure. It is true they are important sources of learning about how to avoid failure. They don't necessarily teach about success. Studying success tells us about what success looks like and how it is achieved.

5. In building relationships it is quality not quantity that counts

Research shows that the quality of our connections and interactions with others varies enormously. What people really value are the high-quality connections where they feel something important is happening in the moment of the conversation. In general, these are two-way conversations where each is able to build on the other's contributions to create something new (as opposed to experiencing a one way downloading of information for example). Each party is left feeling refreshed, energized, valued and recognized. They can be fleeting moments. Over time they build to a resilient relationship that can withstand strain, such as the strain of having to give feedback on poor performance. Use your micro-moments of interaction well.

6. It's a culture not an event

Performance management needs to be seen as a cultural process. The organization needs to create a culture where reviewing group and individual performance after events becomes an unexceptional habit. As each meeting, project or presentation finishes, quickly ask how it was for people and if there was anything different they would like to see next time. After a sales pitch review with colleagues ask how it went. As it becomes part of normal organizational life for everyone to review their own and, when invited, colleagues' performance, so the 'appraisal' meeting will become less of a 'dead' event.

7. Link it to the mission

Make it clear to everyone how these conversations relate back to the organizational purpose so people can see performance management has a bigger purpose than just 'improving' them personally.

8. Use the three top tips

- Keep it simple.
- Equip the managers.
- Avoid forced distribution curves.

And if you are interested in more on this, see our video 'Seven Steps to Effective Performance Management Conversations'[68] produced with Skills Booster for Udemy for Business.

---

68 https://www.udemy.com/performance-management-conversations/learn/v4/overview

44: Appreciative performance management

This chapter offers further reflections on the challenge of making a performance management system achieve its desired function.

So often a process, the very purpose of which is to be motivating and enlivening, turns out to be dispiriting and demotivating. If we have to have these conversations, how can we make them positive and appreciative?

Let's remind ourselves of what we mean by performance at work

Usual suspects include: success i.e. achieving goals and targets; discretionary effort i.e. going above and beyond 'contractual duties'; organizational citizenship behaviour i.e. doing things for the good of the organization; meeting or exceeding standards; and increasing our value to the organization through learning and developing.

And, what affects performance

General features include: clarity of expectation; having the tools to do the job, intrinsic motivation and satisfaction at work; goals, context and rewards; positive and correctional feedback.

An appreciative perspective

Suggests that other factors that make a difference include: organizational culture, and maybe specifically the presence or absence of Cameron's abundance bridge; opportunities to use our strengths; feeling good; the quality of our work relationships; working in reward-rich environments and effective use of questions.

An appreciative perspective includes:

1. The abundance bridge

This is a metaphor used by Kim Cameron to suggest that flourishing organizations create an abundance of generosity, excellence, benevolence, and flawlessness through their culture of positive deviance (learning from success), affirmation (seeking out and affirming the best in people and situations) and virtuous practice (being genuinely and authentically good to each other).[69]

---

69 Cameron, K. (2008) *Positive leadership: strategies for extraordinary performance.* Oakland, CA: Berrett-Koehler.

2. A concentration on strengths

A focus on identifying and using strengths is thought to be key to: optimal performance, accessing potential, enhancing well-being, a sense of fulfilment, learning and growth, motivation and morale, willingness to contribute, sense of energy, goal attainment and the ability to be authentic. [70]

3. Feeling good

When we feel good we are more creative, more sociable, display flexible thinking, cope better with complexity, have good interpersonal relationships, are more motivated and tenacious, and have improved cognitive performance. When feeling good we think wider and better than usual and we discover and build cognitive, psychological, social and physical resources that enhance resilience.[71]

Appreciative approaches

To have an appreciative appraisal conversation use feedforward interviews,[72] the reflected best self-process and/or enthusiasm stories. Focus on identifying and developing strengths, ensure the magic ratio of 3:1 or more positive comments (indeed best to separate out positive and corrective feedback into two different conversations with clear and different purposes). Give diamond feedback. Define win-win goals.

You might find our selection of strengths cards or positive action cards available from our online store useful to support this activity.[73]

---

70 Linley, A. (2008) *Average to A+ realising strengths in yourself and others.* Coventry: CAPP Press.

71 Fredrickson, B. (1998) What good are positive emotions? *Review of General Psychology* **2**(3) 300-319.

72 Kluger, A.N. and Nir, D. (2010) The feedforward interview. *Human Resource Management Review* **20**(3) 235-246.

73 https://www.acukltd.com/shop

45: The psychology of risk and performance-related pay: lessons from micro-finance

A reflection on the complex impact of performance-related pay on behaviour.

The phenomenon of micro-finance in the developing world provides valuable insights into people's attitudes to risk, in particular why seemingly irrational behaviour is in fact perfectly rational once seen within an individual context.

What have we learnt about risk assessment from micro-finance schemes?

Micro-finance provides insight into this field through noting the difficulty encountered in persuading the very poor to borrow money. This reluctance to borrow seems, on the face of it, fairly irrational behaviour. The poor, due to their lack of capital, have a higher level of potential return on investment in such capital than any other group in the economy. They should, according to conventional microeconomic theory, leap at the chance of borrowing money to invest.

For example, a subsistence farmer should be very keen to borrow to invest in simple, proven technology such as chemical fertilisers or irrigation (or even a few extra chickens or goats) which he has been unable to afford so far. These are low risk investments and they will greatly improve his output. However, it was discovered that while in general the poor had an astonishing appetite for debt and other basic financial products, the very poorest (those hovering just above subsistence level), for whom the returns should have been highest, were the least enthusiastic of all the poor to take on debt.

The cause of this reluctance to borrow stems it seems not from an irrational dread of debt itself, but rather a very rational attitude to the risk associated with investing in the loan. The poorest subsistence farmers in the third world had factored into their calculations something which had not occurred to the economists and bankers who were setting up the micro-lending schemes, namely the possibility of starvation. While the potential upside to taking out a loan to invest in their land was large (greatly increased harvests and incomes) and the potential downside (a failure to boost crop yields and then the burden of repaying the loan on the same income as before) was small, and the first outcome was far more likely than the second, they could not afford to take the risk because of the danger that failure would push them over the breadline into actual starvation.

This attitude towards taking risks, that of minimizing the potential downside of any change or decision, rather than simply weighing up the options equally and choosing the one which seems on average the most likely to boost your income or wealth, is known as the Minimax strategy (short for minimizing the potential maximum loss, i.e. of minimizing the chance of the worst happening).

What does this mean for financial incentive schemes?

This brings us to the practical implications for managers of people's behaviour towards risk, particularly in the area of performance-related pay. While most employees in Britain and the West are in very little danger of actual starvation or anything close to it, most have calls on their income which they see as essential for various reasons, and which they will adopt a Minimax strategy to protect. Some common ones might be:

- Being able to afford the repayments on the mortgage.
- Being able to pay monthly bills.
- Being able to enjoy health and leisure activities.
- Being able to invest in material improvements to their homes.

To protect these personal choices many employees will therefore not embrace a switch from consistent pay to a performance-related pay scheme, or any other re-organization of their terms of employment, with the zest which managers may expect. Indeed, it turns out that while the least productive members of any organization will resist the introduction of a scheme which rewards contribution to productivity, so too do many more productive employees who might be expected to embrace it, if they are reasonably close to what they would consider their own 'poverty line', due to the Minimax thinking this engenders.

How does this help explain bank behaviour?

At the lower end of the scale customer service in banks is often shoddy because the branch managers, probably the lowest rank where performance-related pay is a major component of their incomes, are reluctant to risk re-organising the way the branch is run to reduce queues, or to send staff for retraining. This is because such activity may cause major temporary disruption and hit short-term profits, making them miss their quarterly targets even if profits go up later.

Meanwhile in the investment banking division the top traders and their bosses are offered bonuses, which not only come on top of already high pay (making Minimax behaviour less likely), but which are in many cases virtually guaranteed, being tied to short-term profits. More risky behaviour usually increases profits in the short run (by increasing trading and loan volumes) but stores up trouble for later (by increasing the proportion of bad debts) and so encourages risk-taking if remuneration is tied primarily to short term profits.

Thus, the pay structure encourages caution and timidity where you need it least, with front-line lower management, but not in those on the trading floors or steering the ship in head office. In this case, performance-related pay has caused risk-averse behaviour where the potential downsides of risk are small and where innovation is most needed, and risk-seeking behaviour where the potential for disaster, and the consequences of such a disaster, are much larger.

Helping incentives to work

From these observations it should be apparent that calibrating incentive schemes involves more than just putting everyone on bonuses and getting out of the way of the resultant tidal wave of creativity and innovation. It requires a careful analysis of the type of decision making (risk-seeking or risk-averse) which is required and an effort to see things from the employee's point of view. Only then can their, sometimes baffling, refusal to react to incentives in the way intended be rationally understood and accounted for.

Written by Jem Smith.

46: Taking a coaching approach: seven top tips for developing talent in your staff

Guidance on when and how to use a coaching approach to improve performance and build capacity.

A key challenge for leaders and managers is developing the capacity of their staff or team. Taking a coaching approach allows you to focus on drawing out motivation rather than trying to push it in. It allows you to create energy and motivation and it is usually experienced as an empowering process by your coachee. It helps people develop their initiative and a sense of ownership of their work and tasks, and, in general, converts potential into capacity.

Here are seven tips to help make your coaching conversations highly productive.

1. Be clear what you are coaching for

It's important to be clear why you taking a coaching approach rather than just giving information, orders or instruction. Generally, it is worth taking a coaching approach when we want to invest in skill development.

Examples might be:

- To improve problem-solving skills.
- To improve emotional intelligence when interacting with customers.
- To increase confidence in someone's own abilities and so their ability to be proactive and use initiative.
- To increase team collaboration and mutual support.
- To develop expert excel skills.

It is also important to know when not to invest in a coaching approach. For example, while for one person developing expert Excel skills might be key for their job, for another their engagement with Excel may be a very rare occurrence. In which case other ways of solving the problem might be more effective and appropriate.

2. Select appropriate opportunities

Coaching is only one of a number of management interaction styles and is not right for all occasions. In emergency situations for instance, you are better off just telling people what they need to do.

Some indicators of a possibly good opportunity for coaching are when:

- Whatever the person is struggling with, or asking for help with, is going to be a recurring challenge.
- There is no panic. Heightened emotional states, such as panic, can lead to unhelpful learning. For instance, if you try to coach someone who is in a panic, they may 'learn' that you are an obstructive unhelpful so-and-so rather than that you helped them develop a new skill or to think for themselves.
- There is time to assure yourself that they are good to go after the conversation and that you are happy with their next steps. This needn't take long, but there needs to be time to conclude the conversation.
- Someone is asking for help.
- Someone comes to you with a problem, and it's clear they have a solution in mind.
- You are trying to help someone and they are resisting all your suggestions.

3. Use turning questions to get into a coaching conversation

If people come to you expecting you to give them the answer, then you need to turn the conversation into a coaching conversation. These questions will help:

- 'That sounds interesting/challenging/important, what do you think might be the way forward? What ideas do you already have?'
- 'If that is what you are worried about, what do you want to see happen instead?'
- 'If I wasn't here, what would you do about this?'
- 'I can see you are looking for help with this, what is the most helpful question I can ask you to help you with your thinking in the 30 seconds we have here?'

After asking any of those, or a similar question, put an expectant expression on your face and stop speaking! Create a big space full of expectation and hope for them to answer into. Hold your nerve.

These questions work to turn the question away from your resourcefulness towards theirs. It also helps move them from passive recipient waiting for an answer, to active agents in finding a way forward.

4. Help them draw on their existing resources

Questions you can usefully ask to achieve this include such questions as:

- 'When have you tackled something similar? Not necessarily here but in other places you've worked or in other situations. How did that work out? How could what you learnt from that be relevant here?'

- 'Who else knows something about this and might be interested to work with you on finding a way forward?'

- 'What ideas do you have?'

- 'Where else might there be some information on this that might stimulate ideas? Websites, in-house training, forums, professional associations?'

5. Help them explore and develop possibilities. Reality check

This is where you finally get to feed your knowledge, problem-solving skills and expertise into the conversation, but in a different way. You use it to help shape up the idea into the best it can be, making sure they retain ownership of it. For example:

- 'Explain to me more about how that's a good idea. How do you see it working?'

- 'Have you considered/taken into account/thought about...?'

- 'So what will you do if....?'

- 'Hm, I'm just wondering how that might go down with... what do you think?'

- 'Great, what do you see the risks as being? How will you deal with them?'

This is also where you set any boundaries on action. This might range from 'It's a great/interesting/novel/exciting/challenging/provocative idea and I truly am sorry to have to say I can't support it as it will be too expensive/take more time than we have/be seen as too risky'. Then move swiftly too 'However, I think the bit about ... could work, let's explore that more'. Or 'what else have you got?'

6. Road test for readiness

This is a crucially important part of the process where you are testing to see how committed, ready and energized they are to make this happen. Questions you can ask at this point include:

- 'What's your first step?'

- 'Who else do you need to talk to?'

- 'How will I know you are making progress?'

- 'On a scale of 1-10 how ready are you to get going on this?'
- 'What else needs to happen to increase your readiness?'
- 'How can I support you to make this happen?'

Offer encouragement and support, express belief, and agree a 'progress check' process.

7. It's not for every situation and it doesn't work every time

Coaching is not suitable for every occasion. Sometimes people do need to be told what to do. For example when:

- They don't know enough to even start to engage with the challenge.
- They are missing a vital piece of information, and need to be informed of it.
- It's an emergency, you have the answer, and speed is of the essence.
- It's not worth the time or energy e.g. it doesn't fit the criteria of point 1.

Also sometimes particular people or even groups of people get stuck in patterns of belief that makes it hard for them to engage in coaching, for instance:

- They believe it's your job to think, not theirs.
- They're still smarting from some previous managerial behaviour (this can go on for years).
- They have zero confidence in themselves and their ability and are highly dependent on others.
- They are severely depressed, anxious or otherwise cognitively incapacitated.
- They are fully preoccupied with other challenges, maybe outside of work, and have no capacity to engage with being creative.

In this case you need to address these challenges before you can hope to get very far with coaching.

In conclusion

Be aware that coaching isn't for everyone and every situation. Beyond that though, on the whole, once people genuinely believe that you want them to contribute and you will support them in their adventures of learning, they relish it; and they will grow in ability, confidence, initiative and general switched-on-ness before your very eyes!

Our Udemy for Business training video 'Coaching Skills for Managers', produced with Skills Booster[74] offers more on this. And our store offers sets of coaching cubes that support coaching activity with 36 coaching questions.[75]

---

74 https://www.udemy.com/leadership-coaching-skills/learn/v4/overview
75 https://www.acukltd.com/store/coaching-cubes

47: How working with strengths can improve performance

This chapter gives the headline findings about the impact of working on our strengths.

Our strengths are those abilities we have that are hardwired into our ways of doing things. They are a combination of genetics we inherited and the environment in which we were raised. By the time we are adults some neural pathways are much more practiced than others. We have habitual ways of being and behaving that we find effortless; indeed almost irresistible. These, in essence, are our strengths. We might use them for good or evil, with or without much skill, but they are our go-to, default way of being in the world. While they can and frequently do get us into trouble when applied badly or inappropriately, they are also our greatest asset. And yet...

Many of us have been diligently working for years to get better at the things that we are bad at. Time after time the same things come up in the performance appraisal, 360-degree feedback or the personality profile, time after time we resolve 'to work on our weaknesses'. In this we are in good company; '87% of people believe that finding your weaknesses and fixing them is the best way to achieve outstanding performance'.[76]

However, as Buckingham says, *'This isn't development, it's damage control'*.[77] As someone with poor attention to detail, I live in fear of sending out incorrect invoices. My diligent attention to them, checking and double-checking is damage limitation indeed. And it takes me a disproportionate amount of time.

However, recent research suggests that we are wrong in this belief because:

- Excellence is not the opposite of failure.
- Strengths are not the opposite of weaknesses.
- We will learn little about excellence by studying failure.
- We will learn little about our strengths by concentrating on our weaknesses.
- By studying our mistakes, we will learn more about how we make mistakes.

---

76 Buckingham, M. (2007) *Go put your strengths to work*. London: Simon Schuster.
77 *Ibid.*

- By studying our weaknesses, we will learn more about ourselves at our worst.

- If we want to learn about success, we must study our successes.

- If we want to learn about our strengths, we need to study ourselves at our best.

This isn't to say that we don't need to attend to our weaknesses; clearly we do. However, we can be cleverer about how we do that. In an ideal scenario we fit the tasks to the strengths profile. My ideal book keeper (for my invoicing for instance) would be someone for whom attending to detail isn't an anxiety-ridden, fraught activity where a mistake lurks undetected in every line, but is a delight, an engaging dance with perfection. While I emerge from the task with a sense of 'fingers crossed' they would emerge with a sense of 'job well done'. (For those of you who are worrying about my ability to stay in business, I do now have an assistant who helps with the double-checking.) This of course is another way of dealing with weaknesses: getting help.

With the time and emotional energy we save by not 'working on our weaknesses' we can concentrate on understanding and maximizing our strengths. The research demonstrates very clearly that excellence in individual and team performance is related to the awareness of, and exercise of, our strengths, on a daily basis.

- People who get the chance to play to their strengths every day are 50% more likely to work in teams with a low turnover, 38% more likely to work in productive teams and 44% more likely to work in teams with higher customer satisfaction scores.[78]

- In high performing teams, people say they call on their strengths more than 75% of the time.

However, only 17% of people use their strengths at work everyday.[79]

The jury is in – working on your strengths can help achieve great performance.

Please see our selection of strengths cards for support with these conversations.[80]

---

78 Buckingham, M. and Clifton, D. (2002) *Now, discover your strengths: how to develop your talents and those of the people you manage*. New York: Free Press.

79 Buckingham, M. (2007) *Go put your strengths to work*. London: Simon Schuster.

80 https://www.acukltd.com/store?tag=strengths%20cards

48: Developing our potential: capitalizing on existing strengths

This brief chapter introduces a little more about the benefits of working with strengths.

It's great to learn new skills, to stretch and challenge ourselves; the benefits are clear, it's engaging, it extends our resourcefulness and it adds variety to life. In addition, recent research suggesting that doing things that make our brain hurt (that we find hard, in other words) prolongs its useful life. And there is no harm in working on our weaknesses: it is possible to make marginal improvements that might make us slightly less annoying or infuriating to other people. The benefits of working on our strengths are somewhat less obvious though; why invest in getting better at something you can already do well?

Positive psychology research suggests that actually there are clear benefits for individuals and workplaces to knowing people's strengths and helping them find ways to exercise them every day. In addition, exercising strengths is related to performance, authenticity, motivation, and self-confidence.[81]

Our strengths are those abilities and tendencies that are so natural to us they are almost effortless. There are a number of different typographies of strengths in the literature now, many with accompanying psychometrics, all with slightly different definitions.

Figure 48.1: Different strengths suites and how they are measured

Theory	Measure
Character Strengths – Seligman	Values in Action (The VIA measure)
Workplace Strengths – Brewerton	Strengthscope (StrengthsPartnership)
Strengths – Linley	Realise 2 (CAPP – Centre for Applied Positive Psychology)
Talents –Buckingham/Gallop	Strengthsfinder

---

81 Linley, A. (2008) *Average to A+ realising strengths in yourself and others.* Coventry: CAPP Press.

But in essence strengths are the habits of behaviour we have acquired without really noticing. For example, you might have a tendency to tidy everywhere you go, to facilitate communication, to problem solve. Maybe you are a stickler for precision and detail (you can't help yourself). This is a key defining feature of a strength, given the opportunity we find it hard not to do it.

Figure 48.2: Other ways to identify strengths

Other ways to identify strengths
Things you can't not do.
Things you use as a reward for having got other things done.
Things you save to do as a treat.
When you feel motivated and energized.
Things that seem effortless, it puzzles you that others can't 'just do it'.
When you are feeling at your best.

This also highlights one of the downsides of our strengths; used inappropriately they can get us into trouble. Linley[82] has coined the lovely phrase 'the golden mean' of strengths use, which he defines as, 'the right strength at the right time to the right amount'. The development work with strengths is to develop skill in using them.

Teams offer a great opportunity for people to work more to their strengths, as the work required to complete the task can be shared amongst the team members in a way that allows each to exercise their strengths. In high performing teams, people say they call on their strengths more than 75% of the time.[83] And what to do about the jobs or tasks that play to no-one's strengths? Share them out evenly, in small chunks.

Understanding our own strengths, and the strengths of our colleagues is the key to achieving our own best performance, and getting the best from others.

We supply a number of difference strengths cards suitable for different workplace contexts through our online store.[84]

---

82 Linley, A. (2008) *Average to A+ realising strengths in yourself and others*. Coventry: CAPP Press.

83 Buckingham, M. (2007) *Go put your strengths to work*. London: Simon Schuster.

84 https://www.acukltd.com/store?tag=strengths%20cards

49: How does positive organizational behaviour turn into positive organizational performance?

This chapter explains what positive organizational behaviour is and how it impacts performance.

Positive organizational scholarship researcher Kim Cameron[85] reports that flourishing organizations, that is organizations that are successful as well as being described as great places to work, exhibit three key cultural characteristics.

1. A strong interest in learning from positive deviance

All organizations have an interest in learning from negative deviance, that is, when things go wrong. Far fewer have an interest in learning from positive deviance, when things go right. But they are missing a trick. We now know that very often the root causes of success are not just the polar opposite of the root causes of failure. Taking an active interest in learning from exceptionally good performance allows organizations to increase their ability to succeed.

2. The modelling and promotion of virtuous actions

There is still a strong organizational story that suggests that a successful organizational culture is hard, macho and dog-eat-dog with little time for sentiment. By contrast Cameron's research has found that organizations that promote virtuous actions, by which he means things such as kindness, patience, humility, generosity and forgiveness, reap the benefits in organizational performance. A moment's thought suggests this makes sense, as such an environment means people are likely to take more learning risks than in a blame-orientated culture with a minimal tolerance of mistakes or errors. Of course the learning process still has to be managed, but the recognition that people are human and that in any human system error is inevitable helps liberate learning behaviour and reduce blame avoidance and buck-passing.

---

85 Cameron, K. (2008) *Positive leadership: strategies for extraordinary performance*. Oakland, CA: Berrett-Koehler Publishers.

3. A strong bias towards affirming the best in people and situations

Cameron found that his exceptional organizations had a real bias towards noticing and affirming the best in people. We might say they had developed skill with their appreciative capabilities as well as their critical ones. Being affirmed in your essential goodness as well as your particular strengths helps boost confidence and morale. It also affects motivation. People grow towards the best reflections of themselves. Reflecting back the best of people helps them attain their potential.

This collection of behaviour actively promotes two organizational processes that lead to improved performance.

Upward virtuous circles of positive emotion and behaviour

When we see others displaying exceptional virtue, we are inspired to emulate them. People behave better in the company of the better behaved. The kind of culture described above contributes to a self-reinforcing virtuous circle of people feeling good, therefore being more inclined to do good things, therefore more likely to be observed by others behaving well, who in turn are more likely to be inspired to behave at their best, with colleagues, customers and suppliers. All these little bits of behaviour add up to a performance culture.

Social capital

These three key organizational behaviours also contribute to the development of good social capital. Social capital describes the levels of trust and connection between departments or divisions in an organization. High levels of social capital promote good information flow and low-level decision-making and problem-solving, all of which contributes effectively to local and global performance.

50: Forget carrot or stick: try nudging

Another take on how to influence behaviour to create performance.

In any organization there is always a variety of tools available to managers to influence staff towards desired behaviour. This has traditionally been seen as a choice between two general approaches: incentives and coercion, or the carrot or stick approach.

Now there is a new alternative

This third method utilizes the natural inertia of most people when confronted with the choice of accepting the status quo or changing things. Generally, they accept the status quo unless the difference between the two in terms of their perception of their own welfare is very large.

By making the desired state of affairs the norm, but allowing employees the freedom to change this individually if they wish, organizations can gain the benefits of the majority of the workforce behaving in the easy 'default' way. While at the same time, through providing choice, they avoid the resentment and active opposition of the few who summon the energy to choose an alternative.

Interestingly this approach, known as 'choice architecture', or more colloquially as 'nudging', is credited to an economist working at Schipol International Airport in Amsterdam who reduced 'spillage' by men in the airport's urinals by having a picture of a black housefly etched onto the bowl. Spillage declined by 80% as most men are unable to resist aiming at the image, located in the centre of the bowl. Thus he achieved his objective without hectoring passengers with notices or fines or expensive material incentives.

A weightier concrete example of this kind of approach, which also illustrates the kind of situation where it is most appropriate, was the Turner Review's recommendations on reform of the pensions system for the government. It recommended that the most cost-effective method for providing for old age was for people to save for their own retirement by enrolling in a government-sponsored scheme. In order to realize the economies of scale which would make this cost-effective, however, a large portion of the population would have to be involved. To avoid making this compulsory he recommended simply enrolling workers in the scheme automatically while leaving them the option to opt out if they wished.

Is nudging the right option for your desired behaviour change?

To answer this, you need to consider this question: does the behaviour require the participation of most, but not all, of the organization to be effective? If the answer is 'yes', then nudging might be a good approach to take.

This approach offers advantages over more traditional approaches. For example, in some circumstances dictates (stick) might seem petty to some, while cash incentives (carrot) might seem crude and insensitive to others.

Considering these factors should give you an idea of whether choice architecture might be suitable for enabling a change of behaviour in your organization.

With thanks to Jem Smith.

51: Positive deviance: creating and learning from exceptional performance

An introduction to a great methodology for working with seemingly intractable performance issues.

Positive deviance is an exciting methodology emerging from an understanding of organizations as complex adaptive systems. It helps organizations learn from those who manage to achieve better than normal outcomes from within the same resource constraints as their colleagues.

It is one of Kim Cameron's[86] distinguishing features for flourishing organizations: they both learn from and create positive deviance. Flourishing organizations are interested in exceptionally good performance and they learn from it. Some of the earliest examples of how learning from positive deviance can make a real difference comes from community work.

For instance, an early example of positive deviance was in a poor Vietnamese community.[87] In this community there were many starving children, yet some families were doing better than others in feeding their children. A positive deviance investigation by the villagers themselves revealed that the more successful families were taking shrimps and crabs from the rice fields i.e. had realized an additional source of protein. While some others were spreading their children's rice ration out over 24 hours rather than just giving them one daily meal, which is better for young children. These were things that theoretically everyone could do but not everyone did. These are positive deviance strategies. Of course there were also other factors that made a difference, such as having a rich relative that sent supplies. However, these strategies are not available to others and so are known as true but useless strategies.

A key factor for the success of the intervention (i.e. achieving behaviour change) was that the researchers got the villagers to do the investigation. Positive deviance investigations are being used very successfully to reduce super bug infection rates in some hospitals.[88]

---

86 Cameron, K. (2008) *Positive leadership: strategies for extraordinary performance*. Oakland, CA: Berrett-Koehler.

87 Mackintosh, U.,A.,T., Marsh, D.,R. and Schroeder, D.,G. (2002) Sustained positive deviant child care practices and their effects on child growth in Viet Nam. *Food and Nutrition Bulletin* **23**(4_suppl2) 16-25.

88 Kimball, L. (2007) *An inside job: best practices from within. Leading ideas: strategy and business*. McLean, VA: Booz, Allen & Hamilton.

It is a very effective way of 'growing' a better culture. By recognising that small variations in performance always exist, and by focusing on and amplifying the variations in a positive direction, the whole organization can be encouraged to move in the direction of the best.

Appreciative Inquiry as a methodology works on the same principle of identifying positive deviance, learning from it, and increasing its presence in the organization.

When might investigating positive deviance be the way forward in an organization?

With thanks to Lisa Kimball from Plexus.

When...

- There is some existing deviance e.g. some people are doing better than others in a similar situation (performance variation across team or division).
- It's a really intractable problem.
- It involves behaviour change.
- Everyone knows what to do, they are just not doing it.
- The situation is bathed in data. It really helps if the groups can keep track of the changes they are making and their impact.
- There is top leadership support. This means top leadership support the process through releasing resources, being responsive to early efforts and initiatives, and tracking, recording and amplifying results.

How to do positive deviance:

- Ask about success.
- Compare best to near best to tease out small differences that make a difference.
- Encourage peer to peer inquiry (and analysis) into success.
- Identify strategies for success (discounting TBU factors).
- Support with behaviour change strategies.
- Support with top leadership resources: interest, budget, encouragement, action.

52: Diamond feedback

This chapter introduces a metaphor that can be useful for managers struggling to give positive performance feedback.

The ability to give positive feedback is useful on at least two counts.

1. Positive feedback acts as a 'reinforcer' in operant conditioning theory

That is, the receipt of it should increase the likelihood of the behaviour it has just followed being displayed the next time the same or similar circumstances occur. So, we can use positive reinforcement to 'grow' more of the behaviour we want.

2. Positive feedback is a mood enhancer

Most of us respond well to praise and we are now well aware of the many benefits of positive mood states e.g. people are more creative, more able to deal with complexity, more interested in the new, more amenable to working with others and so on. And of course, there are likely to be other benefits such as relationship enhancement, growth in self-knowledge etc.

However, it is noticeable that many managers and leaders not only have strange ideas about giving positive feedback, but also find it hard to give. The strange ideas include the general one that to praise is to 'give something away', as if they have a limited pot of this stuff called positive feedback. This can cause them to set very high performance bars for receiving praise. Another is the idea that it somehow disincentivizes people. And interestingly they are most worried about doing this to their best performers, who are, contrary to the manager's belief, not always full of self-confidence. So, while managers assume they know they are good, and worry about praise spoiling them or going to their head, the people themselves worry about whether or not they are good enough, their self-confidence slowly ebbing away. And then of course there is the 'They get paid, why do they need to be praised as well!' argument.

Beyond this though, even once managers are persuaded to take the risk of giving positive feedback, they can lack the skill. Clive Hutchinson of Cougar Automation introduced me to the idea of diamond feedback that he in turn was given by Peter Taylor, an NLP specialist, of Brilliance Training. I have found it be very useful in helping managers and leaders to look at feedback differently.

It is based on the metaphor of feedback against a pack of cards, which as I understand it runs like this.

Clubs – beating someone over the head with a message of failure but with no explanation as to why the thing, event, behaviour was wrong or a failure.

Spades – giving critical or corrective feedback with information about why the behaviour/ performance etc. wasn't good enough.

Hearts – heart-warming phrases such as 'well done', 'good job', 'good show' without any indication as to what it was that was good.

Diamonds – praise accompanied by detail 'I really like the way you...it had the effect of...it demonstrated...what was really good was the way you...the difference it made was...well done'.

Some managers and leaders find giving positive feedback much easier once they can clearly conceptualize it as being related to data rather than just some weird emotion-based thing. It is also much more helpful for staff as they begin to learn about what is valued about their behaviour or what they bring to the party, and where their perceived strengths lie.

53: Know thyself: what is the point of 360 feedback?

This short chapter makes it clear why we need the feedback of others.

360 degree feedback is a very popular management tool, the question is how useful is it? Recent research on the accuracy of self-perception suggests it can be very useful and can play an important part in distinguishing the best from the rest in terms of leadership during change. The research[89,90] shows that:

- Self-perception of competence and character are frequently distorted by bias, misconception and illusion, resulting in a correlation with reality of around .29 (very low, almost non-existent).

- Self-perceptions tend to be flawed in a particular direction: upwards.

- Other people are frequently better at assessing our competence and prospects than we are.

- We are better at predicting how others will behave in a particular situation than how we ourselves will behave.

- On average people think of themselves as being anything but average.

- Psychologically speaking this over-optimism about our abilities is a useful defence against becoming disheartened. In organizational terms it leads to consistent underestimation of how long it will take to do something, amongst other things.

- People don't know themselves well because they have little comparative data (how someone else would do what they do) and little feedback (about how much better the thing could be done). They don't know what they don't know, and so think they are doing just fine.

- People can be trained to become more accurate in their self-perceptions.

- Peers possess some of the information necessary for accurate self-knowledge

89 Simmons, C. (2006) Should there be a counselling element within coaching? *The Coaching Psychologist* **2**(2) September.

90 Dunning, D. (2006) Strangers to ourselves? *The Psychologist* **19**(10) 600-603.

This is important because...

Research suggests that a key factor that distinguishes those leaders who are more successful at managing change from those who are less successful, is their degree of self-knowledge, self-awareness, and self-acceptance. They are highly aware of how their behaviour can impact on particular others and take care to ameliorate the possible negative effects. They are also aware of how the behaviour of others can affect their own behaviour.

54: Ten top tips for courageous conversations at work

Guidance on how to have that difficult conversation.

Many people at some point in their working lives have to have a difficult conversation with someone. It might be about a performance issues or something more personal. It can be with a peer, a subordinate or indeed a boss. Very often people are highly anxious, understandably so, about having this conversation. They then either avoid it for so long that when they do tackle it, it comes as a complete shock to the other party, or they rush at it like a bull in a china shop just to get it over with. Here are some tips to help produce a good result.

1. Be clear what you are trying to achieve

You need to be clear in your own mind why you are putting yourself through the trauma of having this conversation and what you hope to achieve. Is it an apology, an agreement about something, a change in behaviour in the future, some sort of restorative action or maybe a resubmission of a piece of work? Be clear what the successful outcome is and be listening for it.

2. Be clear what you are listening for

Being highly anxious can make us deaf. We become so focused on saying everything we have planned to say that we fail to hear the other person quietly saying, 'you're right' or 'I know' or even 'you might have a point'. 'You bet I have!' we say, and then return to our carefully prepared speech. You need to stay alert to the first signs that you have made your point and be prepared to switch modes to 'OK what next?' even if you haven't said everything you intended. Otherwise you run the risk of producing a new source of conflict, as your conversational partner feels unfairly berated when they've made a concession. This can sabotage the chances of recovery.

3. Be clear what gives you the right to initiate this conversation

It really helps us reduce our anxiety if we can understand how the conversational intent aligns with our values. For instance, you may have to tell someone that they didn't get the promotion they were after and give some hard feedback as to why. The clearer you are that giving this feedback is, for example, helpful behaviour (and it is important to you to help and develop others) then the easier it is to say what needs to be said about the current shortfall in their experience, manner, etc. that they need to address if they are to succeed in the future. Fobbing them off softly is easier but less helpful to them in the long run.

4. Give thought to how you set up the meeting

There are pros and cons to giving advance notice of wanting to have a difficult conversation with someone. The downside is there may well be a drop-off in productivity as they become distracted wondering what it is about. There is also the danger that their anxiety will drive them to push you to 'just say it now, let's get it over and done with'. On the other hand, springing it on them unexpectedly can lead them to feel ambushed or tricked in some way. It's a judgement call and depends on the situation and circumstances.

5. Look for the positive in the situation

Sometimes bad outcomes are the result of good intentions. Was the behaviour caused by a strength in overdrive? For instance, maybe 'too pushy' can be reframed as a strength of will, zest or tenacity being used with greater force than was appropriate, or where negotiation strengths were needed. Was there an honourable intention behind the behaviour? Many mistakes start out as good ideas or intentions. Be alert to any good consequences that occurred that you want to address, as well as the problematic outcome. All of these give you a way to approach the behaviour that make it more likely the other person can own it, still feel good about themselves, and be open to making changes.

6. Listen first

It is often a good idea, once you have outlined the area/topic/incident that you want to discuss, to give the person a chance to give their view on the situation. Many a manager taking this approach has found the other person is only too aware that there is a problem, or an issue, or that something didn't go right and that they have been making themselves miserable over it. Of course, you'll also have people who take the opportunity to 'get their defence in first' but at least you have the lie of the land before you say your piece, and indeed you may not need to say much at all.

7. Offer reassurance

There is an art to building and maintaining the relationship bridge while trying to convey information or a perspective that the other person might find hard to hear. Think about an opener such as 'I feel this conversation may be difficult, but I am confident it will be to the benefit of both of us'. Or 'My sincere hope is that we come out of this conversation with a shared understanding of what happened and how we can make things better'.

8. Be honest about the effect on you

The more able you are to be honest about your motivation for having the conversation, the more likely you are to be acting and talking with integrity. Authenticity and integrity tend to produce better responses in others. So say something like, 'To be honest I felt really embarrassed when... and I like to feel proud of my team when... that's why I want to...'. This isn't about trying to 'guilt trip' anyone; it's about being honest about your investment in this as well as the favour you are hoping to do them.

9. Use descriptive not evaluative language

Try to stick to an account that articulates what you saw and the consequences in a way that is factual and could be verified by any other observers. Steer away from evaluators like 'aggressive' and say instead something like, 'You were speaking in a louder than your normal speaking voice, leaning in very close to B. Your face was going red and your forehand bulged. I also noticed B leant backwards and raised her hands. She didn't speak for the rest of the meeting. Later B came to me and said she felt intimidated by you in that meeting'. Here you can add your concern, 'My concern is that if B feels like that we will lose her input to the discussion. I know you are very passionate about this topic. I need both your inputs. Let's see if we can find a way where you both feel able to make your points'.

10. Look forward to solutions, not backwards to blame

The aim of the discussion, if possible, is to create a common agreement about the situation now without getting too lost in counter-arguments about blame in the past. It doesn't have to be a complete consensus, just enough to allow the conversation to move productively to the next stage of finding ways forward that are acceptable to you both.

We supply a booklet in both hard and soft copy that takes you through all the stages of preparing and delivering a courageous conversation from a positive perspective.[91]

---

91 https://www.acukltd.com/store/how-to-have-courageous-conversations-the-positive-way-a-booklet-training-guide

55: How to keep your employees engaged at work

Tips on creating work and organizational engagement.

Engaged employees are a business imperative: they perform 20% better and give 57% more discretionary effort.[92] Organizations with a high level of engagement have better quality, sales, income and turnover, profit, customer satisfaction, shareholder return, business growth and success.[93] It is estimated that currently only 19% of employees are highly engaged in their work, while active disengagement costs the UK economy between £37.2bn and £38.9bn a year.[94]

Organizations often struggle to understand what creates engagement. Positive psychology research is revealing that employee engagement is primarily a psychological and social process. There are a number of steps organizations can take to increase engagement.

1. Create a positive culture

Actively introduce processes that increase positivity. For example, start meetings with praise for last week's achievements, celebrate successes and create a work climate of hope and good humour. Introduce ways of measuring people's experience of positivity at work.

2. Learn to affirm the best

Recognize and develop best practice. Encourage virtuous organizational behaviour such as helpfulness. Recognize team and individual strengths, initiative and innovation, both formally through appraisal processes, and informally by leadership interest and focus.

92 Corporate Leadership Council (2004) *Driving performance and retention through employee engagement: a quantitative analysis of effective engagement strategies.* Corporate Executive Board.

93 Stairs, M. and Gilpin, M. (2010) Positive engagement: from employee engagement to work place happiness. In: Linley, P.A., Harrington, S. and Garcea, N. (eds) *Oxford handbook of positive psychology and work.* Oxford: Oxford University Press.

94 Flade, P. (2003) Great Britain's workforce lacks inspiration. *Gallup Management Journal* **11** December.

3. Turn strengths into talents

When people are able to use their strengths they are more engaged and perform better. Introduce processes that help people get to know and own their strengths, using psychometrics or best-self feedback. And help them develop their strengths into high performance talents.

4. Help teams play to individual strengths

The most productive teams are able to share the team tasks according to strengths, so encourage team members to swap tasks that fall in their weakest areas for those that play to their strengths.

5. Help people re-craft jobs around their strengths

Make the job fit the person, rather than trying to make the person fit the job. Most outcomes can be achieved in more than one way. Help people find a way of maximizing their ability to use their strengths and talents, and to minimize the time they spend struggling with tasks for which they have no aptitude.

6. Create opportunities to experience flow

Flow is a psychological state so rewarding that people risk life and health to achieve it (think of mountaineers or starving artists). Find out where people experience flow in their work. Help them recognize it. Help them work out how to increase their opportunities to experience it.

7. Create reward-rich environments

People are motivated and engaged by the opportunity to obtain rewards. Many things can be rewarding for people in their work environment: praise, appreciation and thanks, smiles and opportunities. Create work environments full of small and easily-won rewards that are salient to them.

8. Understand goal seeking

Before you set goals for someone you need to understand what they find rewarding. For example, some people find public recognition rewarding, while others just like to know that what they have done has been helpful.

9. Help people find meaning in their work

People are very good at finding meaning in what they do. Everyone wants to believe they are spending their time valuably. Help them by making it clear why their work is important, what it means for them, you, the department, the organization, a better world.

56: Getting behind your employee survey results

This chapter introduces Roffey Park research on what makes for engaging leadership behaviours.

A three-part model

Roffey Park research suggests that there are three key components to employee engagement: my job, my organization, my value. Their report *The Human Voice of Employee Engagement: Understanding what lies beneath the surveys*[95] gives a full and readable account of the factors that make a difference. A key finding is that pride is at the heart of employee engagement.

They found that people want:

■ To be treated as individuals.

■ To be consulted and informed about things that affect them.

■ To feel valued for themselves and what they do.

■ To be supported with work issues.

■ To have clear and fair process for performance evaluation and development.

They found that people want their leaders to be:

■ Strategic.

■ Visible.

■ Communicative.

■ Trustworthy.

They want a good relationship with their manager. Effectively they want to be able to feel pride in themselves, their work, and their organization. When they do, they are highly likely to be engaged employees.

---

95 Gifford, J., Finney, L., Hennessy, J. and Varney, S. (2010) *The human voice of employee engagement understanding what lies beneath the surveys*. Roffey Park.

Finding out what lies behind the survey data

One way to help explore employee engagement survey data is to assemble focus groups of organizational members and to ask them to record on Post-its the immediate feelings they experience when someone asks them the following questions:

'Where do you work?'
'Who do you work for?'
'What do you do?'

These Post-its are then organized, by question, under red, amber and green headings (traffic lights), and a discussion takes place.

The beauty of this process is that this raw data can be presented to the senior decision makers not able to be present at the focus group. It allows them to get a real feel for the sentiments, practicalities, and personalities behind the bland statistics of the engagement survey results: what they should treasure, what they should notice, and what they need to change.

57: From engagement to flourishing

In this chapter we start to move beyond engagement to positive organizational flourishing as an ambition for our employees.

Creating employee engagement has long been a key focus of organizations. It is known that more highly engaged employees are more productive, take less sick leave, are more likely to stay and are better organizational citizens.[96] The definition of an engaged employee is someone who feels responsible for and committed to superior job performance i.e. job performance matters to the employee.[97] It is a very useful concept and undoubtedly people are better behaved employees when they are engaged then when they are not, however the concept of employee engagement is very focused on the organizational benefit and less on the benefit to the individual.

The concept of human flourishing, by contrast, is focused on benefit to the individual. It allows us to expand on the benefits to the organization of having engaged employees, to the benefits to all of having employees who are positively flourishing. I believe that the concept of human flourishing embraces the concept of active engagement (in life, in work) within it.

Flourishing has been defined by Huppert and So.[98] To qualify as flourishing, an individual needs to experience these core features in their lives: positive emotions, engagement, interest, meaning and purpose. In addition, they need to experience three of these six features: self-esteem, optimism, resilience, vitality, self-determination and positive relationships. By this definition, having measured 2,000 people in 23 countries, they have determined that Denmark leads with 33% of its citizen's flourishing, while the UK lags at 18% and Russia brings up the rear with 6%.

Seligman's[99] PERMA model simplifies and operationalizes this definition down into five key factors that encourage human flourishing: positive emotions, engagement or flow, relationships (positive ones that is), meaningfulness

96 Lewis, S. (2011) *Positive psychology at work: how positive leadership and appreciative inquiry create inspiring organizations.* Chichester: Wiley-Blackwell.

97 Britt, T., Dickinson, J., Greene-Shortridge, T. and McKibben, E. (2007) Self-engagement at work. In: Nelson, D. and Cooper, C. (eds.) *Positive organizational behavior.* London: SAGE Publications Ltd.

98 Huppert, F.A. and So, T.T. (2013) Flourishing across Europe: application of a new conceptual framework for defining well-being. *Social Indicators Research* **110**(3) 837-861.

99 Seligman, M.E.P. (2011) *Flourish: a new understanding of happiness and well-being – and how to achieve them.* London: Nicholas Brealey.

and accomplishment. Flourishing is essentially a positive psychology take on the well-established concept of well-being, extending it to a vibrant sense of growth, vitality, vim and exuberance. It is the +5 end of the -5 to +5 scale of languishing–surviving–flourishing.

We know how to create flourishing organizations thanks to Kim Cameron's[100] work: we need to learn from success, affirm the best in people and be nice to each other (I paraphrase freely here!). Flourishing organizations are likely to create the conditions for human flourishing. We know how to create all the PERMA conditions for people at work. Organizations can be more than places that engage our passions and interests, they can be places that positively foster human flourishing. There is a way, the question is, is there the will?

---

100 Cameron, K. (2008) *Positive leadership: strategies for extraordinary performance*. Oakland, CA: Berrett-Koehler Publishers.

58. The habits of highly creative people

Lessons distilled from the lives of the creative greats.

I have recently been reading *Daily Rituals* by Mason Currey.[101] He has collected short accounts of the daily rituals of some well-known creative people, past and present. His collection includes writers, philosophers, artists and composers. Most are male and white. It makes interesting reading and I thought I would distil my observations from it for you. I'm not sure how, if at all, it relates to positive psychology but perhaps you will be able to find a connection?

1. Most have strict routines, a few more of a binge pattern.

2. Most are early risers, some are not.

3. Quite a few get up and work for a few hours during the night, dividing their daily sleep into two distinct segments.

4. Almost all emphasize the power of graft and routine over muses and inspiration.

5. Most are men.

6. A high proportion seem to have someone to 'do' for them. Particularly preparing food. Many are woken at ungodly hours with a cup of something by someone who regularly gets up even earlier to perform this service.

7. An alarming number use stimulants ranging from excessive amounts of coffee to amphetamines.

8. A high number include a walk of an hour or more in their daily routine.

9. Most have a daily goal of input (number of hours sat at desk) or output (number of words or pages).

10. Almost all had a quiet space, separate from the living space.

11. Despite living the life of a monk, many had friends willing to fit into the two hours a day put aside for such frivolities as friendship.

12. Many describe the agony and the ecstasy of the creative life. Most experience the creative process as hard, for a few it seemed not so.

13. Some induced health problems through their dedication to the creative life.

14. Few are satisfied with what they achieve.

---

101 Currey, M. (ed.) (2013) *Daily rituals: how artists work*. New York: Knopf Publishing Group.

What I take from this:

- All books are written one word at a time.
- That a little done every day adds up.
- Habits of work trump moments of inspiration.
- That no one ever said the creative life was easy.

And that the ability to organize a life free from alarums, anxieties, disruptions and the general mess of the human condition helps create *conditions* conducive to concerted concentration. Oh, and that having someone to 'do' all the boring bits of maintaining body and soul (shopping, cooking, cleaning etc) helps create time.

And that choices must be made and habits formed.

So what's your excuse?

What would you advise a young person keen to engage in the life creative?

59: Why your workforce acts stupid and how to release their intelligence

It can be very frustrating when people don't use their initiative at work to solve problems or to be creative. Equally frustrating, the way people go about solving their problems can sometimes seem incomprehensible. As one manager once reported to me, 'my problem is when people come to work they leave their brains in the car park'. There are a number of reasons why when people come to work they sometimes switch off their intelligence and put on their stupid hat.

1. Our understanding of organizations encourages this

In an unconscious way many people subscribe to the idea of an organization as a head and a body. The head decides what to do and the body follows instructions. Thinking is viewed as a management skill and is rewarded as such. Non-managerial staff refer to this when they say 'I'm not paid to think'. When such a view dominates organizational life then people will find their efforts to contribute discounted as invalid. This shows in meetings when a suggestion made by a non-manager isn't 'heard' until it is picked up and echoed by a more senior person, then suddenly it has value.

2. It is not safe to make suggestions

Sometimes people have discovered that there is too big a risk attached to making suggestions or showing initiative. Maybe in the past someone was publicly humiliated when they made a suggestion that a powerful person thought risible. Or maybe when their idea 'failed', perhaps through no fault of their own, they found themselves being held accountable and blamed for the failure. A few experiences like this and the workforce quickly decides it's safer to keep their thoughts to themselves.

3. There is no effective way to contribute

Sometimes the challenge is the lack of a suitable process or forum to enable a connection between those aware of the problem, those aware of possible solutions, and those holding sufficient power and influence to agree to changes in working practice. Without these connections it is very difficult for people to act as an 'intelligent system'. Instead people struggle on, devising local solutions that may or may not work well in their area, but that don't really offer a long-term way forward.

4. Fruitful interaction is inhibited

While the problem is sometimes a lack of formal coordination, as above, other times it is a lack of an ability to coordinate informally. In some organizational environments it is frowned upon for people to be away from their desks or designated work areas. This can inhibit the ability of people to problem solve at a local level. Instead of talking directly to someone in another work section to resolve an issue, the problem is escalated up the line. It is rarely as pressing to more senior staff as it is to those directly affected and so never reaches the top of their list of priorities.

5. Goodwill has been withdrawn

When people feel badly or unfairly treated by their organization, the low risk silent protest is the withdrawal of goodwill. Goodwill is the fuel for volunteer behaviour. People who have withdrawn goodwill sometimes refuse invitations to engage saying, 'It's not in my job description'. Withdrawal of goodwill can include the withdrawal of critical evaluation of ideas. An attitude can develop of 'Let them (management) make stupid decisions, what do I care?' Once relations have fallen to this low, people will passively implement instructions they know to be potentially damaging, instead of actively contributing their local knowledge.

So what can be done to release the individual and collective intelligence of all organizational members?

1. Change the organizational metaphor

We need to move away from thinking of organizations as machines or as a human body, with a central control mechanism, and think more of them as being like living systems such as flocks of birds or swarms of bees. These living systems use the intelligence of all their members to self-organize in the face of opportunity or danger. Following a few simple principles allows them to act in a coordinated and synchronistic way. 'Organization' is recognized as being a product of the behaviour of the many rather than as a design of the few. These types of metaphor encourage us to recognize the value of the unique perspective of every member.

2. Encourage initiative and contributory behaviour

Calling on our understanding of behaviour change, we can recognize that encouraging people to risk using their initiative or making contributions requires that we recognize and reward very early and tentative attempts. Initially we need to welcome with open arms any idea put forward to grow people's willingness to contribute their ideas. Only when people truly believe that the act of putting forward ideas or making efforts is genuinely welcomed and appreciated can we risk applying some critical evaluation.

3. Use co-creative problem-solving processes

Bring together the people with the problems, the solutions and the decision-making power to create a fully-informed, robust solution or plan for change. Appreciative Inquiry is excellent for this, as is SimuReal. World Café and Open Space also offer methodologies that bring whole systems together to create sustainable change.

4. Encourage local problem-solving and decision-making

A few pre-conditions need to be in place to support this behaviour. People need to have relationships with their counterparts that are strong enough to handle conflict and disagreement as well as creativity and innovation. They need to be confident that their managers value the time invested in both the building of such relationships and the time invested in calling on them to solve problems or generate new ideas. They may also need access to amenities like somewhere to meet, or good quality company information.

5. Build social capital and good relations

Social capital at the organizational level refers to the degree of connectivity between different departments or functions. A good level of connectivity encourages the development of trusting relationships between departments, and also facilitates the flow of information around the organization. Consistently good relations between management and non-managerial staff accumulates in relational reserves that can be called upon in times of trouble. In other words, when people feel they have been well treated by the company over time, they are much more likely to respond very positively to an 'all hands on deck' call to suddenly help with an unexpected catastrophe.

60: Charming devils and the mischief they make

Sometimes it's not the performance, it's the people that are the problem!

It is increasingly becoming apparent that some people with severe personality disorders (narcissistic, psychopathic, paranoid and schizoid) slip through the organizational selection net. The problem is they don't appear in our midst with 'trouble' tattooed on their foreheads, instead they are often rather charming devils who do very well until they fall (and bring everyone else down with them).

How to reduce the chances of appointing a chancer, a megalomaniac, an egoist, a drama queen, or an obsessive, to your team

Beware that their failings come disguised as virtuous traits, as they bring almost an excess of a good thing. So the dimensions can look like this...

- Work focused – workaholic – obsessive/compulsive.
- Team player – dependency on others – can't make individual decisions.
- Action focused – decisive – rushed, rash and impulsive – dictatorial.
- Analytical – paralyzed – unable to act.
- Integrity – strong values – rigidity/cult leader.
- Innovative – enthusiastic/committed – unrealistic.

Spotting trouble in your midst

Someone who has the following characteristics...

- Who is all things to all people.
- About whom people hold deeply divided opinions (seen as saving angel by some and dangerous devil by others).
- Who wields disproportionate power to their status.
- Can skilfully play individuals, telling them what they want to hear.
- Has an uncanny ability to make bad things, things that don't work, and people in their way, disappear (Teflon man/woman).

- Lies and cheats with impunity in the service of some greater goal.

- Demonstrates loyalty only to self.

…just might be displaying strong psychopathic tendencies. As they advance up the organization and external control and non-deferential feedback lessens, the bigger the mess they can create.

How can you lessen the likelihood of this happening to your organization?

- Be brave enough to let go of the problem people early.

- Select for optimal not maximal qualities.

- Do proper biographical tracking history on your top appointments.

- Beware of trading off weaknesses for some great strengths.

- Use 360 degree-feedback, and listen to what those of no current 'use' to the person have to say. The once seduced and now discarded may have a less enamoured view of the charmer.

- Give leaders a stable deputy and make sure this person has adequate power to influence, control, or veto leadership action i.e. make sure the leader doesn't gain absolute power!

- Offer support to help self-management such as coaches, mentors, therapists.[102,103,104]

102 Furnham, A. (2007) *The Icarus syndrome. People and organizations at work*. Spring edition.

103 Trickey, G. (2007) Talent, treachery and self-destruction. Paper at ABP conference, 2007.

104 Babiak, P. and Hare, R. (2007) *Snakes in suits: when psychopaths go to work*. London: Harper Collins.

61: How to screen your high fliers: lessons from Robert Kaiser

Why high fliers derail.

Introduction

Robert Kaiser makes an intriguing argument as to why many executives see their career progress suddenly interrupted. He argues that for many, ambition and inflexibility, which may have contributed to their early success, can become such a handicap in senior leadership positions that it eclipses their intelligence and work ethic, causing them to become a liability.

He argues that many executives reach a point called 'termination', when their career suddenly becomes unstuck. For some this point is never reached: either their talents meet the demands of being part of the top leadership team in the largest organizations in their field or, for whatever reason, they leave before their termination point is reached.

Drawing on research into management going back to the mid-1980s, principally from Sears, Roebuck and Co. and the Centre for Creative Leadership, Kaiser has concluded that for the rest (around 50% of executives) their career hits this point of crisis and never recovers; either levelling out or going backwards from then on. The question is, which executives are affected and why?

The right stuff

The Centre for Creative Leadership research in particular suggests that both successful and derailed executives are very similar in many ways, both being bright, hard-working and motivated with a good track record. The difference, according to their research,[105] was that the successful executives had 'the right stuff', an array of skills, experience and attributes which allowed them to cope with the stresses and difficulties of very high office, namely:

---

105 McCall, M.W. and Lombardo, M.M. (1983) *Off the track: why and how successful executives get derailed* (No. 21). Center for Creative Leadership.

- A wider range of experiences in their career history in terms of the people and environments they had worked with and what they had achieved.

- A greater ability to deal with stress and to be graceful about their own ability to make mistakes.

- A focus on problem solving rather than structures.

- An ability to get along with a wider range of people.

There are many opinions as to what constitutes 'the wrong stuff', i.e. those traits which hold back many executives, but a broad consensus emerged that it was largely due to the lack of the above, namely:

- An inability to delegate efficiently, which becomes more important the greater your responsibilities.

- An inflexibility which, while possibly suited to making sure routine tasks are completed efficiently and to a high standard, becomes a handicap when more creative approaches are needed.

- Most importantly, an inability to get the best out of those they worked with and to attract and retain good subordinates due to a perception of arrogance, aloofness and ambition. This particularly came out under stress, when these executives had a propensity to turn on their subordinates.

It is actually important to have 'people skills'

While other factors have also been pointed to by some, including an inability to learn new things as their executive responsibilities grow, and a lack of technical business skills (which become more of a handicap the further up the ladder they go), the lack of people skills was by far the overriding factor. An unsurprising finding perhaps, when you consider that the main feature of career progression is a lessening of the dependence of executives' success on their own output and a greater dependence on the output of their subordinates.

This handicap, caused by a lack of people skills, becomes greater the further up the ziggurat executives ascend and eventually overwhelms their inherent strengths. Kaiser also acknowledges a role for bad luck in hitting termination; some executives face greater problems earlier on than others. And yet others get all the way to the top before their flaws are revealed.

It also appears that executives are often derailed when they emerge from out of the shadow of a patron, i.e. when they had to take full responsibility for their actions and become true leaders.

Men are from Mars, women are from somewhere very similar to Mars but with a few important differences

The research also shows some interesting gender differences. For women having the 'right stuff' affected their chances of avoiding derailment more. The characteristics of derailed executives was similar for men and women, with the exception that the men tended to have more problems with forming relationships with colleagues, while the women often had an 'image' problem, i.e. they were perceived as not looking like leaders.

Do these findings hold across cultures?

Moving onto the differences between failed executives in different cultures, Kaiser shows how Van Velsor and Leslie[106] found that while derailed executives in Europe and the USA were very similar, it seemed that problems motivating and managing subordinates were more of a handicap in the EU. This research also found that the ability to adapt to change was becoming a more critical determinant of whether executives succeeded or not in both cultures, presumably reflecting the increasing pace of change in business.

Further research by McCall and Hollenbeck[107] has shown that when it comes to expatriate executives, the similarities between failures become far fewer. It seems that traits which are a disadvantage in western business culture (see above) can be an advantage elsewhere. It is thus almost impossible to predict which executives will become successful international managers based on such traits. What does appear to be a good predictor of future success across cultures and positions is self-awareness;[108] when different approaches work in different environments the only real key to success is to be aware of your behaviour as an executive, and be prepared to adapt it if it does not get results.

Conclusion: don't look for a wimp or a tyrant, look for someone who can be both

In his paper *Management Derailment*[109] Kaiser and his co-authors conclude that there are behaviours in four key areas that are good predictors of an executive who is inflexible and insufficiently self-aware and therefore heading for derailment:

---

106 Van Velsor, E. and Leslie, J.B. (1995) *Why executives derail: perspectives across time and cultures. Academy of Management Perspectives*, **9**(4), 62-72.

107 McCall, M.W. and Hollenbeck, G.P. (2002) *Developing global executives*. Boston, MA: Harvard Business School Press.

108 Eichinger, R.W. and Lombardo, M.M. (2003) Knowledge summary series: 360-degree assessment. *Human Resource Planning* **26**(4).

109 Hogan, J., Hogan, R. and Kaiser, R.B. (2010) Management derailment. *APA Handbook of Industrial and Organizational Psychology* **3** 555-575.

- Business skills: they adopt too tactical an approach, aren't strategic enough.

- Leadership: they are unable to develop mutually respectful and trusting relationships with subordinates. They can't delegate properly, inspire or coach their staff.

- Interpersonal: they are incapable of bonding socially with their peers and colleagues.

- Self-management: they are not sufficiently aware of their own behaviour and so when things go wrong it doesn't occur to them that they might be the cause of it.

Fundamentally, when the moment of crisis arrives in an executive's career, they will either rise to the occasion, showing themselves to be adaptable, visionary and a great leader of their staff or the stress will overwhelm them and they will become defensive, bad tempered and rigid in their thinking.

Saving the passengers: how to spot executives before they derail

So how can executives be screened for leadership potential? Surprisingly, research by Kaiser and others when he worked at the Centre for Creative Leadership[110] showed that personality testing is rare in executive level appointments, occurring in only around a third of cases, and in almost all of these the screening focused on the wrong thing, for two reasons:

- It is based on identifying good and bad traits, in the manner outlined above, despite the fact that many of these traits are contentious and can be hard to define in practice. International organizations are also different depending on which culture you're working in.

- It slanted almost entirely towards identifying the 'good' traits in executives and making recommendations based on that. This may miss the fact that someone who is gifted in some areas, e.g. who has a wide range of management styles and an ability to think strategically, may be severely handicapped in others, for example he may also be unable to delegate and loathed by his subordinates.

Kaiser claims that the key, apart from a track record of people skills and a varied career history, is to test executives' personalities for self-awareness and *balance*, i.e. not to concentrate too much on trying to identify traits as 'good' or 'bad' but to see if the executive possesses the capability to recognize that their behaviour can influence the success or not of the organization. To see if they can be both operational and strategic, forceful and empowering, depending on the circumstances, rather than being set irrevocably one way or the other.

---

110 Sessa, V.I., Kaiser, R., Taylor, J.K. and Campbell, R.J. (1998) *Executive selection*. Greensboro, NC: Center for Creative Leadership.

He further recommends that this type of personality testing is combined with a transition plan for executives moving up to new positions, with an integrated feedback system to allow them to spot if their management style is not working.

All very reasonable you might say, but how many of us actually work in an organization that does this?

Written by Jem Smith.

Section Five:

Positive Psychology for Groups and Teams

This section starts by looking at some information about what helps teams work more effectively. We look at the importance of interdependence and the diversity of group membership. We consider ways to help the team work better together and how to create high-performance teams. We also look at specific challenges such as encouraging innovation in team work and working together in a virtual way.

62: Want to know the biggest secret of successful group work?

A short and sweet introduction into one of the key team success factors: interdependency.

It has been convincingly and consistently demonstrated that co-operative groups out-perform individuals working competitively or independently.

However, many group factors (status differentials, tension and stress, social loafing) can act to render a group as ineffective as a bunch of individuals.

So how can you ensure your group works well together?

Make sure they believe their goals are positively linked, so that the progress of one is the progress of all. Then you'll find that:

■ They want each other to be effective, and will invest in each other.

■ They want to collaborate, and will be generous with each other.

■ They want others to succeed, and will be supportive when things are hard.

■ They experience the success of others and will celebrate for each other.

■ They will experience many rewarding moments, and will want to stay engaged.

This chapter is supported by our Udemy for Business video, 'Seven effective ways to maximize team performance',[111] produced in partnership with Skills Booster.

---

111 https://www.udemy.com/building-team-performance/learn/v4/overview

63: Five ways to get your team working more effectively

Teams are the building blocks of organizations. Teams are groups of people who work together to achieve things, but not all groups are teams. Teams are characterized by interdependencies, in other words team members have to work together to get things done. While this interdependency creates the potential for the whole to be more productive and creative than the sum of the parts, it can just as easily be a recipe for frustration and conflict. How can you help your team get the most out of working together?

1. Create a positive working culture

Very few people like to be in an atmosphere that is critical, hostile, unfriendly or cold. Yet many teams manage to create precisely this culture because they focus too much on achieving the task and fail to account for basic human nature. Research over the last ten years has convincingly backed up what many of us intuitively knew; a good working atmosphere makes a huge difference to a team's productivity. What the research found is that the key to the difference between high performing and low performing teams is the ratio of positive to negative comments in team meetings. Interestingly, this doesn't need to be balanced, it needs to be weighted in favour of positive comments, at least by a ratio of 3:1.[112]

A number of things seem to happen once this magic ratio is reached and even more so if the ratio moves closer to 6:1. There is more positive affect; 'good feeling' generated by the group when they are together. When people feel good they are more able to think well, be creative, and to work with others. In addition, people become more willing to contribute ideas, and to work with goodwill through the moments of uncertainty, disconnection or confusion in the conversation until something new emerges. The benefits continue beyond the immediate team meetings, as team members' actions in their own domains are more in sync with their colleagues, and so the departmental interface issues are lessened.

---

112 Losada, M. and Heaphy, E. (2004) The role of positivity and connectivity in the performance of business teams: a nonlinear model. *American Behavioral Scientist* **47**(6) 740-765.

2. Help people play to their strengths

Many people have put much effort into attempting to address their weaknesses over many years to little avail. I know this because I meet them at their 360 feedback sessions somewhere mid-career where they say 'Yes, that always comes up as a weakness, I do try...'. A depressing conversation for both parties.

Recent thinking is that attending more to our strengths will reap greater benefit in terms of performance improvement. This is because when we are using our strengths, work feels effortless, we are energized and confident, we are engaged and probably experience moments of flow. Feeling like this we are more able to be generous and patient with others, so the benefits flow onward. Strengths are an expression of highly developed mental pathways and neutral connections that take minimal effort to enact. Help your team members discover their true strengths and then find ways as a team to utilize everyone's strengths to achieve the team task. Think of your team as an economy of strengths, and work out how to create extra value by trading your strengths.

3. Create commonality amongst team members

Teams are often made up of people with different skill sets and areas of expertise that tend to see the world, and the priorities for action within it, differently. This can lead to a great awareness of difference, and the differences can come to be seen as insurmountable. Yet at the same time there will be areas of commonality amongst team members, often in the areas of core values and central purpose.

A very productive way to access these commonalities is through the sharing of stories. When people are asked to share personal stories of their moments of pride at work, or moments of achievement or success, or the part of their job that means the most to them, they are expressing their values and sense of purpose in an engaging, passionate and easy to hear form. The listener will undoubtedly find that the story resonates with them, creating an emotional connection at the same time as they begin to see the person in a different light. In the best scenarios, as people share their highlight stories, a sense emerges in the room of 'Wow, these are great people I'm working with here, I'd better raise my game!'.

4. Move from the habitual to the generative

Groups can get stuck in repeating dynamic patterns. When this happens listening declines, as everyone believes they know what everyone else is saying, they've heard it all before. And so does the possibility of anything new happening. To break the patterns we need to move from rehearsed speech (which means exactly what it says, speech that has been thought or said so often it just tumbles out) to generative speech (which is the delightful sensation of hearing ourselves say something new).

To help the team make the shift you need to ask questions, or introduce activities, that mean people need to think before they speak, that brings information into the common domain that hasn't been heard before. Positively or appreciatively-framed questions are particularly good for this. So too are imagination-based questions. For example, 'If we woke up tomorrow and we had solved this dilemma, how would we know, what would be different?' 'If we weren't spending our time locked in this conversation, what might we be talking about?' Or 'as if' questions 'If we discuss this as if the customer was in the room with us, what will we be saying?' Sometimes just getting people to all switch from their habitual seating pattern breaks old dynamics and creates new ones.

5. Create future aspirations

When teams suffer a crisis of motivation or morale it is often associated with a lack of hope. A lack of hope that things can get better, a lack of hope in the power and influence of the group or the leader, a lack of hope or belief in the possibility of achieving anything.

Hope and optimism are both great motivators and also key in team resilience. In hopeless situations we need to engender hopefulness. Appreciative Inquiry as an approach is particularly good at doing this, as it first of all discovers the best of the current situation, unearths the hidden resources and strengths of the group, and then goes on to imagine future scenarios based on these very discoveries about what is possible. As people project themselves into optimistic futures clearly connected to the present, they begin to experience some hopefulness. This in turn engenders some motivation to start working towards those more aspirational scenarios of how things can be.

This chapter is supported by our Udemy for Business video 'Seven Effective Ways to Maximize Team Performance',[113] produced in partnership with Skills Booster.

---

113 https://www.udemy.com/building-team-performance/learn/v4/overview

64: Using positive psychology to produce high performing teams

Three key aspects of high performing teams that positive psychology has brought to light.

What is positive psychology?

Coined as a phrase by Martin Seligman as President of the American Psychological Association in 1998,[114] positive psychology is the psychology of exceptionally good living. It embraces areas of study such as happiness; human flourishing; exceptional well-being; energy and vitality, meaningfulness and achievement. The switch in focus from psychology's traditional concern with when things go wrong for people (mental or physical ill-health, poor educational performance etc.) to when things go right for people has resulted in a burst of new streams of research and new knowledge about the psychology of high performance in people.

Three things that make a difference

Three key areas of positive psychology that are relevant to the challenge of team performance are; positivity, strengths and motivation.

1. Positivity

Research in this area can be seen as a quest to answer such questions as: 'What good are good emotions? What purpose do they serve? Why do we have them?' In 2004, Losada and Heaphy[115] discovered that a high ratio of positive to negative comments amongst team members in meetings was a reliable predictor of good performance. They postulate that positive comments lead to positive emotional reactions and we know that positive emotional states are correlated with many group phenomena such as sociability and social bonding; openness to information, creativity, coping with complexity, tenacity and motivation, and virtuous behaviour (patience, generosity etc).

---

114 Seligman, M. (1999) *Presidential address.* The American Psychological Association's 107th Annual Convention, August 21st, 1999.

115 Losada, M. and Heaphy, E. (2004) The role of positivity and connectivity in the performance of business teams: a nonlinear model. *American Behavioral Scientist* **47**(6) 740-765.

All of this acts on the group dynamics in a way that enhances connectivity amongst group members, and promotes greater creative thinking. It also produces an increased ability to act in harmony with other group members and group objectives, even when not in direct contact with each other. The researchers call this dynamic 'synchronicity'. They found that for these effects to be produced, the ratio of positive to negative comments and experiences needs to be between 3:1 and 12:1 positive to negative. Beyond this ratio there is a danger of a lack of critical examination of ideas.

What does this mean?

This means that if we can develop the linguistic habits in our team meetings of: building on the best in the ideas of others rather than knocking them down wholesale; expressing appreciation of helpful comments or contributions; thanking people for pointing out flaws or problems with ideas; laughing together and so on, we can have a direct impact on the performance of the team over time.

2. Strengths

It has always been recognized that people vary in their innate abilities. However, our emphasis in the workplace has often been on trying to help people develop greater skill in their weaker areas. More recently a school of thought has suggested that helping people become better at what they are already good at is a more effective investment. The argument is that a natural strength plus skill in using it, becomes a talent. Helping people understand their particular strengths, and then developing their skill and judgement in using them is being revealed to positively affect performance, well-being, goal attainment, energy levels, authenticity, morale, motivation, fulfilment at work and meaningfulness.

What does this mean?

This means that at least some of your development effort should be focused on helping people understand their strengths profile. That consideration should be given to fitting jobs to people's strengths profiles rather than fitting people to rigid job profiles. That teams should distribute tasks by strengths rather than necessarily by role. It seems likely that the more people are able to use their natural skills at work, a process that people find satisfying and energizing, the more likely they are to deliver dedication and high performance.

3. Motivation

Motivation is a fascinating topic. Why are we motivated to do some things and not others? Why do we find doing some things so rewarding that we will do it for nothing, just for pleasure, and other things you couldn't pay us enough to do? The answers to these questions are many, but a key thought is that it is related to our own unique personality, physiology, history and context. In this way motivation can be understood as a relationship between people's unique needs and values and the environments that satisfy them. Motivation is a response made to an environment that provides opportunities, invitations and incitements to do things that the individual finds motivating. It seems we are motivated to use our strengths and talents because doing so makes us feel 'our best selves': energized, motivated feeling good about ourselves and so able to be at our best with others. If we can find opportunities to use our strengths and talents, we are likely to feel motivated.

What does this mean?

This highlights that motivation is an individual process. Teams have to somehow create opportunities for everyone to feel motivated. This means something in the team process, goal or environment must produce opportunities for people to achieve things desirable to them (their needs and values), and to engage their strengths (energized, committed, meaningful). Appreciative Inquiry as a process facilitates both of these aspects of team working. The discovery phase helps groups and individuals identify existing strengths. The dream phase allows all voices to contribute to the creation of desirable images of the future. While the destiny phase encourages people to volunteer to create movement and progress in areas or projects that are motivating to them.

So how can I use positive psychology to help my team deliver high performance?

- Encourage a positive atmosphere with a good ratio of positive to negative comments.

- Help individuals identify their strengths and enable them to use them in the team endeavour.

- Use Appreciative Inquiry processes to help the team develop a co-created image of the future state towards which they are working, and enable them to contribute to its achievement by using their unique strengths.

65: Five ways to foster innovation using Appreciative Inquiry

A key asset of teams should be their ability to innovate drawing on the diverse range of skills in the team. This chapter suggests how to move to that state.

Appreciative Inquiry is an approach to organizational change and development. Based on five key principles of practice, Appreciative Inquiry helps teams or organizations generate both positive energy and innovative ideas for change.

Appreciative Inquiry is a participative process, and the ideas that emerge from the process have the weight of the group behind them. This active co-creative process means that resistance to change and the need to achieve buy-in are much reduced if not completely eliminated. The action ideas that are generated and agreed are implemented by the very same people who created them.

Here are five ways Appreciative Inquiry can be used with teams or organizations to generate innovative ideas and action:

1. Learn about what stimulates innovation in your context

Discovery interviews are an appreciative process that highlights the best of the past. By exploring past pinnacle experiences of innovation, creativity and inspiring change, you can discover the group's existing resources, skills and knowledge about when, and how, creative and innovative things happen.

Using discovery interviews you can learn about situations, contexts or questions that have been associated with particularly fruitful experiences in the past and actively work to re-create them in the present. In addition, people's current creativity is stimulated by the discussions that follow the questions, and they are likely to feel their creative juices starting to flow.

2. Use stories to jump start imagination

Discovery interviews tend to generate a lot of interesting and often previously untold stories about the topic under discussion. Sharing these stories acts as a spring board to creativity. You can also bring in stories from other contexts that you find inspiring and think might act as a prompt to new thinking.

One way to use stories gathered during a round of discovery interviews is to share the story and then spend time brainstorming what ideas it has stimulated about the particular current context you are working in. Just leave them, or record them as possibilities, and move on to the next story.

3. Ask generative questions

Questions can produce new conversation and insights, or they can stimulate old patterns of conversation. Questions that produce new thoughts, connections and ideas; in other words that are likely to generate innovative insights and ideas for action, tend to have certain characteristics.

Element of novelty and surprise

They have an element of novelty and surprise; they are questions that people haven't considered before and may well be surprised to be asked. Many positively-framed questions are of this nature. However, imagination-based questions, or questions that ask people to combine two seemingly opposed ideas can also have this effect of producing new thought.

Relationship building

They act to build relationships as people discover new things about each other: positive, inspiring and attractive things. They start to develop good feelings about each other and to develop mutual positive connections. Connections to others are key to successful change efforts. People need to feel needed, supported and valued to want to engage with the many challenges of working with others to achieve things.

They are meaningful

Good discovery questions connect to things that are deeply meaningful to the participants. These are questions about important things: my work, my values, my experience. By asking about what matters to people and giving express permission to answer with reference to feelings, they act to ensure that people are psychologically engaged with the question, answer and process, not just rationally engaged.

They cause a shift in understanding of 'reality'

Good generative questions act to reframe reality for individuals and the group. They do this by focusing on aspects of the context that are overlooked or ignored. In the simplest terms this means asking about positive things when 'the reality' is perceived to be wholly negative. The answers reveal many more positive things going on than people believed was the case, so their reality shifts.

Designing questions that have all these characteristics takes thought.

4. Dream together

An important part of the Appreciative Inquiry process is 'dreaming'. This process involves using our imagination to leap out of the present, over the many current, obvious problems and barriers to change, to a time in the future where we have achieved our aspirations to be better.

A good dreaming process acts to fire up the imagination and stimulates people to create attractive and hopeful images of the future. Usually a number of different groups create their own dreams and then the sharing of the dreams is another source of inspiration for individuals and the group as a whole.

In the same way that good science fiction creates impossible ideas that may inspire future scientists, so good dreaming sessions expand the group's sense of the possible. The creative horizon expands.

5. Improvise destiny

And finally, Appreciative Inquiry is attuned to the improvisational nature of creative efforts. At the end of an AI workshop the group as a whole should have a shared sense of where they want to be heading, and the kind of futures they want to be creating. With this shared sense acting as the 'roadmap', people need to be given permission to get on with making it happen, to be enabled to take voluntary and visible action, while the leader's role becomes that of creating coherence and connection.

We stock some excellent Appreciative Inquiry cards[116] at our online store. Very helpful if you are new to this area of practice.

---

116 https://www.acukltd.com/store/a-taste-of-ai-20-appreciating-people

66: What I learnt about virtual team working while preparing for the World Appreciative Inquiry Conference

This was one of my first experience of trying to work virtually with people in different countries and time zones. I found it a most dispiriting experience, with a happy ending. This offers little advice, only observations on my reality and the impact of the experience on me.

At the World Appreciative Inquiry Conference I co-presented a symposium with four other people from three other countries: France, Denmark and The Netherlands. We also originally had a sixth partner from Greece, but the economic situation there meant he had to drop out; another story. In preparing for our presentation across time and country borders, I learnt something about the realities of virtual team working.

The original face-to-face meeting

The six of us originally met up in Manchester after the European Appreciative Inquiry network meeting when Cora, a Dutch colleague, pulled us together with an idea of developing a submission for the World Appreciative Inquiry Conference. As usual at the end of an intense two days I was exhausted. I was flattered to be invited to join the group, and happy just to flop down somewhere with a coffee. I just kept saying yes and so found I had agreed to working together over the internet to get this proposal together. I agreed because with the group I felt warm, included, valued. I didn't know any of the others particularly well but well enough to feel confident in the group's ability to produce something.

Virtual disharmony

So we all went off our separate ways. I think we had three internet meetings. None went smoothly, and I felt bad about each one. The first I arrived late to, partly because of the time difference and partly because it was in the evening and I resented having to be at my computer at 8pm at night. Of course, when I found the others all there I felt bad.

The second one was better and I felt I redeemed myself a bit by volunteering to do some stuff. The last one was awful. No one could get the technology to work and so my evening was ticking by and I was hungry for my dinner. I think it was 30-45 minutes before we were all in contact. Then I got completely distracted as it seemed I hadn't done something I had been asked to do when I was sure I had done everything I had promised. This meant I was searching through past papers and records to justify myself rather than listening. I did not spend these internet meetings in a particularly appreciative frame, it was hard work staying even near an appreciative place. They didn't make me feel good about myself. Eventually we agreed that we would meet on the first evening of the conference to finalize things.

The value of glances

So we gathered. Immediately it felt good to be together. The process continued to be fraught with stress and under pressure yet it still felt good as a process. I was thinking about what made the difference between how it felt face-to-face and how it felt over the internet.

Two key things I noticed

- Face-to-face we could touch each other. It is amazing how much we use casual touch to reinforce, soften, apologize, support etc.

- We could exchange glances with other people as someone was talking, checking out we are still OK, sharing something, catching their eye to communicate something.

In other words, as the words worked to sort out our session, finalize details, raise questions etc, our non-verbals worked to connect, to transmit and create positive affect about and for each other, to sort out and resolve minor misalignments.

I am often asked about virtual team working and don't usually have a very helpful answer. This experience has made it clear to me the high relational value of face-to-face interactions. I know they can't always be arranged and they are expensive, but internet contact is no substitute. No doubt it can be done better than we did it, but it cannot offer the richness of the relational communication of face-to-face interaction.

The difference showed up, for me, in my mood, level of engagement, feelings towards the group, ability to be patient, helpful and so on.

67: Women make groups cleverer! Evidence for collective intelligence

I found this research very interesting.

Fascinating research on group performance suggests two key things:

- That the collective intelligence of a group is more than the sum of its parts.
- That the presence of women in a group is key to high collective intelligence.

How do we know this?

Researchers[117] worked with 699 people, divided them into groups of three to five people and set them various tasks. The wide range of these tasks was designed to measure all sorts of different aspects of intelligence. These included visual puzzles, brainstorming, making collective moral judgments, and negotiating over limited resources. They also measured the individual intelligence of everyone. They then tried to see how the individual intelligence scores related to the team's performance scores.

When they did a factor analysis of the group performance scores and the intelligence measures, they found one factor that accounted for 43% of the variance and that was not related to either average intelligence of group members or the maximum intelligence score. It seemed to be something over and above a simple aggregate of intelligence. They consider this factor to represent a measure of the group's collective intelligence, with collective intelligence defined as 'the general ability of the group to perform a wide variety of tasks'. The suggestion is that collective intelligence is an emergent group phenomenon that is a product of more than just the existing intelligence in the group.

They ran three different studies of this type and compared results. The findings held. On each occasion collective intelligence was found to better account for group performance than measures of individual member intelligence.

---

117 Woolley, A.W., Chabris, C.F., Pentland, A., Hashmi, N. and Malone, T.W. (2010) Evidence for a collective intelligence factor in the performance of human groups. *Science* **33**(6004), 686-688.

So, if individual intelligence doesn't account for group intelligence, what does? The researchers moved on to examine a number of group and individual factors that might be predictors of collective intelligence. Interestingly many of the factors that are thought to be associated with group performance, such as group cohesion, motivation and satisfaction, didn't predict group performance.

The findings

Instead they found:

- That there is a group factor of collective intelligence, conceptually similar to the idea of the individual factor of general intelligence, that has a global effect on performance on many different tasks, and accounts for 43% of the variance in performance. It is also strongly predictive of performance.

- That collective intelligence is not strongly correlated with the average or maximum intelligence in the group.

- That collective intelligence is strongly correlated with the average social sensitivity of the group members. This is the strongest predictive factor of group collective intelligence, which, in turn, is a strong predictor of group task performance on a wide range of tasks.

- That collective intelligence is strongly correlated with the equality of distribution of turn taking.

- That collective intelligence is strongly correlated with the proportion of women in the group.

It is suspected that the last correlation is related to the others e.g. that the presence of women tends to increase the social sensitivity and the equality of turn-taking in the group.

What to do to improve or enhance the collective intelligence of your project or work groups?

- Help the group recognize that collective intelligence in group decision making and performance is an emergent phenomena of group interaction patterns.

- Help the group recognize that the emotional life of the group is as important as its intellectual life.

- Ensure their discussion processes allow all voices to be heard, and that people take turns to talk, and to listen.

- Ensure that the group is mixed by gender.

Section Six:

The Importance of Positive Emotions at Work

This section makes clear the impact of our emotional state on our behaviour and work performance, while also suggesting many ways to help people feel good at work. We look at how happiness relates to success, performance and productivity. We look at the impact of politeness and rudeness at work. We explore the impact of gratitude and forgiveness on relationships at work. We look at hope and its importance in creating change. And finally we explore the idea of willpower: what affects it and what it affects.

68: What good are positive emotions?

This chapter offers a brief outline of Fredrickson's broaden and build theory of positive emotions.

Emotions can be conceptualized as short-lived experiences that produce co-ordinated change in people's thoughts, actions and physiological responses; that is, when we feel a certain way, we are more or less inclined and prepared to act a certain way. With negative emotions some of the thought-action-physiological responses are well documented e.g. the fight/flight response. When we experience strong negative emotions our perceptual field and our range of thought-action repertoires narrows. Essentially this works to increase our chances of survival in win/lose situations: negative emotions[118] can be seen as a way of signalling that we are in a win/lose situation. But what about positive emotions?

The broaden and build theory of positive emotions

Fredrickson[119] suggests that when we experience positive emotion, our repertoire of thought-action responses and our scope of attention broaden, rather than narrow. This means:

■ We become more playful, exploratory, and integrative (that is, able to process our experience as it is happening).

■ We have an increased preference for variety.

■ We have access to a bigger range of behaviour.

■ We become are more able intellectually to deal with complexity and diversity.

■ We can cope better with chronic stress.

This behaviour in turn allows us to build our resources such as:

■ Physical resources e.g. skills and our health.

■ Social resources e.g. friendships and social support networks.

---

118 We no longer refer to emotions this way, preferring to refer to 'unpleasant', 'less pleasant' or 'unhelpful' emotions, depending on the context.

119 Fredrickson, B. and Branigan, C. (2005) Positive emotions broaden the scope of attention and thought-action repertoires. *Cognition and Emotion* **19**(3) 313-332.

■ Intellectual resources such as knowledge, understanding of others, intellectual complexity.

■ Psychological resources e.g. optimism, creativity, resilience.

These outcomes are durable, persisting after the transitory emotional state. The resources, built while we are feeling good, are available to us in times of adversity. Feeling good indicates to us that we are in a win/win situation.

The message for managers?

It's good for your people to feel good, and it's good for your organization's ability to be creative, innovative, flexible, communicative, deal with stress, think outside the box, and to look beyond the obvious. What have you done today to help someone experience a burst of positive emotion?

69: Does happiness contribute to success? Reasons to be cheerful

This chapter outlines the exciting research suggesting that happiness influences success, as well as vice versa.

While much research confirms that successful outcomes can foster happiness, it has tended to be seen as a one-way linear relationship: you have to be successful to be happy. But might it be more of a circular relationship? A virtuous circle where being happy makes it more likely you will succeed? In 2005 Sonja Lyubomirsky, Ed Diener and Laura King[120] pulled together all the research they could find that addressed the question: does happiness contribute to success?

What does it mean to be happy?

Happy people are those who frequently experience positive emotions such as joy, interest and pride. They experience negative emotions such as sadness, anxiety and anger less frequently. It is this ratio of time spent in positive rather than negative moods that predicts those who define themselves as 'happy people'. From other research we know that the ratio needs to be 3:1 or above to start to move us to describe ourselves as generally 'happy'.[121]

One suggestion is that happy people feel positive emotions more frequently because they are more sensitive to rewards in their environment. In other words, they find more reasons to be cheerful.

How might feeling happy help us succeed?

It seems that experiencing positive moods and emotions leads us to think, feel and act in ways that add to our resourcefulness and that helps us reach our goals. Positive emotions, it appears, are a signal to us that life is going well, that our goals are being met and our resources are adequate. Since all is going well, we feel we can spend time with friends, learn new skills, or relax and rebuild our

---

120 Lyubomirsky, S., Diener, E. and King, L. (2005) The benefits of positive affect: does happiness lead to success? *Psychological Bulletin* **131**(6) 803-855.

121 Fredrickson, B. and Losada, M. (2005) Positive affect and the complex dynamics of human flourishing. *American Psychologist* **60**(7) 678-686.
Authors note – while the statistical methods in both this and the Losada and Heaphy papers have been criticized, the general ratio finding still holds, being supported by other research.

energy reserves. We are also likely to seek out new goals, to plan a new project, or get started on booking that holiday, for instance. We can compare this with when we are in a negative mood state, when our concern can become to protect our existing resources and to avoid being hurt or damaged in some way.

Lyubomirsky and colleagues reviewed 225 papers and found that feeling good is associated with things like feeling confident and optimistic, feeling capable, sociability, seeing the best in others, activity and energy, helpfulness, immunity and physical well-being, effectively coping with challenge and stress and originality and flexibility. We can easily see how these would help with motivation and tenacity in achieving goals.

Some of their findings

- Positive affect and job performance is bi-directional e.g. each affects the other.

- Happy people seem to be more successful at work, in their relationships and experience better health.

- Happy people set higher goals for themselves.

- Happy people are more willing to do things beyond the call of duty.

- Happy people are more successful across domains of marriage, friendship, income, work performance and health.

So effectively yes, happiness does lead to success.

What does all this mean for us?

The key to happiness is frequent positive mood states that outweigh negative mood states by at least a 3:1 ratio. When we are happy, good things are more likely to happen and we can generally cope with life better. To proactively manage our mood states is a good investment for us and our organizations.

Some questions to help you think how to use this information:

- How well do you know your mood boosters?

- How do you find reasons to be cheerful, and how do you help others to do that?

- How effectively do you build them into your daily, even hourly life?

- How good are you at spotting when the ratio is slipping and finding a way to boost your mood?

- How can you help others with this?

70: Happy workers are more productive

A short account of the findings of a meta-analysis with advice on how to apply it.

Psychologists have long struggled to support their humanist belief that happy workers offer more value with any evidence. A recent review of research in this area suggests we can now confidently assert that looking after your employees makes good business sense.

Recent meta-analysis of research[122] in this area suggests:

- There is a positive relationship between worker satisfaction and production.

- This correlates with higher customer loyalty, lower staff turnover, and higher revenue or sales.

- This also shows in behaviour such as being more co-operative, helpful, punctual, time-efficient, and taking fewer absences.

So how to achieve this marvellous state of affairs? The answers lie with the growing understanding of positive psychology, from which we know:

- Leaders' positive emotion levels predict the performance of the entire workforce.

- High performing teams have a ratio of positive to negative interactions of greater than 3:1 and less than 10:1.

- Positive mood, humour and appreciation affect team climate and productivity.

- Excellence is based on maximising the use of strengths, not remedying deficits.

So the message for leaders is:

- Be positive and upbeat, encourage the same mood amongst your employees.

- Adapt and grow jobs around people, don't modify people to fit jobs.

- Make sure your people feel good at work.

---

122 Page, N. and Boyle, S. (2005) Putting positive psychology to work. *Selection and Development Review* **21**(5) 18.

71: Did you know: facts about the impact of emotional states on performance

Sometimes we want the data. This chapter collects together some key persuasive research findings about the benefits of positive psychology at work.

Lots of people feel instinctively that happiness and well-being at work must be important. But are they a business necessity or a 'nice to have'? Surely it makes more sense to ensure your business is profitable and thriving before you start worrying about how people feel?

Increasingly research suggests that investing in employee well-being by ensuring positive work relationships, an emphasis on strengths-based development and worker happiness, has productivity pay-offs. So why delay, start promoting positive psychology practices at work today.

Here is a selection of evidence-based support for the promotion of positive psychology e.g. happiness and well-being at work. It is clear from the evidence that a large component of the happiness we feel is within our control, and that many, more than 50% of the population, are functioning at a less than optimal state. And that our emotional state affects our performance and productivity at work.

- 40% of the variation we experience in our sense of happiness, compared to others, is within our control. 10% is due to circumstances beyond our control and 50% due to our genetic make-up and inheritance which dictates our set point of happiness. Our 40% variance is influenced by 'intentional activity'. In other words we can affect the happiness of ourselves and others. The research behind this assertion is based on twin studies (the genetic component) and the long-lasting effect of changing circumstances on happiness levels (the circumstances) leaving 40% of the variation due to individual actions.[123]

---

123 Lyubomirsky, S., Sheldon, K.M. and Schkade, D. (2005) Pursuing happiness: the architecture of sustainable change. *Review of General Psychology* **9**(2) 111.

- 54% of Americans are 'moderately mentally healthy' meaning they aren't mentally ill but they lack great enthusiasm for life and are not actively and productively engaged with the world. 11% languish, i.e. they are functioning just above the level of clinical depression.[124]

- Exercise can be as effective at treating clinical depression as medication, and have an effect for longer.[125]

- People whose managers focus on their strengths are 2.5 times more likely to be engaged at work than those whose managers focus on their weaknesses.[126]

- Highly engaged employees take, on average, three sick days per annum, actively disengaged employees, six or more per year.[127]

- On average employees take six days absence a year, although it can be up to 20 days in the public sector, the most happy average only 1.5 days absence a year, in the UK and USA. Liking your colleagues produces the same correlation with absence.[128]

- Engaged employees give 57% more discretionary effort at work.[129]

- Doctors in a positive mood before making a diagnosis make the correct diagnosis 19% faster than those who were in a neutral state.[130]

- In a major fast food company an intervention to reduce management turnover (the retention of managers being a major problem for this sector) using Appreciative Inquiry led to a retention rate 30% higher than when problem-solving techniques were used.[131]

124 Keyes, C.L. (2005) Mental illness and/or mental health? Investigating axioms of the complete state model of health. *Journal of Consulting and Clinical Psychology* **73**(3) 539.

125 Blumenthal, J.A., Babyak, M.A., Moore, K.A., Craighead, W.E., Herman, S., Khatri, P. and Doraiswamy, P.M. (1999) Effects of exercise training on older patients with major depression. *Archives of Internal Medicine* **159**(19) 2349-2356.

126 Rath, T. (2007) *Strengthsfinder 2.0*. New York: Gallup Press.

127 Stairs, M. and Gilpin, M. (2010) Positive engagement: from employee engagement to work place happiness. In: Linley, P.A., Harrington, S. and Garcea, N. (eds) *Oxford handbook of positive psychology and work*. Oxford: Oxford University Press.

128 Pryce-Jones, J. (2010) *Happiness at work: maximising your psychological capital for success*. Chichester: Wiley-Blackwell.

129 Stairs, M. and Gilpin, M. (2010) Positive engagement: from employee engagement to work place happiness. In: Linley, P.A., Harrington, S. and Garcea, N. (eds) *Oxford handbook of positive psychology and work*. Oxford: Oxford University Press.

130 Estrada, C.A., Isen, A.M. and Young, M.J. (1997) Positive affect facilitates integration of information and decreases anchoring in reasoning among physicians. *Organizational Behavior and Human Decision Processes* **72**(1) 117-135.

131 Jones, D.A. (1998) A field experiment in Appreciative Inquiry. Organization Development Journal **16**(4) 69.

- The happiest people at work are 180% more energized than the unhappiest, they contribute 25% more and achieve their goals 30% more. They are 47% more productive, meaning they are contributing a day and a quarter more than their least happy colleagues per week.[132]

- The happiest are 50% more motivated than the least happy.[133]

- People who are happier are 25% more effective and efficient than those who are least happy.[134]

- Feelings and behaviour are contagious: negative behaviour has a ripple effect to two degrees, but positive behaviour can reach to three degrees.[135]

- The more you want recognition, the less you want money in its place.[136]

- We lose 40% of our productivity flip-flopping between tasks – three lost hours in a typical eight hour day.[137]

132 Pryce-Jones, J. (2010) *Happiness at work: maximising your psychological capital for success*. Chichester: Wiley-Blackwell.

133 Pryce-Jones, J. (2010) *Happiness at work: maximising your psychological capital for success*. Chichester: Wiley-Blackwell.

134 *Ibid* Pryce-Jones.

135 Barsade, S.G. (2002) The ripple effect: emotional contagion and its influence on group behavior. *Administrative Science Quarterly* **47**(4) 644-675.

136 Pryce-Jones, J. (2010) *Happiness at work: maximising your psychological capital for success*. Chichester: Wiley-Blackwell.

137 APA (2006) *Multi-tasking: switching costs* [online]. Available at: https://www.apa.org/research/action/multitask.aspx (accessed March 2019).

72: Did you know that seeking happiness can make people unhappy?

But be aware, the pursuit of happiness can produce paradoxical effects

While we recognize that in general happiness is a crucial ingredient of well-being and health, happiness is not valued to the same extent by everyone. For some people it is a 'nice to have' while for others it is the stuff of life, a state to which they constantly aspire. Goal pursuit theory suggests that if we value something and actively pursue it we should experience more of it.

However, there is a sting in the tail. The more highly we value something, the higher the standards are likely to be against which we evaluate our achievement of it. So, for instance, if I value academic excellence and strive hard to achieve it, I'm not going to be very satisfied with just a 'pass' grade: it hasn't met my standards of a great mark.

Importantly, while my disappointment with my mark doesn't change it, if my goal is to achieve happiness, my disappointment with the level of happiness I am experiencing DOES affect my level of happiness. To be disappointed is incompatible in the moment with feeling happy. Of course, expectations are context specific: most people don't expect to feel happy at a funeral, but might well expect to feel happy at a party.

If I'm at a party and DON'T feel as I expected I would, e.g. happy, then I am likely to feel disappointed. And the disappointed feeling will lower my happiness. If I had not had any expectations of feeling happy then I wouldn't feel disappointed by not feeling happy and, paradoxically, might actually feel happier than the disappointed person!

In other words, by valuing happiness very highly, and making it a goal and measure of value, we produce the very circumstances that raise the likelihood of disappointment and adversely affect our chances of achieving happiness. The pursuit of happiness may cause decreased happiness.

Considering all this, Mauss *et al* [138] concluded:

'... *valuing happiness is not necessarily linked to greater happiness. In fact, under certain conditions the opposite is true. Under conditions of low (but not high) life stress, the more people valued happiness, the lower were their hedonic balance* [ratio of positive to negative emotional states], *psychological well-being, and life satisfaction, and the higher their depressive symptoms.*'

In short, an overly-focused pursuit of happiness is unlikely to lead to greater happiness.

We need to recognize that we experience all sorts of emotions and while happiness can be encouraged by the way we live our lives it can't be produced to order: it is not a guaranteed outcome of any activity.

I wonder if the huge increase of reported depression in the world is in any way related to this strange paradox. Have we somehow, with our twenty-first century interest in and emphasis on happiness, raised expectations about how much happiness people should feel, maybe even to the extent that all non-happy feelings are experienced as strong failure and disappointment? My mother used to say to me '*I don't mind what you do* [as a career], *as long as you are happy*'. For her happiness was the goal and measure of success. Even then I struggled to understand the advice as I didn't understand how to 'be happy': I didn't know what made me happy. Finding that out has been a life-long journey.

My father, conversely, pointed out to me long before it became a poster slogan, '*Happiness is a journey not a destination*', or to misquote John Lennon: '*Happiness happens while you are concentrating on something else*'. And finally, my own resolution of this paradox: happiness is a happy by-product of the life lived and the choices made.

---

138 Mauss, I.B., Tamir, M., Anderson, C.L. and Savino, N.S. (2011) Can seeking happiness make people unhappy? Paradoxical effects of valuing happiness. *Emotion* **11**(4) 807.

73: The hidden costs of rudeness

Manners matter.

We all know rudeness is an unpleasant aspect of life, did you also know it has a cost attached? Two researchers, Porath and Erez,[139] have spent years exploring the effect of rudeness on people at work, this is what they have found:

- Between 1998 and 2005 the percentage of employees who reported experiencing rudeness once or more in a week doubled from almost 25% to almost 50%. Indeed in 2005 25% of employees reported experiencing rudeness at least once a day.

- Surveys reveal that after experiencing rudeness most people lose time and focus, make efforts to avoid the person, work less and slack off more, and think more about leaving the organization.

- Experiments by Porath and Erez have demonstrated direct adverse effects of experiencing or even just observing rudeness on cognitive performance e.g. problem-solving, flexibility of thinking, creativity and helpfulness. Experiencing rudeness also increases a propensity to aggressive and violent thoughts and actions.

- In addition, 94% of people get even with the rude person or with their organization (88%).

- It seems that 'processing' the rude encounter engages brain resources so that less is available for attention and memory, making us temporarily 'less clever'.

- These effects occur even in a culture of habitual rudeness, in other words even if a level of rudeness or incivility is normal in your organization it doesn't mean people are inured against the effects.

- Rudeness has a contagion effect: it makes us less likely to help people not even involved in the incident, and to be ruder and more aggressive than we might have been.

So, a culture of rudeness in an organization has hidden costs of:

- Reduced performance.
- Poorer problem solving.
- Rigidity of thinking.

---

139 Porath, C.L. and Erez, A. (2011) How rudeness takes its toll. *Psychologist* **24**(7), 508-511.

- Less 'citizenship' behaviour e.g. general helpfulness.

- Reduced creativity.

- People avoiding contact with certain others (who might have information they need).

- Heightened tendencies to aggressive words or even actions.

- 'Vendettas' of getting even being played out in the organization.

The effect of this on suppliers and customer relationships, as well as internal relations, is not hard to imagine.

Politeness pays

Interestingly, Kim Cameron[140] and others at the University of Michigan have been examining the effect of 'virtuous behaviour' on employees and organizations. They have found a similar but polar opposite effect, that is, the more people experience virtuous behaviour from others: helpfulness, forgiveness, generosity, courage, honesty, support etc., or indeed just witness it, the more likely they are to demonstrate such behaviour themselves. Such behaviour also has the effect of raising levels of 'feeling good', which is strongly associated with flexible and complex thinking, creativity, good team work and so on.

How much are poor manners costing your organization? And what can you do about it?

1. Create a culture of civility and politeness, led right from the top.

2. Treat 'manner' of management as a performance issue, as well as outcomes.

3. Keep stress levels down for people: stressed people are more likely to 'lash out' at others.

4. Have a code of conduct that makes it clear that people have a right to be treated in a civil manner, and act on complaints.

5. Take bullying seriously.

6. Help those who have a hot head to develop compensatory tactics, particularly the ability to eat humble pie and to seek forgiveness after an uncontrolled outburst.

7. Encourage managers to recognize power as a privilege, not a stick with which to beat others.

---

140 Cameron, K.S. (2003) Organizational virtuousness and performance. In: Cameron, K.S., Dutton, J.E. and Quinn, R.E. (2003) *Positive organizational scholarship: foundations of a new discipline*. Oakland, CA: Berrett-Koehler Publishers.

8. Beware those who are deferential to those above them and demonic to those below.

9. Emphasize that difficult issues can be tackled without resorting to shouting or belittling, and model how.

10. Beware of the hidden costs of the 'high performer' who is also known to be consistently aggressive and rude to his or her staff: the cost of the means might actually outweigh the benefits of the ends.

74: Thank you makes a difference

On the other hand...

We are all taught that it is polite to be grateful, but does it make any other difference? Recent research suggests yes, including in the workplace. Most people feel gratitude frequently and it makes them feel good to feel grateful. Gratitude motivates reciprocal aid giving. It can be considered as an emotion, a behaviour and a personality trait.[141]

As an emotion

- As an emotion, gratitude acts as a moral barometer, drawing attention to help received; it can also encourage a behavioural response (offering help). And the expression of gratitude can act as an effective positive reinforcer to the behaviour for which it is expressed.

- How likely we are to feel grateful also seems to relate to our estimates of the value of the help, how costly it was to provide and whether it was altruistically intended.

- Expressing sincere gratitude can raise happiness levels for up to a month. Conscious cultivation of feelings of gratitude by identifying three good things about your life each evening is very self-reinforcing and increases happiness levels. The effects seem very durable.

As a personality characteristic

- As a personality characteristic it seems that some people feel much more gratitude than others.

- People who express extensive gratitude are more likely to have higher levels of happiness and lower levels of depression and stress.

- It has one of the strongest links with mental health of any personality variable.

---

141 Emmons, R. and Mishra, A. (2011) Why gratitude enhances well-being: what we know, what we need to know'. In: Sheldon, K., Kashdan. T. and Steger, M. (eds.) *Designing positive psychology: taking stock and moving forward.* Oxford: Oxford University Press.

As an aid to social relations

■ Gratitude is uniquely important in social relationships, contributing to an upward spiral of helping and mutual support.

■ People who do not experience gratitude may not notice they have been helped and may not reciprocate, thus decreasing the likelihood that they will receive help in future.

■ Grateful people are seen as more empathetic, agreeable and extroverted. They are more likely to be seen as helpful and unselfish with others.

■ Those who express gratitude are more likely to see the world as friendly and hospitable.

So the moral of the story for managers is...

■ Be grateful.

■ Encourage others to be grateful and to directly express their gratitude sincerely to anyone to whom they feel grateful.

■ Encourage people to notice when they have been helped and to express their appreciation of the help.

■ Offer help to others to encourage the creation and maintenance of mutual reciprocity.

75: Why it is important to learn to forgive those who trespass against us

This chapter explains why cultivating forgiveness is essential to our well-being, never mind that of our transgressor.

Why this is an ability we should all cultivate

Forgiveness has an image problem. Asked to forgive people say: 'But I can't forget what they did' or 'I can't imagine ever being friends again' or 'But I want them punished'. These responses show a confusion between forgiveness, reconciliation, forgetting and justice.[142]

To forgive doesn't mean forgetting, it doesn't mean reconciling and it doesn't mean letting people off e.g. ignoring, minimizing, tolerating or excusing the offending behaviour. Nor does it mean minimizing an injustice, putting up with ill-treatment or allowing an offender to harm again. It is not about meekly turning the other cheek. It is a personal process that may or not be expressed directly to the offender. While knowing you have been forgiven is clearly likely to have an impact on the offender, I want to focus here on the benefits to us of learning to be more forgiving of others, whether we tell our offender about it or not.

Forgiveness is a gracious and courageous response that enables the forgiver to lessen the power of the transgression to define him or her. Forgiveness remembers the past in a way that opens up positive futures.

It tends to be a process that unfolds over time, slowly replacing the desire for revenge or avoidance and replacing unforgiving emotions such as bitterness and fear.

Techniques that help foster forgiveness

- One thing that helps induce feelings of forgiveness is focusing on the offender's humanity: to err is human.

- Another is to see the action as distinct, not defining. Thus we might say: 'they lied' rather than 'they are a liar'.

---

142 Van Oyen Witvliet, C. (2013) Forgiveness. In: Lopez J.L. (ed.) *The Encyclopaedia of Positive Psychology.* Chichester: Wiley-Blackwell.

- Developing feelings of compassion or mercy also helps, reflected in sentiments such as, 'I can't condone what they did but I can see how they were driven to it', or perhaps, 'I can see there were some muddled good intentions in there, but that doesn't excuse what they did to me'.

- These are pro-social responses of empathy and compassion that express a desire for genuine and ultimate good. Such responses act to edge out the hurt and bitter responses. Forgiveness responds to harm with grounded hope. Hope is a key positive emotion for moving forward in life.

What helps us to forgive?

- Forgiveness begins (and this is unexpected to many) by accurately naming and blaming the offender for the harm done.

- A strong religious identity and commitment helps (but not just 'being spiritual'), as does feeling empathy or compassion for the offender.

- Having a more agreeable personality and having a closer and more committed relationship before the offense (with the exception as outlined below) also aid forgiveness.

What makes it harder to forgive?

Having a hostile personality or narcissistic tendencies makes it harder to forgive in general, while depression adversely affects the ability to forgive in close relationships.

Why should we forgive?

- Correlational research suggests that people with more forgiving personalities have less anxiety and lower blood pressure. Those with unforgiving personalities have worse self-esteem, greater depression and anxiety, and often exhibit post-traumatic stress disorder symptoms e.g. nightmares, sleep difficulties. Those who have trouble forgiving themselves suffer the worst!

- Experimental research demonstrates that as people learn to forgive they show increased self-esteem, hope, positive attitudes towards their offender and a desire for reconciliation. They also generally experience reductions in grief, depression, anxiety and anger. They also experience increases in positive affective responses, that is, they are better able to experience positive emotions.

- Interestingly, those who focus first on forgiveness to restore their own happiness (rather than focusing on the offender), make faster progress. However, in the long run, those who seek to forgive out of altruistic compassion and concern for the offender ultimately experience greater self-benefits.

- Other lines of research have shown that unforgiving reactions, such as mental rehearsal of the painful event, arouse strong negative emotions such as fear, anger and sadness; create muscle tension around the eyebrows and eyes; and are associated with higher levels of blood pressure, heart rate and sweating. Empathetic and forgiving reactions have significant positive and calming effects.

So what to do?

- Attempt to understand the transgressive behaviour without minimizing or excusing it.

- Focus on compassion for the humanity of the offender (to err is human, and none of us are perfect).

- Forgive, e.g. replace the hurt and bitter feelings with a genuine attempt to wish the offender well.

These empathetic and forgiving responses prompt greater positive and relaxing emotions, joy and a sense of having more control in the situation, with a calmer physiological profile.

76: Creating hope in a hopeless situation

This chapter presents Cooperrider's equation for elevation.

In the summer of 2015 I presented a workshop at the World Appreciative Inquiry Conference. Hot from seeing David Cooperrider[143] at the World Positive Psychology Congress in Orlando, I started by introducing his positive power equation:

The experience of elevation = $\dfrac{\text{willpower + waypower + wholepower}}{\text{experience of deficit}}$

Elevation is the emotion that empowers us to reach for, and bring to the world, the best in ourselves. It is the process by which we are inspired by others displaying exceptional virtue. It is a process released by the Appreciative Inquiry processes, particularly the discovery process, which releases stories of people, teams, and organizations at their best, in a shared space where they can impact on the consciousness of others.

This emotion is released and this state is enacted when hope (made up of willpower and 'waypower': a desire to do something and a way of doing it) is experienced by a whole system in a way that overwhelms the experience of deficit, that is, the experience of problems, fatalism, isolation and a lack of hope.

It explains how it is possible to create proactivity, hope and optimism in seemingly hopeless situations.

---

143 Cooperrider, D. (2015) *Mirror flourishing: Appreciative Inquiry and the designing of positive institutions.* Keynote talk at Fourth World Congress on Positive Psychology, Orlando, Florida June 25-27th.

77: How to not eat that chocolate bunny all at once!

This chapter was produced around Easter one year, it explains how willpower works (or not!).

Few events encourage us to indulge our chocoholic sweet tooth quite as extravagantly as Easter. Chocolate eggs the size of rugby balls, filled with more chocolate, fill the shelves of even the meanest corner shop. As our children assemble their chocolate hoard from generous friends and relatives, we admonish them not to eat them it at once, indeed we may even put some aside in a place only we can reach so we can ration their consumption.

But what about our own hoard of chocolate, who is going to act as quartermaster for us? For most of us the answer is our own willpower, and recent research suggests willpower to be an unreliable friend. Ever wondered why, immediately after you have eaten a sensible few chunks putting the rest away until next week seems an eminently sensible and easy idea, yet three hours later as you open the fridge to get the milk for your tea, the chocolate nestling in its silver foil leaps into your hand?

Willpower, it turns out, is like a muscle. Indeed, it is sometimes known as the moral muscle. Every time we resist doing something we want to do, or make ourselves do something we don't want to do, we wear it out a little bit and have less left to resist the next temptation. It turns out that thinking hard, making complex decisions and using our initiative also all drain our reserves of willpower.

The effect of using willpower in one area is immediately evident in another. Hungry students sat waiting for an experiment in the presence of biscuits they were told not to eat, persevered less with the difficult task that followed: drawing on their willpower to resist the urge to grab a biscuit they had less left to make themselves persist with a difficult task.[144]

It gets worse. It transpires that willpower strength is related to body glucose levels: eating refreshes our glucose levels and restores a level of willpower. It was discovered that judges adjudicating on parole boards were statistically more likely to grant parole requests at the start of the day (after breakfast)

---

144 Baumeister, R.F., Vohs, K.D. and Tice, D.M. (2007) The strength model of self-control. *Current Directions in Psychological Science* **16**(6) 351-355.

and after lunch. Assessing risk and saying 'yes' is harder than playing safe and saying no. Judges were more able to grapple with complex decision making involved in saying yes when their willpower levels were high after eating.

The good news is it is a muscle that can be strengthened through practice. We also know that good self-control is a key factor in success at school and work, so it is a muscle worth working out. Be aware that immediately after exercise it is, as we have seen, weakened; the strengthening benefits only show over time. Willpower is one of the things that keeps us good. We are more likely to cheat, steal, relapse into our addictions, be aggressive, sexually misbehave or overindulge in our chocolate hoard when we have used up all our available willpower. Perhaps this could be one reason why occasionally people who make hard decisions all day, such as judges and captains of industry, have spectacular losses of judgement and self-control.

So how can you resist eating that chocolate bunny all at once and keep your family safe from harm?

Willpower tends to deteriorate during the day and will be tired or depleted by the end of the day. If you put your excess chocolate somewhere hard to reach early in the day when you have the energy to do so, for example locked in a garden shed or up in the attic, then you are both less likely to stumble across it accidentally while looking for milk, and less likely to summon the energy to find the key, put on a coat and wellies, go out in the cold and dark, to get some should the thought of it cross your mind.

If you eat sensibly and regularly, you are less likely to be assailed by sudden irresistible urges for sweet things (glucose hits). Give yourself some easy rules to follow; for example 'I can only eat the chocolate bunny as a substitute for some other sweet thing e.g. dessert, or my biscuit with tea'. Then at the beginning of the day, when you have the energy for complex decision-making, decide which pudding or biscuit will be substituted by chocolate, prepare the amount of chocolate and put only that where you can easily get it later and put the rest in the shed.

Of course, as we all know it is easy, full of willpower in the morning, to decide to just throw the excess chocolate away to remove all temptation. Just be sure to throw it in someone else's bin way down the street. It is not unknown for people to find themselves going through their bin three hours later looking for that carefully-wrapped-before-disposed slab of chocolate!

Other options are: take it all into work and share it with everyone who comes your way. Give it to your partner or your hollow legged children. Take it, untouched, to your local charity shop to sell or raffle. Or eat it all in one sitting and be damned, life is for living and willpower is too precious a resource to be squandered on chocolate rationing when there's a job to be done, children to be raised, new adventures to be had and a life to be lived!

78: Willpower as a source of success

More on the importance of willpower.

Research over the last twenty years has confirmed that two of the most important predictors of success in life are intelligence and willpower (or self-control). We now know a number of important things about willpower:[145]

- It is a form of energy that can get 'used up' over the day. It is a limited resource. At our best we deal with this by conserving our efforts to match the available resource. So if we have to write an important document when we are tired, we may prioritise that over resisting having biscuits with that cup of tea. At our worst we have nothing left to manage a temptation; hence we break the 'alcohol free week' resolution on Wednesday with one glass that turns into half a bottle.

- Many different activities draw on it: resisting impulses, making decisions, taking the initiative. All self-control tasks draw on the same energy source.

- People use it in four different spheres: regulating thoughts (e.g. resisting distracting thoughts, concentrating); regulating mood or emotion (e.g. not allowing ourselves to fall into despair, bolstering ourselves up); regulating impulse (e.g. resisting temptation); and regulating performance (e.g. trading off speed and accuracy).

- Exertion in one area affects availability of this resource in another area: so resisting that piece of chocolate cake at break will adversely affect your perseverance at a difficult task.

- It tends to be more tired (or depleted) at the end of the day.

- It is like a muscle in that it can be strengthened through practice (like a muscle the fatigue effect of use is immediate, the strengthening effect is delayed).

- Virtue deteriorates when this resource is depleted; cheating and stealing rise for example, as do aggression, sexual misdemeanours and addictive behaviours.

- Intelligence declines when this resource is depleted, as do other cognitive functions.

- People are worse at decision-making when this resource is depleted; they are less prone to compromise and more prone to fall back on irrational bias (rather than engaging with current material and thinking). They may also duck or postpone decisions.

---

145 Baumeister, R. (2012) Self-control – the moral muscle. *The Psychologist* **25**(2) 112-115.

- Initiative declines.

- Willpower is tied physically to glucose. This has real life effects: as previously described, judges are more able to deal with the complexity of parole decision-making after lunch, and the chances of getting parole increase dramatically.

What does this mean for leaders?

- Think about when you ask people to do complex decision-making; earlier in the day is likely to be better. And probably earlier in the week.

- Develop a true appreciation of diversity. When people can truly be themselves at work, they can put their energy into their work, not in hiding or disguising their 'difference'.

- Encourage people to work reasonable hours and to recover and refresh overnight so they aren't exhausted all the time. This may positively affect pilfering and fraud rates as well as interpersonal relations.

- Use your willpower effectively to set up your life so that you don't have to make dramatic draws on it. Organize workload to work steadily and so avoid last minute panics, shop when you aren't hungry and buy only 'good' food to have in the house. Approach your most challenging work first thing in the morning and leave 'easy' stuff to the end of the day.

- Build up your own self-control muscle, practice self-control.

- Use this resource wisely, prioritize your activities, for instance don't start an aggressive new exercise regime that involves rising at 5am every morning just as you are about to initiate a big project at work. Start new habits (exercise, diet, email control) when work is going well and smoothly and you have spare capacity.

Section Seven:

Developing Positive Psychology Skills, Creating Positive Experiences

This section brings together chapters that range from how to run a gratitude exercise, to how to run a training session, to understanding how to listen appreciatively. Along the way we consider the challenges of getting the best from performance management, strengths-based development, how to have productive meetings, the importance of the quality of our conversation and the challenge of obtaining compliance. We also think about how to apply positive principles to delivering training programmes and to creating effective evaluations. We look at practical activities like the success round and the 'time to talk round'. We focus on how to craft appreciative questions and how to listen appreciatively. We end by thinking about problems from a positive psychology perspective.

79: Positive psychology: a useful tool for human resource directors

This chapter outlines how human resource directors can begin to apply positive psychology to some of their core activities.

What is it?

Positive psychology is the study of 'strengths, virtues, excellence, thriving, flourishing, resilience, optimal functioning in general, and the like'.[146] It was introduced as a field of study by Seligman[147] at his inaugural address to the American Psychological Association in 1999 and has grown rapidly since. Positive psychology is at heart the study of human excellence and flourishing, and as such has clear application to the work of human resource directors and other organizational leaders.

Implications for human resource directors

Research in this area demonstrates the difference organizational features such as social capital, positivity ratios and the utilization of individual strengths, can make to an organization's profitability and productivity and to the well-being of its staff. For example, Gittell and colleagues[148] were able to demonstrate that the authentic leadership of Jim Parker of South Western airlines and the goodwill his leadership had built amongst staff was a key factor in their exceptional resilience as an organization in the wake of 9/11, despite being in the most adversely affected category of 'domestic airlines'. It seems that high social capital (organizational trust and interconnectivity by other names) and relational reserves (goodwill towards leadership) positively affect the ability of organizations to bounce back from adversity e.g. organizational resilience. Further, Hodges and Asplund[149] demonstrated that a developmental focus on

---

146 Donaldson, S.I. (2011) Determining what works, if anything. In: Donaldson, S. I., Csikszentmihalyi, M. and Nakamura, J. (eds.) *Applied positive psychology: improving everyday life, health, schools, work and society.* Oxford: Routledge.

147 Seligman, M. (1999) *Presidential address.* The American Psychological Association's 107th Annual Convention, August 21st, 1999.

148 Gittell, J., Cameron, K. and Lim, S. (2006) Relationships, layoffs and organizational resilience: airline industry responses to September 11th. *The Journal of Applied Behavioral Science* **42**(3) 300-329.

149 Hodges, T.D. and Asplund, J. (2010) Strengths development in the workplace. In: Linley, P.A., Harrington, S. and Garcea, N (eds.) *Oxford handbook of positive psychology and work.* Oxford: Oxford University Press.

understanding and utilizing people's strengths at work can reap dividends of reduced turnover and greater productivity. Understandably, atmosphere and work culture affect well-being, and happier people tend to have stronger immune systems and better cardio-vascular health.[150] Positive ways of working and behaving at work appear to positively impact engagement, staff retention, sickness levels and organizational capacity.

Two key concepts

Two key concepts from positive psychology that are readily applicable in organizations and human resources processes, are positivity and strengths.

1. Positivity

Positivity refers to the ratio of positive to negative affect experienced by people. Studies in a number of domains, including team performance[151] and marital harmony[152] have consistently found that a ratio of at least 3:1 positive to negative interactions are needed to reach a threshold where creative ways forward can be found. At ratios below this interactions get stuck in non-productive conflict and relationships deteriorate. In more general terms positive affect is shown to positively affect our cognitive abilities, our sociability, our innovation and our resilience; all of these are important for organizational performance.

2. Strengths

Strengths are essentially our natural and innate abilities, borne of physiology, hereditary endowment and environmental influences. Studies in neuroscience consistently demonstrate that although the brain has greater plasticity than once thought, we still develop patterns of ability based on repeated use of certain neural pathways. What this effectively means is that by adulthood, and certainly by our late twenties, we have both well-established and poorly established neural pathways. These differences impact the ease with which we can access the whole line connection, the smoothness of thought to action. The quality of this connectivity is thought to be associated with our areas of strength, or non-strength.

Research in positive psychology shows how investing in areas of existing strengths can reap dividends. For example, when we are using our strengths we are likely to be more energized, motivated, engaged and successful. We find it less tiring so our productivity is likely to be

---

150 Diener, E. and Biswas-Diener, R. (2011) *Happiness: unlocking the mysteries of psychological wealth*. Chichester: Wiley-Blackwell.

151 Losada, M. and Heaphy, E. (2004) The role of positivity and connectivity in the performance of business teams: a nonlinear model. *American Behavioral Scientist* **47**(6) 740-765.

152 Gottman, J.M. (1994) *What predicts divorce? The relationship between marital processes and marital outcomes*. Hove: Psychology Press.

higher. People need to learn how to use their strengths effectively and appropriately. It seems strength plus skill equals exceptional performance or talent. So the invitation is to work more to shape jobs around people and less to fit people into roles.

Practical application

Our understanding of the beneficial effects of both increasing positivity in an organization and of helping people to understand and use their particular strengths has many practical applications.

1. Performance management

For instance, appraisals or performance management conversations are supposed to be motivating, yet often have the opposite effect. The use of enthusiasm stories,[153] feed-forward interviews[154] and best self 360 feedback[155] techniques all offer alternative approaches to helping people understand when and how they are at their best and how to make that more possible. These are inherently positive and motivating processes. They also reveal a lot about a person's particular strengths.

2. Management development

Management training and development can be revised to take into account these positive psychology insights, helping managers and leaders understand the importance of the 'feel good factor' as well as introducing ways of achieving it. They can be taught how to identify strengths, and how to address team tasks in ways that create opportunities for people to play to their strengths and complement each other. They can also be introduced to change processes that make use of positive psychology such as Appreciative Inquiry.

3. Recruitment and selection

Recruitment and selection can be revised to reveal natural strengths and enthusiasm rather than past experience or skill sets. While these may be important, they can also be misleading as sources of motivation. When people are recruited to do what they love doing, less management energy has to go into motivating them to do it.

153 Bouskila-Yam, O. and Kluger, A.N. (2011) Strength-based performance appraisal and goal setting. *Human Resource Management Review* **21**(2) 137-147.

154 Kluger, A.N. and Nir, D. (2010) The feedforward interview. *Human Resource Management Review* **20**(3) 235-246.

155 Cameron, K. (2008) *Positive leadership: strategies for extraordinary performance.* Oakland, CA: Berrett-Koehler.

4. Downsizing

Positive psychology also offers help with some of the more difficult human resource tasks such as downsizing. Gittell's[156] research has demonstrated that existing levels of social capital and relational reserves make a huge difference to the ability of an organization to bounce back from difficult situations. High levels of social capital and relational reserves are produced by positive and appreciative leadership and organizational behaviour.

5. Leading through uncertainty

Finally, I believe that positive psychology offers support to leaders that are faced, as many currently are, by the challenge of offering leadership during times of uncertainty. Pulling together what we know about motivating people using positivity, strengths, and meaningfulness with participatory processes such as Appreciative Inquiry, creates ways of maintaining motivation and morale through difficult times.

For more about bringing positive psychology into the workplace, see our positive organizational development cards. Introducing 20 key concepts, they contain 60 questions to stimulate discussion and 60 starting points for action.[157]

156 Gittell, J., Cameron, K. and Lim, S. (2006) Relationships, layoffs and organizational resilience: airline industry responses to September 11th. *The Journal of Applied Behavioral Science* **42**(3) 300-329.

157 https://www.acukltd.com/store/positive-organizational-development-cards

80: How to add life to your years

This chapter distils the research about how to increase the likelihood of having a healthy old age.

Mae West famously suggested that it's not the 'men in your life' you need to worry about so much as 'the life in your men'; and as the celebration of another birthday reminds me that more of my life is behind than in front of me, I feel I'd be wise to focus on 'the life left in my years' rather than the 'years left in my life'. And so, I turn to George Valliant[158] for advice.

Valliant has been a key researcher in the study of adult development. This study has tracked hundreds of white, American college men since the 1940s, and a similar group of what the study called 'inner-city men' (i.e. men of different classes, cultures, races, ethnicities etc.), were tracked since they were school children in the 1950s. Reporting research conducted when the men were in their 70s or 80s, he asks, 'What predicts a good quality of life, as subjectively and objectively defined, at that age?'

Factors that don't predict good quality of later life

Interestingly, Valliant identifies six factors that, contrary to popular belief, are NOT shown by this study to have any impact of the chances of being classified as 'happy-well' at 70 or 80, rather as than 'sad-sick', 'prematurely dead' (died after age 50 but before general life expectancy) or 'intermediate' (neither definitely happy-well nor definitely sad-sick, but still definitely alive!).

- Ancestral longevity.

- Cholesterol.

- Parental social class.

- Warm childhood environment

- Stable childhood temperament

- Stress levels.

---

158 Vaillant, G. (2015) Positive ageing. In: Joseph, S. (ed.) *Positive psychology in practice.* Chichester: Wiley-Blackwell.

Since these are things we have little control over, their lack of influence on the quality of our old age is good news. Also good news is the fact that the factors that do make a difference are within our control.

The less good news (for those of us who are older already) is that these predictive factors need to be in place by age 50 to affect quality of life 30 years later.

Factors that do predict good quality of later life

The factors that are shown to positively predict happy-well status at 70 or 80 are:

- Not smoking or stopping young (best to stop before 45).

- Mature defences adaptive coping style. This essentially means you use 'all about the other' coping mechanisms such as altruism, sublimation, suppression or stoicism, and humour, rather than 'all about me' mechanisms such as passive aggression, dissociation, projections, fantasy, or acting out, when coping with adversity. Or, as Valliant says, to put it another way you are good at turning lemons into lemonade and not turning molehills into mountains when dealing with the slings and arrows of life.

- Absence of alcohol abuse e.g. alcohol not causing multiple problems with family, law or life.

- Healthy weight e.g. BMI 22-28.

- Stable marriage e.g. without divorce, separation or serious problems.

- Exercise e.g. that burns more than 500 calories per week, regularly.

- Many years of education. Interestingly this isn't about the correlation with social class so much as an apparent association with increased self-care, future orientation and perseverance.

Of the first six, at least four need to be present at 50 years old to reap the benefits 20 to 30 years later.

Unfortunately, we are all subject to the whims of bad luck: being stuck by lightening, injured by the stupidity of others, crippled in an accident, or derailed by malignant genes. So, no guarantees.

This is undoubtedly a terrific and valuable study, the question for many of us, of course, is how generalizable it is across gender and ethnicity, culture and class? Even so, for now I'll gamble that it is and be cautiously optimistic that there will be 'life in my years' yet.

81: How to increase your effectiveness as a manager with strengths cards

Strengths cards are a useful tool for helping with development conversations. This chapter gives some ideas about how to use them in different types of development conversations.

Increasingly, being an effective manager is about helping others to be their best. People's natural strengths are at the heart of great performance. While there are great psychometrics around to assess people's strengths, they aren't always available, suitable, or affordable. A pack of strengths cards is portable, re-useable and infinitely applicable. Below are eight ways managers can use a pack of strengths card to enhance their effectiveness.

Ideas for using your strengths cards

1. Coaching: creating confidence, resilience, motivation and performance

Coaching for performance is an important part of any manager's role. Bringing strengths cards into the coaching conversation can help create a positive focus and stimulate a conversation about an individual's particular strengths. By exploring past successes and helping an individual recognize the particular personal strengths that consistently underlie their successes, you enhance their self-confidence and resilience as they recognize and own their own particular performance assets. By focusing on how these assets can be realised in future performance, you both create motivation for the challenge and enhance their likelihood of succeeding.

For example: ask someone to share their greatest achievement or success in the area under discussion then spread the cards out on the table and together identify the strengths that allowed them to achieve that success and then identify with them the ones that really resonate with them as being an essential contributor of their successes. The strengths they are happy to own.

2. Coaching: for personal and career development

Managers are increasingly responsible not just for an individual's 'in-role' performance, but also for their career development. An exploration of an individual's real highlights of their career so far, and an analysis of the strengths at play in those moments, can help someone understand what they need to develop a satisfying career: ever more opportunity to play to, and utilize, their strengths in the service of personally important goals. Assessed from this perspective, different future paths can open up, and existing ones become more or less attractive.

For example: invite the person to talk to you about their career highlights, spend some time identifying the strengths that contributed to these highlights, then imagine what their future career will look like if they can use these strengths to achieve things that are important to them. Ask them to imagine what they will be doing, where they will be working and who with, how they will be spending their time. Then together you can identify a possible future career goal and how to get there.

3. Team development: creating an economy of strengths, increasing capability

Team members can find themselves restricted in using their strengths by the division of work by role. In the worst case scenario a particular task falls to someone because it's 'in their remit', despite the fact that they have no natural talent (or strengths) to support them in this task. Usually the result is that the task is done very slowly (or rushed) using tremendous energy and effort (or none) to at best a mediocre standard. Once a team understands all its members' natural strengths, they can operate as an economy of strengths. This means the team can allocate and share tasks according to the strengths-fit, increasing both the effectiveness and efficiency of the team and the productivity of individual members.

For example: help each team member to identify their strengths using questions like 'When have you felt most alive at work?' Then follow the processes as above. Once everyone has identified their strength, create a map of the strengths of the members of the team. There will be overlap. Then they can then analyze the tasks the team has to perform against what strengths are needed for each task and allocate them accordingly.

4. Performance appraisal: motivating people to be their best

Performance appraisals are meant to be motivating. Too often they are the exact opposite. This is partly due to an over-emphasis on analysing problems and failures in the past, and partly due to an emphasis on creating a list of future tasks. Shifting the focus to helping people identify the best of the past, and the strengths they display in achieving those successes, and then constructing a vision of the future based on how they could access and utilize those strengths even more in the future, will help switch the conversation from de-motivating and de-energizing to motivating and energizing. This is because people find using (and the anticipation of using) their strengths motivating and energizing. Use the cards to help someone explore, name and own their particular strengths that allow them to succeed.

For example: invite the person to share when they have been most excited about their work or what they are working on (not whether it succeeded or not). Spread the cards out and together identify the strengths that underpin these most motivated moments. Help them identify future goals, targets or projects that create the same sense of excitement because they will call on the same strengths. Help align these to organizational priorities, so everyone wins.

5. Motivating micro-moments

Effective managers know that every interaction with someone acts to motivate or de-motivate them, to encourage change or to support the status quo. By increasing your strengths spotting skills and your appreciative ear, you can increase the motivational encounters your staff experience with you. By understanding your people as a profile of strengths (rather than as their job profile) you can notice when they are using their strengths, or help them access them when they aren't. With an appreciative ear you can help them notice what they did right, or what went well, even in difficult situations.

For example: spread the cards out and think about one of your staff and about the most clear memory you have of being impressed with something they did at work. Look at the cards and think about what strengths the staff member was using when they did this. They will have been motivated both by their success and the very process of using their strengths, so if you spot the next time they are using these strengths and mention it, they will be motivated by the fact that you can see when they're at their best. Practice 'spotting' the different strengths as you encounter your staff at work, you'll soon get the hang of it!

6. Elevate mood to elevate performance

As a generalization people perform better when they feel better. This isn't about job satisfaction, this is about momentary states of well-being. When people feel good they are more curious, more tenacious, more sociable, and better able to cope with complexity. They have more energy, they are more generous with others. Having a conversation with an individual or a team that is focused on past or present successes is likely to elevate mood in the moment. By going a step further and identifying the strengths at the core of the success you are increasing the likelihood of a replication of these success, as people understand better what made them possible. This is also likely to elevate mood.

For example: have a session where members of a team are asked to recount a time when another team member made a big contribution towards the success of the team. Use the cards to help people offer feedback to each other about the strengths they were struck by in this person's account. Take it from there.

7. Leadership: know thyself

It is well known that effective leaders recognize their own shortcomings, and work to limit the damage they can cause. It is less appreciated that great leaders also know their strengths, and how to use them well. When a leader knows and owns their strengths, they are more able to use them wisely and judiciously. They also better understand that other people don't have this strength: that what is easy for them can be harder for others. They can become more forgiving of others. They can gather people around them that can help them exercise their strengths appropriately, and ameliorate their weaknesses. Use strengths cards to help leaders understand their own strengths and develop control and skill in using them, and to understand that other people are blessed differently.

For example: sit down with the leader of one of your teams and explore with them which of their strengths contributed to a recent success of the team (see point 1). Then go a step further and ask them to name someone who also contributed to this success and explore their strengths. It should dawn on the leader that the reason they were both instrumental in this success wasn't just that they had some of the same strengths, which were suited to the job at hand, but also that they had some different but complementary strengths, and so each to some degree offset the weaknesses of the other.

8. Recasting problematic behaviour: strengths in overdrive

Sometimes difficult behaviour is caused by an out of control strength. The person who never gets their own work done because they are too busy helping others: empathy in overdrive. The person who seems to want to have a say in every issue whether it concerns them or not: leadership in overdrive. Understanding that sometimes people aren't in control of their strengths, that their very strengths are the things that lead them into trouble, gives us a different place to go with the conversation. We can recognize the strength as a general asset, then focus on how to use it wisely. Strength plus skill in using the strength is key to great performance.

For example: this is a damage limitation exercise: someone has caused problems and needs to be told that they need to modify their behaviour. What you can do is start the conversation, not with the problems they've caused, but by investigating their strengths (see point 1) and then have a look at the cards and see if the behaviour in question can be recast as a strength in overdrive. If so, then you have somewhere different to take the conversation and should have a better chance of getting an actual genuine attempt to modify behaviour and not just sullen temporary withdrawal.

We stock a range of strengths cards on our online store suitable for different audiences and contexts.[159]

---

159 https://www.acukltd.com/store?tag=strengths%20cards

82: Strengths-based development: how to do it

This chapter gives advice on how to apply strengths-based thinking in a more general way to encourage development.

Appreciating Change has long been an advocate of strengths-based development, finding it to be more effective and more motivating than deficit-based development. These findings have been supported by research and development in the area of positive psychology.

Recent research suggests:

■ That in the UK those who choose to focus on their strengths and manage around their weaknesses are in a minority (suggesting that most choose to focus on their weaknesses).

■ That the strength of our neural connections is at the root of our 'talents' (things we can do almost effortlessly) and our weaknesses (things we don't do or do badly).

■ That it takes a lot of repetition and effort to change established neural patterns. One group that do this successfully are trainee taxi drivers acquiring 'The Knowledge', and we all know the dedication they put in to achieve that degree of neural connection growth.

It seems that in general terms there is a greater return on investment on development activity aimed at strengthening synaptic connections that are already strong i.e. focusing on strengths.

Individual-strengths development involves three stages: identification of talent, integration into how the individual views himself or herself and behavioural change.

Individuals who focus on identifying and developing their strengths report increases in satisfaction and productivity. It is also suggested that they experience more positive psychological states such as hopefulness, confidence and subjective well-being.

Research suggests also that there is increased employee engagement, which in turn can link to increased profitability, turnover, safety, customer satisfaction and more.

So, what does this mean for managers and leaders?

- There are several ways to identify talents: spontaneous reactions (e.g. people who automatically take the lead in confused situations, people who automatically introduce order into dis-order), rapid learning (things we pick up quickly), yearnings (what people want to do, often showed as their private passions e.g. learning a new language for fun, for instance), and satisfactions.

- Always be alert to these cues. Remember, people often can't actually identify their own talents (as in, 'but doesn't everyone work like this?').

- Help people understand where their talents lie.

- Create opportunities for people to work to their talents. Fit the job to the person not the person to the job.

- Ensure that acknowledgement of an area of weaknesses is seen as effective self-awareness that allows something positive to be done to help.

- Create workarounds for areas of weakness that might cause difficulties. Make sure people know the areas in which they might be vulnerable to error, and that help is at hand.

This development activity can be further supported by Positive Action card packs, available through our online store.[160]

---

160 https://www.acukltd.com/store/positive-action-cards-positran

83: Building for the future: strengths-based organizations

This chapter thinks about strengths-based development from a whole organization perspective.

As the business world becomes ever more competitive, just being able to fix problems in production, supply lines etc. as they arise is no longer sufficient to ensure competitive success. An exciting new way of thinking offers an alternative approach to achieving organizational development, innovation and success.[161] This approach calls on strength-based management and leadership, appreciative innovation, positive organizational design and positive psychology to develop strengths-based organizations.

So what are strengths-based organizations?

They are organizations that:

■ Know their collective and individual strengths and build excellence from them.

■ Build a focus on strengths into all aspects of organizational life.

■ Recognize the need for work to offer life-affirming experiences and ensure that it does for everyone.

■ Recognize that the organizational heart is held in conversation and so ensure consistently high-quality evolving conversation that keeps the organization fresh, energized and alive.

How do you design a strengths-based organization?

By recognizing that people engage and excel, personally and collectively, when they 'work' or 'play' to their strengths, and by designing organizational processes that allow people to experience active involvement in the evolution of their organization.

---

161 Whitney, D. (2008) Appreciative Inquiry: a process for designing life affirming organizations. *AI Practitioner* **November**.

To achieve this you need to ensure that people:

- Know their strengths.

- Know their colleagues' strengths.

- Know how to use their strengths productively together.

- Experience appreciative leadership that illuminates and brings out strengths in individuals and teams.

- Recognize it is this unique configuration of strengths that creates market advantage.

How can this be achieved?

Skilled use of a strengths psychometric, such as strengthscope,[162] combined with strengths-based coaching, helps individuals identify and apply their strengths. While Appreciative Inquiry, an organizational development methodology:

- Creates opportunities for people to tell their stories and be heard, which they find enlivening and energizing.

- Allows everyone involved to be an author of the future.

- Creates positive energy, enthusiasm and inspiration as people are inspired by hearing about what works.

- Allows everyone, through the design phase, to participate in designing organizations that work for them.

---

162 https://www.strengthscope.com

84: Five top tips for having great meetings

This chapter gives advice to help you make better use of your meeting time.

Many people find meetings challenging. These five tips will help your meetings be more successful, enjoyable and productive.

1. Start with something positive

How? Ask everyone a question like 'What's been your greatest success, big or small, since we last met?' or, 'Which of your achievements over the last month are you most proud of?' or, 'Which of your staff do you feel most grateful too, and why?'

Why? Because sharing good news boosts mood (and shares resources) which enhances creativity and problem-solving abilities.

2. Ask more questions than you make statements

How? Consider the question to which your statement is an answer, and ask the question rather than make your statement. So, if you are thinking 'that won't work' ask, 'What might be the downsides and how could we guard against them?' If you are thinking, 'We need to raise sales', ask 'How can we turn this around?' or, 'How can we improve revenue?'

Why? Because statements tend to offer people a binary position of either agreeing or disagreeing. Questions encourage people to engage in a different way which can produce a richer conversation, with more room for nuance, opinion shift and resourcefulness.

3. Think beyond the boundaries of the group

How? Ask questions that bring other stakeholders to the topic under discussion into view, for example 'How might finance react to that suggestion?' 'How would we accommodate customers who...?' 'What will marketing need to know to create a great pitch for us?'

Why? Because considering the needs and perspectives of the whole system even when it is not in the room leads to better, more sustainable, decision-making.

4. Focus on the people who are there not those who aren't

How? Start the meeting on time (unless known exceptional circumstances are affecting a large proportion of the group, in which case rearrange if only by 15 minutes). Make the most of the people present. Assess if the meeting will be able to fulfil its purpose, or do something else that is still valuable. If not, then explain and let people do something useful with their time.

Why? Because it is very easy to get caught up with people who are late or absent and to end up taking frustration out on those present, or to have an hour's meeting because that is what was planned in the hope that others will appear or because it was scheduled for an hour. So those who came on time have their time wasted waiting for others or in an ineffectual meeting, and get berated for the sins of others for their trouble.

5. Find positive things to say about ideas presented and people present

How? Thank people for attending. Look for the positive in what people say, 'Well that is an unusual idea, tell us more about what you are thinking?' as well as lots of 'Good thinking' and 'Good idea' etc.

Why? Because lots of research shows that people generally thrive in a positive atmosphere and creativity improves. A positive atmosphere requires a ratio of positive to negative expressions and emotional responses of about 3:1 or higher.[163] Left to our own devices with our well attuned critical faculties, meetings can fail to achieve this tipping point of positivity.

We have produced an Udemy for Business video in partnership with Skills Booster that addresses this challenge.[164]

---

163 Losada, M. and Heaphy, E. (2004) The role of positivity and connectivity in the performance of business teams: a nonlinear model. *American Behavioral Scientist* **47**(6) 740-765.

164 https://www.udemy.com/leading-productive-meetings/learn/v4/overview

85: What kind of conversation are you having today?

This chapter helps us think about the quality of the conversations we have at work, and their impact.

In many work places conversation is regarded as an adjunct to the real work of getting stuff done. All too often a request for a conversation is experienced as an interruption, a distraction from real work. Seen as a necessary evil, the objective is to complete the conversation as quickly as possible so all involved can get back to work. While the topic of conversation may be regarded as important, the quality of conversation doesn't even register. This is very unfortunate, as the quality of any conversation will have an impact beyond the moment.

The information and ideas that follow come from an excellent recent publication, *Conversations Worth Having* by Jackie Stavros and Cheri Torres,[165] bar the table and graph which I generated from their writing. I have found this classification extremely helpful in thinking about the nature of conversation.

The quality of conversation affects people's emotional state, their ability to learn or take advice, their creativity in problem-solving or generating initiative, their motivation, and their action potential e.g. the likelihood of them doing something appropriate and useful after the conversation. It will also affect their willingness to engage in future conversations. In this way every conversation is potentially an investment in the culture, creativity and productivity of the organization.

This means every conversation has an impact on the quality of organizational life. Each conversation, while a small thing in itself, is part of huge construction: the organizational culture. How it feels to be a member of the organization, to work in the organization, to attempt to improve the organization is determined by our day-to-day interactions: our daily work conversations.

So we are wise to give some thought to the nature of conversation in organizations. Conversations in the workplace can be classified along two key dimensions or axes: inquiry to statement and appreciative to depreciative, as the table overleaf shows. Each combination of dimensions generates a different quality of conversation.

---

165 Stavros, J.M., Torres, C. and Cooperrider, D.L. (2018) *Conversations worth having: using appreciative inquiry to fuel productive and meaningful engagement.* Oakland, CA: Berrett-Koehler Publishers.

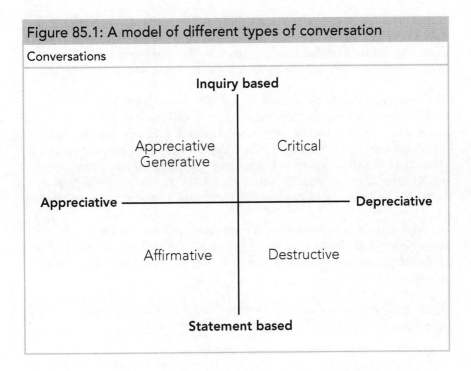

Figure 85.1: A model of different types of conversation

Conversations

Inquiry based

Appreciative
Generative

Critical

Appreciative — — — — — Depreciative

Affirmative

Destructive

Statement based

For example, conversations can be conducted from an *appreciative* or *depreciative* stance. In general terms, those conducted from an *appreciative* stance are likely to add value, as people share ideas and build on the ideas of others. In addition, people's contributions will be acknowledged, opportunities identified, new perspectives generated and possibilities for action created. Such conversations create upwards spirals of confidence and optimism. These conversations serve to strengthen connections, enhance relationships and expand awareness. People experience meaningful engagement.

By contrast, conversations conducted from a *depreciative* perspective, where people advocate for their own ideas and ignore or actively criticize those of others, are likely to be experienced as belittling and critical. In such conversations people are focused on pointing out why things won't work. They may be dominated by a few strong characters. Such conversations are likely to weaken connections and strain relationships, to reinforce existing assumptions and to eclipse people's potential i.e. to limit possibility and movement forward.

Inquiry-based conversations are based on questions. Conducted from an *appreciative* perspective, the aim of the questions is to generate information, to reveal hidden assumptions, perspectives or knowledge, or to expand awareness. They aim to make room for the emergence of possibility and opportunity, or to deepen understanding and initiate change. Such conversations are likely to build relationships, awareness and connections. People are likely to feel valued in such conversations. We can see that this is where the practice of Appreciative Inquiry is located. From a *depreciative* perspective they are likely to consist of rhetorical and negative questions that are pejorative. People are likely to feel that they and their efforts are devalued in such a conversation.

Statement-based conversations consist mostly of comments. Offered from an *appreciative* perspective these are likely to be experienced as affirming. The comments will be positive as well as add value in the way they respond to questions or point to important facts. They are likely to be experienced as validating and to have a positive impact on people and situations. Statement-based conversations conducted from a depreciative perspective are likely to be focused on criticism and blame, they are likely to be a non-validating experience.

In general, the two appreciative-focused conversations are likely to be more beneficial to individuals and the organization. The different characteristics of the two appreciative-focused conversations are interesting, as reflected in the table below.

Figure 85.2: A comparison of appreciative and generative conversations with affirmative conversations

Appreciative and Generative	Affirmative
Meaningful	Genuine, mutual admiration
Mutually enlivening and engaging	Acknowledgement
Geared to generating information, knowledge and possibility	Focused on identifying the positives in plans and aspirations
Solution or outcome focused	Motivating and encouraging
Uplifting and energizing	Feel good
Positive	Reinforcing positive relationships
Productive	Unlikely to generate new knowledge or innovation

The important difference being that *appreciative* and *generative* conversations are more likely to result in change. The difference lies in the power of questions to promote change in thinking and action.

The tell-tale signs of an appreciative conversation are recognized as the presence of energy, creativity and positive emotions. Importantly, critical conversations can be effective when balanced with strong relationships formed as the result of predominantly appreciative conversations. Destructive conversations are likely only to be damaging to those present and the wider organization.

86: How to improve compliance in organizations

This chapter looks at the challenge of achieving compliance from a psychological perspective.

When people don't comply with legal requirements, organizations can face penalties and fines running into the thousands. To take just a few examples current at the time this chapter was written:

- A Greater London pizza manufacturer was fined £15,000 after failing to respond to warnings about an unsafe doorway.

- Hertfordshire County Council accidentally faxed details of two cases it was dealing with to a member of the public and was fined £100,000 for breaching the Data Protection Act.

- Sheffield-based company A4e was similarly fined £60,000 for losing an unencrypted laptop with the details of thousands of people.

- Osem UK, a kosher food company owned by Nestle, was fined £27,372 for not complying with the packaging waste regulations.

- The UK's biofuels watchdog fined three companies a total of £60,000 for failures to comply with environmental legislation designed to reduce carbon emissions from the transport sector.

Many compliance breaches occur in human resources and at the time of writing the compensation limit for unfair dismissal is £65,300 while the compensation limit for breach of contract is £25,000. Over 20% of all UK business are fined due to non-compliance issues. Non-compliance can be a costly business.

To avoid these penalties, organizations put a lot of time and effort into ensuring that people comply with regulations and requirements, however many psychological factors work against them.

1. The overwhelming attractiveness of short-term goals in an immediate context

Faced with the choice between achieving an immediate, positive outcome now, and incurring a probable negative outcome at some point in the future, people are drawn to the short-term immediate outcome. Smoking is a classic example. Smokers know full well that at some point in the future it may have a negative consequence, but right now they really want that nicotine hit. Similarly, in organizational terms, people know that taking a shortcut through the lengthy process of getting rid of someone in the organization opens us up to the risk of a possible financial penalty, but the short-term attraction of solving the problem right now can be overwhelming.

2. The belief that success recognition depends on goal achievement

We usually congratulate people on the achievement of a goal, getting that job, getting promoted, making that sales figure etc. We are not overly practiced at recognizing progress towards a goal, except when we know we are in a teaching situation, for instance when helping our children learn to read. Here we offer praise and celebration at every possible point; if we waited until they were fluent readers before we offered a word of praise or encouragement they would long since have given up.

If we set a goal of perfect compliance and offer no reward or encouragement or celebration of success until it is achieved, we are unlikely to reach the goal.

3. A lack of alignment of organizational objectives

All too often in a particular context within the organization it can appear as if choices have to be made between being compliant and 'getting things done'. These two organizational demands appear to people to pull in different directions. Some classics are: filling the job quickly by 'just appointing someone' and going through a proper recruitment and selection process; keeping production going and taking down time for regular machine maintenance checks; and dutifully recording every contact with a client, however short, and getting on with the next task. Given these conflicting priorities, people usually consider 'getting the job done' by far the most important.

4. Actions speak louder than words

It is a truism that what people do, or how they behave, is a clearer indication of their belief system than what they say. People in organizations watch who actually gets recognized, praised, promoted and rewarded, and assume their behaviour to be that which the organization truly values. So if an organization preaches adherence to standards of practice, but rewards those who achieve goals by any means, then people will see little value in being the mug who adheres to standards and gets left behind in the race to the top.

5. People are strongly influenced by local culture norms of behaviour

The classic example here was the members' of parliament expenses scandal. Spoken more or less loudly by everyone involved was the fact that 'everyone was doing it'. In practice it was highly condoned by the organization. It was a well-accepted 'bending of the rules' to correct a perceived injustice over members' of parliament pay. It is highly likely that there was an underlying message of 'you're a fool to yourself if you don't'. It is a highly principled person who can clearly see the wood for the trees here.

This sort of situation exists in many organizations where the left hand doesn't allow itself to see what the right hand is doing. So one part of the organization can say 'hand on heart' they are complying, while another part is busy bending rules to produce outcomes.

What can be done?

1. Strengthen weak feedback loops

In essence the negative effects of non-compliance need to be brought nearer to the action of non-compliance. Many organizations do understand this and have internal mechanisms for coming down heavily and immediately on breaches of compliance. However, too much of this can create a very coercive environment, which ultimately leads to people hiding breaches, errors, mistakes etc.

So, in addition, the positive consequences of compliance need to be brought much more strongly into view. To take our smoking example, helping people visualize a healthy older age, still able to play sports, play with their grandchildren, with clean lungs, more money to help their children, well-flowing blood, breathing easy etc. brings the long-term benefits of healthy living now more clearly into view. As we can see it also connects to their values, in this example family.

In the work setting things that positively influence behaviour now are likely to be: being able to feel proud of where you work, knowing you are helping the environment, strongly believing that work is fair, valuing the organization's reputation, and receiving prizes and recognition for doing the right thing.

2. Reward effort and progress as well as achievement

Again some organizations already do this. They have charts that demonstrate levels of compliance in different areas, congratulate people who come to ask how to do it right, publicize the best enquiry of the week and so on. Essentially they celebrate when things get better and when they go right. Highlight the benefits of doing it right at every opportunity.

3. Move from either/or to both/and

Help people understand the highest priority is, for example, creating a sustainable business, and that compliance and task achievement are both important for this overarching goal. Therefore their challenge is always to be thinking how can we do what we need to do, and do it right?

4. Model what you want

The lead has to come from the top, otherwise your compliance officers have a thankless task. If senior management don't truly believe that compliance is an important investment in a sustainable future that affects everyone, and is not just a bureaucratic inconvenience, then why should anyone else?

For leaders it can be very tempting to pull rank to bypass procedures. Just remember that people take their cue about what is important from what you do more than what you say. If you are aligned in word and deed, then the message is very powerful.

5. Build the culture to support your objectives

You want to create a culture where people do the right thing when no one is watching. For this to happen there needs to be good alignment between organizational values and practices. People need to know what is required of them, and how to spot when they are being asked or being led into being misaligned, and what to do about it.

87: Seven tips for running your own training sessions

Many managers are asked to train others in what they know. This chapter gives some tips for creating an enjoyable and effective learning experience.

How do we make training stick? We know that investing in the human capital of our workforce by upping their skill level is vital to any organization, but if you've ever sat through a boring training session, or one that brought back unpleasant memories of school, you know that there is a significant chance such investment of time and money will be wasted. Here I list and explore seven tips to help your training sessions be impactful and enjoyable, for you and your trainees.

1. Step out of the expert role

Often we are asked to run a training session due to our expertise in an area. Strangely this can be a challenge, as we encounter what is known as the 'expert problem'. Essentially our own knowledge and skill are so integrated that we can't easily separate out the elements to construct a good training path; and we have forgotten how new and challenging this all is to the novice. The danger is that we inadvertently overwhelm or confuse with our expert knowledge.

The trick is to step out of the expert role. Resist the pressure to download everything you know about the subject, and instead focus on co-creating a learning experience with your participants. The old adage 'start where your people are at' still holds true. Establish their baseline of knowledge and skill and go gently from there. It can help to think of yourself as 'a guide from the side' rather than a 'sage from the stage'.

2. Limit the teacher talking time

If you love your subject and know lots about it, you will have lots to say about it. One of the hardest challenges isn't deciding what to share but what not to share. People learn better when they are active in the process. Try to limit yourself to short bursts of input followed by some participant activity. Get them to work with what you are sharing, to roll it around in their brain, to manipulate it. In this way the learning is much more likely to stick with them. When I am designing a workshop, keen to share this amazing field, I constantly have to remind myself that sometimes 'less is more'.

3. Ask good questions

Questions tickle the brain, questions trigger thought. Pepper your
training with good questions and encourage people to engage with them in
discussion before you build on that foundation with your own knowledge.
Having discussed the question themselves people are keen to have
their knowledge validated by you, the expert. We learn by linking new
information to what we already know. By helping people bring what they
already know to the fore you make that foundation accessible. People learn
as much by hearing what they think about something as hearing what you
think. When people hear themselves saying new things, making new links,
and, seeing new possibilities, the brain really fires up with learning.

4. Grow the engagement

Not everyone loves learning or being in a classroom type situation.
Memories of school can cast long shadows. The transfer of information is
a relational activity. It needs engagement from both parties. To grow the
engagement you need to be positively responsive to any tentative sign of
engagement, for example a first question, or a complaint about the room,
or a challenge to your knowledge. Deal with the content in as generous
a manner as possible and appreciate the engagement. As people see that
you are supportive, encouraging and not in any way punitive, they will get
braver about expressing their views. In a word: be generous dishing out the
sweeties of your goodwill.

5. Create a visible before and after measure

These days I almost always create a before and after measure for a group
session. Take the objectives for the session and turn them into some sort
of scale question. Good starters are expressions like 'To what extent...'
'How clear am I...' 'How confident am I...' and ask people to give you their
baseline measure on a scale of 1-10 at some point during your 'beginnings'.

It is best to ask people to write down their self-scores individually so
they aren't influenced by any group norms. Record them all publicly,
emphasizing that low initial scores are a great sign of potential success
for the session. If appropriate, discuss what this starting point tells you.
Repeat the exercise at the end of the session.

It is highly likely that scores will have shifted to the right and spreads will
have narrowed. In this way you can all see the impact of the session. Again,
encourage discussion of the shifts and what that means. I find that doing
this affirms for both me, and my participants, that learning has taken
place. It also weakens any sense that 'nothing happened and it was all a
waste of time' that anyone might be harbouring.

6. Draw out learning

At points during your session, and certainly at the end, encourage people to verbalize their key learning from the session. Questions that do this include 'One thing I'll take away from today' 'My biggest insight today' 'The biggest surprise of the day'... you get the idea. It is also often a good idea to ask a question that helps them focus on how they are going to use their learning immediately after the session. The biggest loss of the training investment comes at this point of transfer, so encouraging people to think and articulate 'next steps' can be very powerful. I often ask 'What is the thing you can do differently from tomorrow to put today's learning to work?' Time permitting I might also ask about opportunities they can see to apply the learning over the next three months.

88: Working with the need for convergence in a divergent conversation

This chapter addresses one of the challenges of creating permission or a commission to work in these more co-creative divergent ways.

Appreciative Inquiry and other co-creative methodologies are essentially divergent ways of working together; the emphasis is on the value of diversity and variety. Commissioners and participants unfamiliar with this way of working can exert a pressure to converge on a few key points very early in the process, indeed sometimes before the event has even begun. This pressure can be the expression of various different needs, for example:

- The need for a sense of coherence and co-ordination.

- The need for a sense of moving forward or making progress.

- The need for reassurance that there is a degree of commonality amongst the differences and divergence being expressed (that the group isn't going to splinter).

- A request for amplification of points of agreement (a visibility of commonality).

- A need for a convincing story for other audiences of the value of the day.

- A desire for a record of the intellectual learning, to accompany the experiential learning of the participants.

- A request for tangibility.

- A demand for a guarantee that something different will now happen.

At its root this is often a request for a reassurance that there is a positive, sustainable momentum to action that won't die the moment the session ends; this fear is often based on prior experience of away days. There is often a fear that the day is 'just a talking shop' and that unless clear outcomes and actions are written down 'nothing will happen'.

In addition, our 'emergent', 'exploratory' 'unfolding' description of how the day will run can feel very alarming to those commissioning our work, such as leaders, who are used to much more controlled 'facilitation'. A focus on the need to converge can be a request for reassurance that the 'complexity and diversity' they are agreeing to work with can, in the end, be drawn back to somewhere safe and contained.

Ways to moderate this demand, so that it doesn't distract from the day's activities

■ Bring the leaders and other audiences into the event so they experience the change in the room, in the system, in the moment. This reduces the reliance on 'planning' as the driver of change.

■ Work to help leaders understand that their role in this kind of change is to 'ride' the energy it produces; to co-ordinate activities rather than to command and control them. This reduces their feeling of needing to understand everything all at once.

■ Work with leaders on their unchallenged or unquestioned stories of leadership, help them behave differently around change and leadership. This can help reduce anxiety about being solely responsible for achieving change.

How to meet the need without compromising the spirit of our endeavours?

In discussing this with Appreciative Inquiry colleagues we realized that there are two slightly different aspects to this. The first is a need to create sufficient coherence so that the system can move forward. This can be done very much in the same spirit as the rest of the day, with questions and activities focused on creating coherence amongst the group.

The second is the need to create a tangible or visible record of the level of agreement.

1. Make visible patterns and levels of coordination and coherence amongst the divergence

■ Use reflecting teams to reflect key points of agreement or action.

■ Use commitment and request conversations.

■ Have a last 'action round', for example in Open Space. Or a last 'linking' round of 'golden nuggets' from conversations in World Café.

■ Move into the domain of production: acting 'as if' we know the world and therefore can have certainty.

■ Ask those present questions such as, 'What story are we going to tell ourselves (and/or others) about what we have done here today and are going to do tomorrow and in the future? Who else needs to know?' And 'How will you get the resources to do what you now believe needs doing?'

Ask people to make individual commitments to what they are now going to do differently.

- Ask people 'Given all we have discussed today, what is possible?'

- Ask the group what else needs to happen for them to go away convinced that something is going to change.

2. Create a very tangible or visible record of the level of agreement

- Use dots or ticks to get individuals to select which are most important (or some other criteria) to them out of all the ideas or points that have emerged. Gives an instant 'weighting' picture.

- Popcorn. Get people to write on a Post-it the most important thing that has come out of the last conversation, for them. Sort and theme.

- Pyramid. Start people in pairs identifying four or five top things. Then pair up with another pair and produce a new list of top four or five etc. until whole group are narrowing down the last few contenders.

- Get projects (with a first draft name) and what it is going to achieve, onto flip charts, with interested parties and a first step to making something happen.

- Help groups prepare something for absent sponsors who appear at the end of the day, about the best of the day and intentions for the future.

A few further helpful hints

- Everything is everything else. In this instance how you work with commissioners and leaders from the beginning affects the helpfulness or otherwise of the hunger for convergence later on.

- Life is always a compromise.

- That the leader focused on how convergence will be achieved is essentially asking: 'How will I, and my organization, survive the diversity, complexity, confusion, multiplicity and richness, you are proposing to unleash? Please reassure me that we won't fly apart, that it will be safe, that it will be productive.'

This is a very reasonable request for reassurance. It is a strong sign that the person wants to go forward yet has concerns. The challenge lies in offering sufficient reassurance so that we are able to continue moving towards the day, while maintaining sufficient freedom of movement to be able to work with the balance of need in the room on the day.

89: The success round

This chapter introduces a very useful and versatile positive exercise.

As much research has now confirmed, happiness has many benefits. One easy way to use positive psychology to bring these benefits into the work place is by opening a meeting with a 'success round'. All too often in meetings we plunge straight into the business of the day. Starting the meeting by giving people a chance to share a recent success not only boosts people's mood in the moment, it also prepares them to engage more productively with whatever is to follow. As an added bonus, we learn a lot about what makes our colleagues tick.

The exercise is very easy. Essentially as you open the meeting you say something like:

'Before we plunge into the agenda, let's just take a few minutes to reflect on what is going well at the moment. What I'd like is for us all to take a moment to think of a recent success we've experienced at work. It doesn't have to be anything huge, just something that gives you a little glow of achievement or success. Then I'd like us to share them.'

Depending on the size of your group you can do this as a whole round, or just ask people to do it in threes or fours and then share a few examples across the groups.

What you do next is up to you. You could just say:

'Thank you, it's great to hear so many good things are happening even as we …. [are experiencing challenges of some nature]'.

Alternatively you might ask:

'Who else needs to hear about any of this good news and how can we do that?'

Or:

'So what have we just learnt about ourselves?'

You may have other ideas of how to build on what you hear.

Either way you should find that the meeting goes a little better for this early investment. And over time you may notice that people start noticing their 'reasons to be cheerful' more of the time, ready to bring them to your meeting, and that in turn the group's sense of themselves becomes more positive.

90: Gratitude exercise

This exercise creates the experience and emotion of gratitude in the moment.

Context

I used this recently with a group of managers as part of a workshop on positive and appreciative leadership. It is an effective way into the virtuous practices aspect of flourishing organizations and into the topic of authentic leadership. It could just as well be used as an exercise in individual executive coaching or development.

Objective

The brief moment of reflection on blessings that the exercise invites helped these leaders remember that they are connected to, and dependent on, many others. Some left resolved to make their (previously somewhat hidden?) sense of gratitude and appreciation more obvious. This exercise could be built on with individuals with the suggestion of the keeping of a gratitude journal. (The clue is in the title, it's a journal in which you write down things you are grateful for every day. This exercise is proven to lift mood in a short space of time.)

The exercise

Form people into groups of 4-6 people and invite them to introduce themselves. Then invite them each to share three things they feel grateful for:

1. To their colleagues (individual or collective.)

2. To their organization as a whole, or the leadership of their organization.

3. And finally offer them a free choice (anything or anyone of their choice to whom or for which they feel gratitude).

Suggest they might like to start their sentences:

'I want to express thanks..'
or
'I'm very grateful that/for…'

Encourage them to enlarge on what difference the thing they are grateful for, or person they are grateful to, has made to their lives.

Once everyone has been around and shared their stories encourage the group to reflect on the experience of the exercise and, as ever, their learning from it.

Feedback from the recent workshop included the observation that it was easy to overlook the things that one is grateful for amongst the hurly-burly, frustrations and challenges of organizational life, and that to reflect on reasons to be grateful was both a pleasant and a humbling experience.

In addition, people commented on the value of taking time to experience gratitude, noticing that this led, in some cases, to a resolve to say something to someone. In a coaching session one could build on this to suggest that they write the person a gratitude letter, and then arrange a time to read it to them. This again is proven to be an excellent mood-boosting exercise.

When to use

It worked well as an opener to a session exploring what leadership is and means. It could also be used:

- As an exploration of virtuous practices in flourishing organizations.

- In workshops focused on authentic, ethical and moral leadership.

- As part of individual or executive coaching.

91: Time to think: how I became a convert

This chapter introduces a useful exercise to transform the quality of listening in a group.

Time to Think is the title of a book by Nancy Klein.[166] It was recommended as a resource by people I trust.

The first time I read it I didn't really get it, it seemed like a variation on what I already knew and did. Yet people I valued kept referring to it as being a terrific resource and method. I had another look, still not convinced it was so exceptional.

Then an opportunity arose. I was asked to work with a large-ish management team of 12 people. A few preliminary interviews suggested, in a vague way, that group 'behaviour' was an issue. Also that perhaps there were some past issues that were unresolved.

While the day was essentially focused on future strategy, I thought it might be an idea to get a 'time to think' round in early on so everyone could say what needed saying without interruption.

So after a few preliminaries, and a quick round of 'What is most exciting about your work at present?' I introduced the idea, suggesting it might take a while and inviting everyone to make themselves comfortable before we began.

A few words of explanation.

'*In turn, you will get to speak without interruption about "what is the most compelling vision I have for the future of.... and what do we need to focus on to make that happen?" until you are finished. While one person is speaking the rest of us support by listening, clearly showing that we are by our eyes, face and body language.*'

I gave people a couple of minutes to make any notes they wanted about what they wanted to say and then off we went.

Well the first thing I noticed was that after the first speaker had finished he pushed his chair back from the table, very clearly settling into a good, comfortable and attentive listening position. This continued as each speaker spoke, in a very slow Mexican wave effect.

---

166 Kline, N. (1999) *Time to think: listening to ignite the human mind*. London: Ward Lock.

Second, it was very hard for me to assess how valuable this might be. I couldn't tell whether people were rapt or bored.

Third, I did throw in the occasional support for the quality of the listening as we switched speakers. They were doing very well.

Unprompted, people started to link their contribution to those that had gone before, always a sign of attentive listening.

And finally I noticed for myself the transition to a meditative/zen-like state where it became harder and harder to speak.

Immediately afterwards, just before coffee, I asked for feedback on the process. Some of the comments made were:

'What's that been, 40 minutes? An hour? I think there has been more value in the last hour than we would ever achieve in an hour in our meetings. I mean, we might not have made any decisions but just in terms of information transfer – I've learnt so much.'

'It was really hard not to jump in. I've bitten my tongue so hard I think I've drawn blood.'

'Me too!'

'It's strange, I've heard .... say that loads of times before and ...going on about.... But I've never really realized how much it matters to him; how important it is to him.'

'It's made me realize how much I speak for speaking's sake. I am resolved to say less and listen more in future.'

What I can't convey through their words was the sense of discovery and wonder (and deep learning) in their tone of voice as they made some of these comments.

They were knocked out by the power of this simple discipline. The effects of it could be seen throughout the rest of day, as they themselves said. In the final round, reflecting on the day, a lot of people referred back to that hour as being the most thought-provoking or impactful of the day.

I admit I was astonished. I thought it would be a good exercise for them, but I had no idea how powerful it would prove to be.

I am a convert, I shall be using it again. (I am also resolved to try to finish reading the book!!)

92: Crafting appreciative questions

A key appreciative skill is that of crafting questions. This chapter gives pointers on how to create appreciative questions.

1. Direct towards the positive

Appreciative Inquiry is focused on learning from success and using what works as a springboard to new futures. Use superlative emotion words in your questions: 'the most moving', 'the most proud' 'the best experience of...'

2. Unleash new accounts, generative stories

Appreciative questions should bring new, previously untold (at least in this context) stories about the resources and best experiences in the organization into the organizational conversation. It is this introduction and sharing of new accounts of life in the organization that allows new ideas, possibilities and visions to flourish

3. Focus attention on what you want more of

By inquiring into a particular topic you focus attention on that topic or feature. As the question directs people to go looking for examples of the 'best of...' they will look harder and see things they didn't see before. Their awareness of the presence of the topic of inquiry grows.

4. Bring different aspects of organizational life into focus

Think about what people aren't talking about, what isn't being noticed right now. This is where some of the new accounts, knowledge and perception shifts might lie.

5. Identify strengths

Appreciative questions should help people and organizations understand their strengths. Knowing and using strengths helps with motivation, engagement, commitment, performance and confidence.

6. Identify the positive core of the organization

Good appreciative questions expose core values and beliefs as they inquire into meaningful experiences of people. By looking for common themes across a round of discovery interview stories, you can begin to identify the positive core of the organization.

7. Are context specific, resonating with language meaningful to the organization

While I do offer some 'generic' question shapes below, the most impactful questions are context specific, carefully crafted for the particular situation, connecting to the organizational language or 'grammar'.

Some 'starters for ten' question shapes (taken from various sources as well as my own)

- Tell me about a time when... who, how, what, when, where...?
- If you had three wishes for this organization/system, what would they be?
- If by a miracle we woke up tomorrow and the system was running as we dream, how would we know, what would we notice?
- Tell me about how we got from there to here, what was the first thing that changed?
- What is the smallest thing we could change that would make a difference?
- What is the unimaginable thing we could do?
- If we could do absolutely what needs doing, what would we do?
- How will our customers know things are changing here?
- If our success were completely guaranteed, what bold steps might we choose?

We have designed a set of coaching cubes that offer a fun and tactile way to introduce 36 positive and appreciative questions into the coaching or indeed any conversation. These are available from our website.[167] In addition, our positive organizational development card pack contain another 36 questions useful for stimulating discussion.[168]

---

167 https://www.acukltd.com/store/coaching-cubes
168 https://www.acukltd.com/store/positive-organizational-development-cards

93: Using open dialogue to create appreciative questions

This chapter introduces a methodology that could be useful for increasing the quality of the question to be addressed in many different situations.

At the Association for Business Psychology conference in May 2011, John Turner from the University of Hertfordshire led a session on open dialogue: 'a simple methodology for initiating and facilitating a free-flowing dialogue'.

During his session he introduced 'A collaborative method for defining the dialogue focus'. Once we had decided on a broad topic, he asked us to get into small groups and come up with ten questions relevant to the topic.

We were then to sort the questions into 'factual' and 'philosophical'. Factual are those to which there is a right answer that can somehow be ascertained. Philosophical are those to which there are many possible answers. Clearly in Appreciative Inquiry we are often dealing with questions of this nature.

Each group then chose their favourite question out of the ten they had generated and fed it back. During the feedback the group started to look for the commonality amongst the questions. The idea was to narrow it down to two or three broad themes of possible discussion.

Once that had been achieved, we voted for the question theme we found most interesting, using the 'clapometer' measure of popularity. You can clap for all three questions if you want; it's the strength of your clapping that you vary.

Having selected the most popular theme, we then selected the best expression of the question from those initially put forward by the group, and worked to improve it in the light of the other variations.

The group then had a lively and energizing discussion.

It struck me that this was an excellent technique for helping groups to co-create useful, energizing questions. I thought it particularly relevant. It is useful for:

- When working with the planning team to generate good questions for the AI event.

- In team meetings or team development when a contentious issue arises to help create a constructive discussion.

- During AI events or summits, not only during the discovery phase, but also possibly during the design phase.

- When there has been little opportunity for planning and the first activity of an event is forming some questions.

- To help audiences in large organizational briefings to create useful and illuminating questions.

I have also used this at the beginning of a workshop to help create a sense of unity around the key discoveries people hope to make during the process of the workshop.

94: From active listening to appreciative listening

This chapter explains how to listen in a more purposeful way.

Active listening as a set of activities

The popular model of 'active listening' is often presented as a set of behavioural 'mechanics' that if employed judiciously will demonstrate to an audience that 'listening' is taking place. The recommended behaviours include: good eye contact; not interrupting, clarifying; summarising; and displaying other visible signs of attending. It is very easy for these behaviours to become de-contextualized; to become a list of 'to do' behaviours. At which point it can become the 'nodding donkey' school of listening. I certainly have experienced the disconcerting effect of talking to someone who is showing all the right behaviours but behind whose waterfall-mist eyes it is clear that disconnected thoughts are crowding and cascading. I am not being 'heard', although he or she may be hearing what I say.

How might the spirit of Appreciative Inquiry, the desire to 'grow more of what we want' help create more effective listening? And how might this help reposition 'active listening' as a systemic, dynamic, creative act?

Active listening as an intention

We need to recognize that listening is always an act of intent: we are listening to some purpose or for some reason. There are many different possible purposes, for example:

- To bear witness.
- To provide space for someone to think.
- To provide help.
- To provide encouragement.
- To help sort confusion.
- To share an experience.
- To find fault or spot flaws.
- To appreciate.
- To amplify and fan early successes.

And so on. Each might require listening for different things. So at a meta level we could ask ourselves, first, what might be our own personal default intent when we listen? And second what do we particularly need to be listening for in this conversation, what sort of listening is appropriate here? There is a shift from an emphasis on body language to an emphasis on integrity of intention.

What might help

These things might help in all situations:

- Feeling peaceful in ourselves, aligned in mind and body.

- Not worrying about 'the next thing to say' or 'getting it right'.

- Allowing that whatever kind of listening shows up is the right kind.

- Recognising that intense listening can be full of activity – asking many questions, reformulating a lot, reacting. It is not necessarily a passive activity.

- Having the ability to say 'I'm not able to offer you my full attention, or to listen well right now because… [I'm getting anxious about time, I'm distracted by…]'.

- Recognizing that the concept 'I must be 100% present' is precisely that, a concept that may be unobtainable at any given time.

In general, in a spirit of appreciative listening we might find ourselves listening for:

- What is working?

- What are the resources available here?

- What good is in this?

- What is the broader picture, and how can we connect to that?

We might ask ourselves questions such as:

- What arouses my curiosity in this?

- What do I connect to?

- What excites me in what is being said?

- What can we grow from this?

Thanks to the other participants in the source conversation for this line of thought: Madeline Blair, Suzanne Quigley, Pauline Doyle, and Claire Lustig-Roche, which took place at a Blore AI Retreat event hosted by Anne Radford in the UK in 2011.

95: How to use Appreciative Inquiry under less than ideal conditions

This chapter is drawn from experience and marvels at the robustness of the Appreciative Inquiry approach. It draws out some principles of practice.

A while ago I was running a series of one-day Appreciative Inquiry events as part of an ongoing culture change in an organization. On one particular day so many things seemed less than ideal for 'doing' Appreciative Inquiry that I compiled an 'I wouldn't start from here list'.

I wouldn't start from here if:

- Only part of the system is in the room.
- People have been 'sent' by managers with no briefing about what to expect.
- This is perceived as unwelcome time away from working to achieve their production targets.
- They have no idea what they are coming to.
- The link to the 'bigger agenda' of change is not clear to many participants.
- There is no management present.
- They have just received late news of an announcement briefing everyone was expected to attend that day.
- Twenty people are present rather than the 30 expected.

In other words the group that assembled was confused and were not happy about being pulled off the line at short notice to attend some strange event, with work on their mind.

Faced with this disconsolate, grumbling, restless group that felt they would rather be somewhere else I:

- Explained what we would be doing, encouraged them to stay but also offered them the possibility of leaving.
- Get them to mingle with a good mix of introductions and sharing successes.
- Shaped the workshop delivery around their need to attend the briefing – and to absorb its implications.

- Bent with the wind – agreed management should be present, but didn't amplify, and seized any positives to build on.

- Stuck with the voluntarism principle.

- Was prepared to come away with nothing.

I stayed with appreciative principles of working throughout the day. And I did take them through the 5D cycle.

- I kept the focus on who was there rather than who wasn't.

- I emphasized the volunteer principle and stuck with it.

- I meet the needs of the group to be in two places at once.

- I gave time to the adjustment needed to the news delivered in the briefing.

- I adjusted the plan for the day to accommodate less people.

- I acknowledged the frustrations of the lack of 'whole system' representation.

- I trusted the process to produce engagement.

People stayed, people engaged, the day got progressively better and by the end good ideas had emerged with people enthused to take them forward. Appreciative Inquiry really is a most robust process!

Our colleagues at Appreciating People have produced an excellent set of introduction to Appreciative Inquiry cards that we sell through our online store.[169]

---

169 https://www.acukltd.com/store/a-taste-of-ai-20-appreciating-people

96: Getting the most out of the evaluation investment

This chapter addresses the challenge of evaluation from a social constructionist and positive perspective.

Introduction

To design the most impactful evaluation process for your project, workshop or other intervention, there are some questions that need careful consideration.

1. Who is the audience?

Who is the audience for the data or information you are intending to produce? Some possible answers to this question include: the participants, the process or project commissioners, participants' managers, future participants, the event designers, or some other outside audience such as regulatory bodies or external funders. In each case the information they regard as valuable is likely to be different. They will be looking for different things from your evaluation process. You need to be clear about who this information is for before you can begin to answer these other questions.

2. What is the purpose of the evaluation?

There are more answers to this question than may at first be apparent. Sometimes the answer is the straightforward one of measuring some change, but not always. For instance, if the audience is future participants then the purpose of the evaluation may be to create interest, curiosity or excitement about the workshop. If the audience is the event designers then comparative impact of different sections may be of prime importance. If the audience is participants' managers then consequent actions maybe more important to capture than internalized learning.

3. What to measure?

This choice needs to be made in the context of the first two questions. For example, if my primary concern is the participants in a team building exercise, then my priority is to demonstrate the improvement in team relations or dynamic. For this I will take a before and after measure of the things we are supposed to be working on. Any objective for a workshop can be framed as a question. Any question can be designed so that people can give a rating answer. For example, 'On a scale of 1-10 how well do we understand how to get the best out of each other?' The questions can be asked and scored before and after a workshop. It is a rough and ready, highly illuminative measure that creates a shared awareness of both current state and progress made on 'touchy-feely' topics.

Alternatively, if your workshop is about safe handling of dangerous materials then your priority will be to measure knowledge gained through an end of course test. If it is more about on-going performance, for example supervisor coaching skills training, then your evaluation will need to extend into the post workshop time.

4. How long a time period does your evaluation need to cover?

The shorter the time period the more confidently you can say that the changes observed are to do with the specific intervention. With team development workshops I want to demonstrate that change has already taken place by the end of the day to demonstrate the value of the time everyone has invested in working together. So I design an evaluation around the day's events: the audience is me, the participants, and to a lesser extent the HR commissioner.

If I was the team's manager, I would be much more interested in longer term changes in team behaviour. The evaluation would need to extend over a period of months. Regular conversations would need to be had with the participants, asking, 'Give me an example of how you have used the experience of ... in the last two weeks'. People don't automatically make these connections, so if you just ask the bald question 'Have you put that learning into practice?' you may well get a false reading of the impact of the event.

5. How can you triangulate your evaluation data?

The problem with extended evaluations is that the variables become ever more confounded. In other words, as time passes, you can say with less and less confidence that the outcomes you are seeing are to do with your intervention and not some other intervening factor.

One way around this is to triangulate your data. This means that before you do your training you predict a number of ways in which the impact will show. For example with phone sales training these might be: more time spent researching and preparing each phone call, less phone calls made but of longer duration; lots of short phone calls when the right contact is not available; more time spent talking to budget holders; clearer articulation of product benefits; specific needs-assessment questions being asked; a higher percentage of calls leading to meetings and so on. If you measure all of these, and they move in the anticipated direction of a successful intervention, then you have a better basis for saying it was the training that made the difference.

6. How can you direct people's attention to the value created?

The questions you ask in your evaluation will direct people's attention to specific features of the experience more than others. It helps to be clear what effect or knowledge you are hoping to create. If you are running a pilot, and it is important to effect improvements, then ask people to discriminate between sections of the event, and to suggest improvements. However if it is more important that they put what they learn into action, then direct your evaluation questions to usefulness and intended use. If you need to demonstrate change then before and after measures are crucial. When a change is likely to unfold over time, it a good idea to measure small initial changes in behaviour to help people notice that change is happening. If it is about creating a vibe or a buzz about an event or experience, then ask people about highlight moments, feelings, excitement and so on.

Evaluation is a socially constructed process. Understanding it as a co-created social, dynamic, value-laden process means that we can thoughtfully design evaluation processes that give information, add value, affect perceptions, and create potential for action.

97: 'Houston, we have a problem': what does it mean to have a problem?

Here we look at the interesting organizational effect of labelling something a problem.

At the 2012 World Appreciative Inquiry conference I fell into conversation with Stefan Cantore (Sheffield University Management School). Stefan was busy thinking about 'our love affair with problems' in preparation for writing a chapter for a forthcoming publication.[170] We had a great discussion about this that stayed with me and caused me further thought.

How do we know when we encounter a problem? While completing a personality profile questionnaire recently I noticed that I have a problem with the word 'problem'. As the questionnaire asked me variations on how I deal with problems, I struggled to answer: the questions just didn't connect. It would seem that I just don't think in terms of problems and problem-solving: I don't notice when I encounter them.

Trying to answer the questions I found it very hard to think of instances of recent problem solving to help me. Did this mean I led a problem free life? All became clear a few days later when I was working out how to fix something that had broken. I was going through a process in my mind of possible alternatives, seeking the resources and trying the solution out. Yes, you've guessed it, I was problem solving, only the word problem never entered my mind as the name for the activity I was involved in, and probably wouldn't have occurred to me at all if not for my recent struggle with the questionnaire.

Problems and 'Problems'

Talking to Stefan, and thinking about this, I wondered if we have problems and Problems. That is, things we sort out all the time, almost without noticing are 'problems', and some other challenges that are similar but different: 'Problems'. This led me to ask, what happens when we label something a 'Problem'? What is the purpose, impact and outcome of naming some particular

---

170 Cantore, S.P. and Cooperrider, D.L. (2013) Positive psychology and Appreciative Inquiry: The contribution of the literature to an understanding of the nature and process of change in organizations. In: Skipton, L.H., Lewis, R., Freedman, A.M. and Passmore, J. (eds.) *The Wiley-Blackwell handbook of the psychology of leadership, change, and organizational development*. Chichester: Wiley-Blackwell.

thing a 'Problem'? *'Houston, we have a problem'* came to mind as one of the greatest examples of this act of labelling. What did it do? I suggest:

- It called attention to something. In this case the world's attention.

- It suggested this something was beyond the capacity of those so far involved to fix.

- It extended the system around the situation.

- In this way it attracts resources to a situation.

- It caused creativity – the creativity of the Apollo community in this instance is the stuff of legend.

- It acted to focus attention: I'm guessing many other activities at the Apollo base station were put on temporary hold!

So when someone in an organization calls 'Problem' we might argue that they are attempting to get focus, attention, resources and creativity applied to a situation to move it forward. They are also implicitly stating it is beyond the capacity of the existing system to move forward; that they need to connect to a bigger system. It's an acceptable way of asking for help.

Problems from heaven

David Cooperrider[171] suggested that those who bring Problems are a gift, because they also bring a Dream. By labelling something a Problem and so asking for help, the problem-bringer or namer is implicitly suggesting that there is still hope that things can be better, with the help of the wider system. So naming something a Problem also creates the possibility of hope.

So where does that leave us? I think we need a different word for the small stuff that we do every day that gets caught up under the umbrella of 'problem-solving'. It makes it look as if problems are everywhere.

I think the word Problem, used wisely, can act as a clarion call for resource and action. I think it needs to be recognized as a call for wider system involvement. The Apollo astronauts couldn't resolve the situation developing on their spacecraft with their resources, they knew that and called the developing situation a Problem. The wider system responded. They responded emotionally and experimentally. They tried things out and then they tried other things out. They involved everyone with all their different skills to find a way forward that would allow the astronauts to live. People may have used their rational

---

171 Cooperrider, D. and Whitney, D. (2001) A positive revolution in change: appreciative inquiry. In: Cooperrider, D.L., Sorenson P.F. Jnr., Yaegar, T.F. and Whitney, D. (eds) *Appreciative Inquiry: an emerging direction for organizational development*. Champaign, IL: Stipes Publishing.

skills, but they were motivated by their emotional connection to the whole project and to the individuals in danger.

Problem gets a bad name in organizations because it is not recognized as a call for an emotional and relational response. Rather it is seen as a call for a rational analysis, devoid of emotional content. Appreciative Inquiry as an approach is tailor made for helping organizations create a response to the clarion call of a Problem. A response that is emotional and relational while utilizing all the rational abilities of the organization as appropriate. There is nothing wrong with calling Problem when the circumstances warrant it, only in our response.

Section Eight:

Concluding Thoughts

This short concluding section presents my selection of some of the nuggets of interesting ideas or practice that I have picked up from the major conferences I have presented at and attended over the last few years. We finish with a chapter about eulogy virtues.

98: Highlights from the World Appreciative Inquiry conference 2013

Here I share a few highlight moments of my conference experiences at the World Appreciative Inquiry conference in Ghent in 2013.

At a conference attended by over 500 people from 42 nations, with nine keynotes by names like David Cooperrider, Diane Whitney, Ken Gergen, Gervase Bushe and Ron Fry, and innumerable workshop sessions and poster presentations, my experience of the conference could only ever be partial. Here are some of the best bits for me.

Ken Gergen: generativity

'It's the micro-moments of practice within an organization that give vitality to the organization.'

He says it's the little things that keep an organization alive, vital and generative rather than fossilized. I love this observation as it supports my increasing conviction that both flourishing and change in organizations is to do with patterns and shifts in the moment-by-moment interactions more than any grandstanding brouhaha of a big plan.

'An interchange can be generative or degenerative.'

Degenerative exchanges narrow down to the end of meaning, that is, communication ceases. Effectively, someone either refuses to speak anymore or they leave the room. Generative exchanges open up meaning and possibilities. Generative conversations need and create room for improvisation and for mistakes.

In organizations generally we need to encourage more generative interactions. During change it is particularly important.

The importance of generativity to organizational life was one of the key themes of the conference.

Ron Fry: business as agents of world benefit[172]

This caught my eye, the idea that business can be the saviour of humankind at the same time as being a blot on the landscape. Cooperrider and Fry's neat trick was to focus their search on the good done by business on specific practices, not specific organizations. Thus it is possible to say that Walmart, through the power of their supply chain, are revolutionizing the production of cotton, shifting it from a product that is so toxic it burns children to one that is organic, while also acknowledging that some of its business practices are very sharp.

Business as agents of world benefit practices are those that help the markets align with the strength of universal values: business innovations that create mutual benefit. It is about practices, not organizations.

The criteria for inclusion as an example of a business as an agent of world benefit are:

■ Revolutionizing the way the world eradicates poverty.

■ Restoring the biosphere.

■ Building stronger communities.

■ Shaping sustainable peace.

Diane Whitney: appreciative leadership[173]

'We manage complexity through organizational dexterity.'
Brilliantly put!

She also helpfully illuminated the relationship between some positive emotions and behaviour useful in change:

■ **Joy**, through play, imagination and experimentation leads to **Innovation**.

■ **Interest**, through involvement, investigation and exploration leads to **New Knowledge**.

■ **Optimism** through opportunity-spotting, confidence and perseverance leads to **Achievement**.

■ **Contentment** through savouring, integration and complex ideas, leads to **Deeper Insight**.

■ **Love** through connection and relatedness leads to **Cooperation**.

---

172 https://aim2flourish.com

173 Whitney D., Trosten-Bloom, A. and Rader, K. (2010) *Appreciative leadership: focus on what works to drive winning performance and build a thriving organization.* New York: McGraw-Hill.

Steve Oynett: difficult fools

In this highly stimulating and fun workshop session, Steve mentioned the *'children's fire'*. Apparently this is the Native American practice of having a fire lit in the middle of the circle of discussion to symbolize the lives of children for seven generations. It serves to remind the discussants that the impact of any of their decisions must not harm the children for seven generations. A metaphor for sustainability by any other name.

I am sure this metaphor has a use in organizational change.

'The more of a good isn't necessarily more good.'
Planning and efficiency spring to mind!

Sadly Steve has since died, but his wisdom lives on.

Ron Fry and Gervase Bushe: generativity

'Few arrive wanting more work, few leave without having volunteered for cooperative action.'

This is their account of what happens at a generative event. I couldn't agree more, and it confirms my conviction that the proof of the pudding (in terms of how successful your AI event has been) is in the volunteering element at the end e.g. the destiny phase.

From this, they talked about successful organizational transformation. Bushe's research found two key things for successful transformational change.

1. The ideas emerge from within the organization.
2. A new idea (at least to this group, this organization) that is compelling.

While agreeing that the positivity created by Appreciative Inquiry is important, they argue that the heart of change lies with the generative activity of Appreciative Inquiry. In other words, an event could be very positive but if not also generative would be less successful in achieving transforming change.

They added to our repertoire of appreciative questions the idea of the generative question, for instance:

'Tell me about the most provocative experience you have had at the conference, when you felt more challenged (perhaps when your thinking was upended, your values were confronted, your emotions were provoked or your choices were questioned by you)?'

I found this a really useful extension of my understanding of Appreciative Inquiry.

Leo Bormans: happiness

He talked, amongst other things, about green and red dots.

Red dots are the pessimists amongst us – focused on themselves, the past and problems. They are driven by fear and are reluctant to do anything.

Green dots are the optimists amongst us – focused on 'we', the future, and solutions. They are driven by hope and so take action.

He suggested we need to connect the green dots so the red dots become irrelevant.

Again I can see this as an organizational exercise. Not quite sure how; clearly there is a danger of upsetting the red dots!

99: Highlights from the World Appreciative Inquiry conference 2015

More highlight moments, this time from the conference in Johannesburg in 2015.

For those of you unable to attend here are some of my key moments of impact.

Dr John Anderson: geologist
Idea of 'co-curation' of the planet.

David Cooperrider: elevation of strengths
His idea has progressed from *'elevation to conscious elevation to conscious co-elevation'* of strengths.

His concept of 'mirror flourishing' is about moving from the idea that we benefit from getting, to the idea that we benefit from giving. As we give to enable others to flourish, so we benefit ourselves in terms of our flourishing.

Barbara Fredrickson: positive emotions
Positioned positive emotions as *'a reset button for negative emotions that are no longer useful'*. Positive emotions create temporarily expanded mind sets. Flourishing people are set apart from neutral or depressed people in their positive emotion reactivity to everyday events (thus they create a 3:1-5:1 ratio positive to negative events in their own lives every day). The most impactful positive emotions are those co-created with others. They produce 'biological behavioural synchronicity' – both at gestural level but also at the neural firing level. *'Positive emotion makes positive action (altruism) more probable'* – very good session and by skype!

Blagoja Pardulski: dreaming
'No walkabout – no dream – no story – no life.'

The importance of dreaming. Super-teams dream effectively drawing on social sensitivity and ensuring every voice is heard.

'Not icebreakers but firestarters.'
(! – love it)

Dreaming stimulated by novelty (otherwise frontal lobes provide same old same old): new people, new spaces, new data, new body posture.

Chene Swart and Yabonne Gilpin-Jackson: narrative

Great session on narrative. *'Connection before content' 'What is the next wise action?'*

Ron Fry and Jo Kane: business as agents of world benefit

Really interesting project *'50% of the world's top economies are businesses'*. Lyell Clarke talking about the transformation of his company Clarke said, as leader, *'I don't know where we're going, I just know we have to go'*. (Fantastic!! What positive, appreciative, emergent leadership is all about.)

'Somewhere in the world, it is already tomorrow'

Johann Roux, Dirk, Nicki, Theresa, Elonya, Estelle from ITD: mining company case study[174]

An inspiring and moving account of change at a mining company. Many highpoints, just a couple are *'Transformation comes through participation'* and the idea of 'appreciative witnesses' when identifying each other's strengths.

My thanks to all the presenters for these many pearls of wisdom.

---

174 The case study is in Lewis, S., Passmore, J. and Cantore, S. (2016) *Appreciative inquiry for change management: using AI to facilitate organizational development.* 2nd ed. London: Kogan Page.

100: Highlights from the World Congress on Positive Psychology 2015

A further collection of nuggets of comments or ideas that caught my attention at the bi-annual positive psychology conference.

Tal Ben-Shahar: growing tip

Talking about learning from the growing tip of the exceptional.

'The average describes, the best prescribes.'

'Growing tip statistics' are more useful to us for development aspirations than 'the psychopathology of the average'.

Martin Seligman: hope circuit

He spoke on neuropsychology research that demonstrates 'a hope circuit' in the brain that acts to mitigates against the likelihood of 'learned helplessness' occurring. The expectation of control is the key factor. Therefore, he says, to help those depressed etc *'Don't undo the bad stuff, build the good stuff'*. He was very excited about the discovery of these physical coordinates for the philosophical basis of positive psychology.

Cooperrider: PERMA

He used the term 'PERMA cultures' (PERMA is the five key characteristics identified by Seligman as key to flourishing). The term was new to me at the time.

The positive development organization has an 'appreciative mindset' – so experiencing the exponential inquiry effect that works to establish the new and eclipse the old.

$$\text{Positive change i.e. experience of elevation} = \frac{\text{wholepower} + \text{waypower} + \text{willpower}}{\text{experience of deficit}}$$

Kiko Thiel: transcendental deviance

Beyond positive deviance is transcendental deviance.

Kim Cameron: emphasis on the extraordinary vs the excellent. The extraordinary is the ability to 'see the exceptional'. We have some sense of excellence and what it looks like. We don't know the extraordinary until it happens.

Michele Deeks and others: strengths

Michele Deeks from Work Positive and Michelle McQuaid, Shannon Polly, Katherine Britton discussing strengths at work:

'*Manager intervention makes a difference* [to the effect of knowing strengths on performance].'

'*68% of managers are having the wrong conversations.*'

Strengths as basis for 'performance of a life time'. Strengths take us to the 'zone of proximal development'. Shannon has a new book out: *Character Strengths Matter.*[175]

Tom Rath: meaning and work

'*Lives are the sum of all our days.*'

The question leaders aren't asking: 'How do we ensure our people have the energy they need for sustainable performance?'

'*Only 20% of people spent some time doing meaningful work yesterday.*'

'*If you spend a little bit of time being good at everything you reduce your chances of being really great at anything.*'

'*Great leaders are not well rounded, but great teams are.*'

We have 19,200 three second moments in a day; only 16% of people had a positive interaction yesterday:

'*The quality of your manager is more important to your physical health than the quality of your doctor.*'

'*People with a best friend at work are 7x more likely to be engaged in their job.*'

---

175 Polly, S. and Britton, K.H. (2015) *Character strengths matter: how to live a full life.* Positive Psychology News.

'Vacation frequency is a better predictor of well-being than income.'

Only '11% of people had a great deal of energy yesterday.'

'Sleep is an investment.'

101: Resumé virtues or eulogy virtues

My attention was caught by a book review that included the concept of eulogy virtues. Given the positive psychology context of virtues and strengths, I thought the idea interesting and worth pursuing. It seemed a fitting chapter with which to end this book.

Coaches have long suggested that when struggling with life's decisions people consider what they would like others to be saying about them at their funeral, how they want to be remembered, to help them identify some guiding principles for how they live their lives.

Interestingly, this concept resurfaced recently in an article in The Guardian when Oliver Burkeman interviewed David Brooks about his new book *The Road to Character.*[176] Below are some of the ideas or thoughts I found interesting in the article.

■ Brooks, a very successful political lobbyist and commentator, noted that his own life of well-paid worldly success, plus regular meetings with the president, was missing something essential inside.

■ He realized or learnt that success doesn't make you happy. Indeed, Shawn Achor[177] has been arguing for some time that the equation works the other way and that happiness is likely to increase your success. Even so I always feel that these 'I've been there don't do it' talks, be it about success, drug-use or spending five years on a PhD are less than convincing when uttered by those that have already achieved the goal (or had the pleasure and survived). Is that just me?

■ He realized he'd spent too much time cultivating the *'resumé [CV] virtues'*, racking up impressive accomplishments, and too little on the *'eulogy virtues'*. I thought this a very interesting distinction.

■ 'Eulogy virtues' he defines as the character strengths for which we would like to be remembered.

■ He suggests that our 'market driven meritocracy' rewards outer success while discouraging the 'development of the soul'. In the UK at least this seems a reasonable indictment of the current school curriculum debate.

---

176 Brooks, D. (2015) *The road to character.* London: Random House.
177 Achor, S. (2011) *The happiness advantage: the seven principles that fuel success at work.* London: Virgin Books.

- He suggests that we have lost a 'moral' vocabulary. I think certainly in organizations this can be an underdeveloped conversation. The dominant conversation seems often to be about success, profit etc., with any conversation about ethical behaviour, 'doing the right thing by people' and so on to be a much more subservient conversation if it is 'permitted' in the organizational space at all. Which isn't to say that leaders and others in organizations don't have thoughts, doubts and indeed conversations about these aspects of life, just not often in the 'public' organizational conversations.

- He observes a universal tendency to 'get our loves out of order', suggesting that we end up prioritizing what doesn't matter most. I wonder if it is more that sometimes we fail to notice key moments when it might be an idea to revisit, revise or adjust our sense of priorities.

- He frames the notion of life's 'small sins' and gives as an example: *'Thinking more about how you are coming across* [in conversation] *than on what the other person is saying'.*

What do we think about these ideas? How might they relate to our work?

References

Achor, S. (2011) *The happiness advantage: the seven principles that fuel success at work*. London: Virgin Books.

APA (2006) *Multi-tasking: switching costs* [online]. Available at: https://www.apa.org/research/action/multitask.aspx (accessed March 2019).

Avolio, B., Griffith, J., Wernsing, T.S. and Walumbwa, F.O. (2010) What is authentic leadership development? In: Linley, P., Harrington, A.S. and Garcea, N. (eds.) *Oxford handbook of positive psychology and work*. Oxford: Oxford University Press.

Babiak, P. and Hare, R. (2007) *Snakes in suits: when psychopaths go to work*. London: Harper Collins.

Baker, W., Cross, R. and Wooten, M. (2003) Positive organizational network analysis and energizing relationships. In: Cameron, K.S., Dutton, J.E. and Quinn, R.E. (2003) *Positive organizational scholarship: foundations of a new discipline*. Oakland, CA: Berrett-Koehler Publishers.

Barsade, S.G. (2002) The ripple effect: emotional contagion and its influence on group behavior. *Administrative Science Quarterly* **47**(4) 644-675.

Baumeister, R. (2012) Self-control – the moral muscle. *The Psychologist* **25**(2) 112-115.

Baumeister, R.F., Vohs, K.D. and Tice, D.M. (2007) The strength model of self-control. *Current Directions in Psychological Science* **16**(6) 351-355.

Blumenthal, J.A., Babyak, M.A., Moore, K.A., Craighead, W.E., Herman, S., Khatri, P. and Doraiswamy, P.M. (1999) Effects of exercise training on older patients with major depression. *Archives of Internal Medicine* **159**(19) 2349-2356.

Bouskila-Yam, O. and Kluger, A.N. (2011) Strength-based performance appraisal and goal setting. *Human Resource Management Review* **21**(2) 137-147.

Britt, T., Dickinson, J., Greene-Shortridge, T. and McKibben, E. (2007) Self-engagement at work. In: Nelson, D. and Cooper, C. (eds.) *Positive organizational behavior*. London: SAGE Publications Ltd.

Brooks, D. (2015) *The road to character*. London: Random House.

Brown, J. and Issacs, D. (2005) *The World Café, shaping our futures through conversations that matter*. Oakland, CA: Berret Koehler.

Buckingham, M. (2007) *Go put your strengths to work*. London: Simon Schuster.

Buckingham, M. and Clifton, D. (2002) *Now, discover your strengths: how to develop your talents and those of the people you manage*. New York: Free Press.

Bunker, B. and Alban, B. (1997) *Large group interventions: engaging the whole system in rapid change*. San Francisco: Jossey-Bass.

Bushe, G. (2001) Five theories of change embedded in appreciative inquiry. In: Cooperrider, D., Sorenson, P.F. Jnr., Yaegar, T. and Whitney, D. (eds) (2001) *Appreciative inquiry: an emerging direction for organizational development*. Champaign, IL: Stipes Publishing.

Cameron, K. (1998) Strategic organizational downsizing: an extreme case. *Research in Organizational Behavior* **20** 185-229.

Cameron, K. (2008) *Positive leadership: strategies for extraordinary performance*. Oakland, CA: Berrett-Koehler Publishers.

Cameron, K. (2003) Organizational virtuousness and performance. In: Cameron, K.S., Dutton, J.E. and Quinn, R.E. (2003) *Positive organizational scholarship: foundations of a new discipline*. Oakland, CA: Berrett-Koehler Publishers.

Cantore, S.P. and Cooperrider, D.L. (2013) Positive psychology and Appreciative Inquiry: The contribution of the literature to an understanding of the nature and process of change in organizations. In: Skipton, L.H., Lewis, R., Freedman, A.M. and Passmore, J. (eds.) *The Wiley-Blackwell handbook of the psychology of leadership, change, and organizational development*. Chichester: Wiley-Blackwell.

Cooperrider, D. (2015) *Mirror flourishing: Appreciative Inquiry and the designing of positive institutions*. Keynote Talk at Fourth World Congress on Positive Psychology, Orlando, Florida June 25-27th.

Cooperrider, D. and Srivastva, S. (2001) Appreciative inquiry in organizational life. In: Cooperrider, D., Sorenson, P.F.Jnr., Yaegar, T. and Whitney, D. (eds.) (2001) *Appreciative inquiry: an emerging direction for organizational development*. Champaign, IL: Stipes Publishing.

Cooperrider, D. and Whitney, D. (2001) A positive revolution in change: appreciative inquiry. In: Cooperrider, D.L., Sorenson P.F.Jnr., Yaegar, T.F. and Whitney, D. (eds) *Appreciative Inquiry: an emerging direction for organizational development*. Champaign, IL: Stipes Publishing.

Corporate Leadership Council (2004) *Driving performance and retention through employee engagement: a quantitative analysis of effective engagement strategies*. Corporate Executive Board.

Currey, M. (ed.) (2013) *Daily rituals: how artists work*. New York: Knopf Publishing Group.

Diener, E. and Biswas-Diener, R. (2011) *Happiness: unlocking the mysteries of psychological wealth*. Chichester: Wiley-Blackwell.

Donaldson, S.I. (2011) Determining what works, if anything. In: Donaldson, S. I., Csikszentmihalyi, M. and Nakamura, J. (eds.) *Applied positive psychology: improving everyday life, health, schools, work and society*. Oxford: Routledge.

Dunning, D. (2006) Strangers to ourselves? *The Psychologist* **19**(10) 600-603.

Dutton, J.E. and Spreitzer, G.M. (2014) *How to be a positive leader: small actions, big impact*. Oakland, CA: Berrett-Koehler Publishers.

Ehrenreich, B. (2009) *Brightsided: how the relentless promotion of positive thinking has undermined America*. New York: Metropolitan Books.

Eichinger, R.W. and Lombardo, M.M. (2003) Knowledge summary series: 360-degree assessment. *Human Resource Planning*, **26**(4).

Emmons, R. and Mishra, A. (2011) Why gratitude enhances well-being: what we know, what we need to know'. In: Sheldon, K., Kashdan. T., Steger, M. (eds.) *Designing positive psychology: taking stock and moving forward*. Oxford: Oxford University Press.

Estrada, C.A., Isen, A.M. and Young, M.J. (1997) Positive affect facilitates integration of information and decreases anchoring in reasoning among physicians. *Organizational Behavior and Human Decision Processes* **72**(1) 117-135.

Flade, P. (2003) Great Britain's workforce lacks inspiration. *Gallup Management Journal* **11** December.

Fredrickson, B. (1998) What good are positive emotions? *Review of General Psychology* **2**(3) 300-319.

Fredrickson, B. and Branigan, C. (2005) Positive emotions broaden the scope of attention and thought-action repertoires. *Cognition and Emotion* **19**(3) 313-332.

Fredrickson, B. and Losada, M. (2005) Positive affect and the complex dynamics of human flourishing. *American Psychologist* **60**(7) 678-686.

Fredrickson, B., Tugade M.M., Waugh, C.E. and Larkin, G. (2003) What good are positive emotions in crises? A prospective study of resilience and emotions following the terrorist attacks on the United States of America September 11th 2001. *Journal of Personality and Social Psychology* **84** 365-376.

Furnham, A. (2007) The Icarus syndrome. *People and Organizations at Work*. Spring edition.

Gable, S.L., Reis, H.T., Impett, E.A. and Evan, R.A. (2004) What do you do when things go right? The intrapersonal and interpersonal benefits of sharing positive events. *Journal of Personality and Social Psychology* **87**(22) 228-245.

Gawande, A. (2011) *The checklist manifesto: how to get things right.* London: Profile Books.

Gawande, A. (2014) *Being mortal: medicine and what matters in the end*. New York: Metropolitan Books.

Gifford, J., Finney, L., Hennessy, J. and Varney, S. (2010) *The human voice of employee engagement understanding what lies beneath the surveys*. Horsham, UK: Roffey Park Institute.

Gittell, J., Cameron, K. and Lim, S. (2006) Relationships, layoffs and organizational resilience: airline industry responses to September 11th. *The Journal of Applied Behavioral Science* **42**(3) 300-329.

Gladwell, M., (2005) *Blink: The power of thinking without thinking*. London: Penguin.

Goffee, R. and Jones, G. (2000) "Why should anyone be led by you?". *Harvard Business Review* **63**.

Gottman, J.M. (1994) *What predicts divorce? The relationship between marital processes and marital outcomes*. Hove: Psychology Press.

Hammond, S. (1996) *The thin book of appreciative inquiry.* Bend, OR: Thin Book Publishing.

Hodges, T. D. and Asplund, J. (2010) Strengths development in the workplace. In: Linley, P.A., Harrington, S. and Garcea, N (eds.) *Oxford handbook of positive psychology and work*. Oxford: Oxford University Press.

Hogan, J., Hogan, R. and Kaiser, R.B. (2010) Management derailment. *APA Handbook of Industrial and Organizational Psychology* **3** 555-575.

Huppert, F.A., and So, T.T. (2013) Flourishing across Europe: application of a new conceptual framework for defining well-being. *Social Indicators Research* **110**(3) 837-861.

Jones, D.A. (1998) A field experiment in Appreciative Inquiry. *Organization Development Journal* **16**(4) 69.

Keyes, C.L. (2005) Mental illness and/or mental health? Investigating axioms of the complete state model of health. *Journal of Consulting and Clinical Psychology* **73**(3) 539.

Kimball, L. (2007) *An inside job: best practices from within. Leading ideas: strategy and business*. McLean, VA: Booz, Allen & Hamilton.

Kimball, L. (2011) The leadership 'sweet spot'. *AI Practitioner* **13**(1).

Klein, D. (1993) SimuReal: a simulation approach to organizational change. *Journal of Applied Behavioural Science* **28**(4) 566-578.

Kline, N. (1999) *Time to think: listening to ignite the human mind*. Ward Lock: London.

Kluger, A.N. and Nir, D. (2010) The feedforward interview. *Human Resource Management Review* **20**(3) 235-246.

Lewis, S. (2011) *Positive psychology at work: how positive leadership and appreciative inquiry create inspiring organizations.* Chichester: Wiley-Blackwell.

Lewis, S. (2016) *Positive psychology and change: how leadership, collaboration and appreciative inquiry create transformational results*. Chichester: Wiley-Blackwell.

Lewis, S., Passmore, J. and Cantore, S. (2016) *Appreciative inquiry for change management: using AI to facilitate organizational development*. 2nd ed. London: Kogan Page.

Linley, A. (2008) *Average to A+ realising strengths in yourself and others*. Coventry: CAPP Press.

Losada, M. and Heaphy, E. (2004) The role of positivity and connectivity in the performance of business teams: a nonlinear model. *American Behavioral Scientist* **47**(6) 740-765.

Lyubomirsky, S., Diener, E. and King, L. (2005) The benefits of positive affect: does happiness lead to success? *Psychological Bulletin* **131**(6) 803-855.

Lyubomirsky, S., Sheldon, K.M. and Schkade, D. (2005) Pursuing happiness: the architecture of sustainable change. *Review of General Psychology* **9**(2) 111.

Mackintosh, U.A.T., Marsh, D.R. and Schroeder, D.G. (2002) Sustained positive deviant child care practices and their effects on child growth in Viet Nam. *Food and Nutrition Bulletin* **23**(4_suppl2) 16-25.

McCall, M.W. and Hollenbeck, G.P. (2002) *Developing global executives.* Boston, MA: Harvard Business School Press.

McCall, M.W. and Lombardo, M.M. (1983) Off the track: why and how successful executives get derailed (No. 21). Center for Creative Leadership.

Mauss, I.B., Tamir, M., Anderson, C.L. and Savino, N.S. (2011) Can seeking happiness make people unhappy? Paradoxical effects of valuing happiness. *Emotion* **11**(4) 807.

Nyberg, A.J. and Trevor, C.O. (2009) After layoffs, help survivors be more effective. *Harvard Business Review* **87**(6) 15.

Owen, H. (1997) *Open space technology, a user's guide.* Oakland, CA: Berret Koehler.

Page, N. and Boyle, S. (2005) Putting positive psychology to work. *Selection and Development Review* **21**(5) 18.

Polly, S. and Britton, K.H. (2015) *Character strengths matter: how to live a full life.* Positive Psychology News.

Porath, C.L. and Erez, A. (2011) How rudeness takes its toll. *Psychologist* **24**(7) 508-511.

Pryce-Jones, J. (2010) *Happiness at work: maximising your psychological capital for success.* Chichester: Wiley-Blackwell.

Rath, T. (2007) *Strengthsfinder 2.0.* New York: Gallup Press.

Rowland, R. and Higgs, M. (2008) Sustaining change: leadership that works. West Sussex: Jossey-Bass.

Seligman, M. (1999) *Presidential address.* The American Psychological Association's 107th Annual Convention, August 21st, 1999.

Seligman, M. (2011) *Flourish: a new understanding of happiness and well-being – and how to achieve them.* London: Nicholas Brealey.

Sessa, V.I., Kaiser, R., Taylor, J.K. and Campbell, R.J. (1998) *Executive selection.* Greensboro, NC: Center for Creative Leadership.

Shaked, D. (2013) *Strength-based lean six sigma: building positive and engaging business improvement.* London: Kogan Page.

Simmons, C. (2006) Should there be a counselling element within coaching? *The Coaching Psychologist* **2**(2) September.

Sisodia, R.S., Sheth, J.N. and Wolfe, D.B. (2014) *Firms of endearment: how world-class companies profit from passion and purpose.* 2nd ed. Upper Saddle River, NJ: Prentice Hall.

Smith, C. (2007) *Making sense of project realities: theory, practice and the pursuit of performance.* Hampshire, UK: Gower.

Stairs, M. and Gilpin, M. (2010) Positive engagement: from employee engagement to work place happiness. In: Linley, P.A., Harrington, S. and Garcea, N. (eds) *Oxford handbook of positive psychology and work.* Oxford: Oxford University Press.

Stavros, J.M. and Hinrichs, G. (2009) *The thin book of SOAR: building strengths-based strategy.* Bend, OR: Thin Book Publishing.

Stavros, J.M., Torres, C. and Cooperrider, D.L. (2018) *Conversations worth having: using appreciative inquiry to fuel productive and meaningful engagement*. Oakland, CA: Berrett-Koehler Publishers.

Taleb, N.N. (2008) *The black swan: the impact of the highly improbable*. London: Penguin.

Trickey, G. (2007) *Talent, treachery and self-destruction*. Paper at ABP conference, 2007.

Vaillant, G. (2015) Positive ageing. In: Joseph, S. (ed.) *Positive psychology in practice*. Chichester:Wiley-Blackwell.

Van Oyen Witvliet, C. (2013) Forgiveness. In: Lopez J.L. (ed.) *The encyclopaedia of positive psychology*. Chichester: Wiley-Blackwell.

Van Velsor, E. and Leslie, J.B. (1995) Why executives derail: perspectives across time and cultures. Academy of Management Perspectives **9**(4) 62-72.

Vogel, B. (2017) Experiencing human energy as a catalyst for developing leadership capacity. In: Vogel, B., Koonce, R., and Robinson, P. *Developing leaders for positive organizing: a 21st century repertoire for leading in extraordinary times*. Bingley, UK; Emerald Publishing Ltd.

Watkins, J. M. and Mohr, B.J. (2001) *Appreciative inquiry: change at the speed of imagination*. San Francisco: Jossey-Bass/Pfeiffer.

Weick, K. and Sutcliffe, K. (2007) *Managing the unexpected: resilient performance in an age of uncertainty*. San Francisco: Jossey Bass.

Wheatley, M. (1999) *Leadership and the new science – discovering order in a chaotic world*. Oakland, CA: Berrett-Koehler Publishers.

Whitney, D. (2008) Appreciative Inquiry: a process for designing life affirming organizations. *AI Practitioner* **November**.

Whitney, D., Trosten-Bloom, A., Cherney, J. and Fry, R, (2004) *Appreciative team building: positive questions to bring out the best of your team*. Lincoln, USA: iUniverse, Lincoln.

Whitney D., Trosten-Bloom A. and Rader, K. (2010) *Appreciative leadership: focus on what works to drive winning performance and build a thriving organization*. New York: McGraw-Hill.

Woolley, A.W., Chabris, C.F., Pentland, A., Hashmi, N. and Malone, T.W. (2010) Evidence for a collective intelligence factor in the performance of human groups. *Science* **33**(6004) 686-688.

Yaeger, T.F. and Sorensen, P.F. (2001) What matters most. In: Cooperrider, D., Sorenson, P.F.Jnr., Yaegar, T. and Whitney, D. (eds) (2001) *Appreciative inquiry: an emerging direction for organizational development*. Champaign, IL: Stipes Publishing.

About Appreciating Change

Appreciating Change helps individuals, groups and organizations with change. We do this through offering services such as coaching, thinking partnerships, team development, organizational development, and through running developmental workshops.

We understand change as a psychological, people-based process which takes place both within people as individuals and between people as group dynamics. We help people both initiate and adapt to change by taking a strengths-based approach. This means we draw our resources, knowledge and skills, particularly from Appreciative Inquiry and positive psychology.

In addition we have an online shop that supplies various tools we use ourselves to the wider trainer, developer and managerial community. This includes our own tools such as a positive organizational card sets and our coaching cubes, and also many resources from other suppliers such as a happiness game, strengths cards and feeling magnets. You will also find Sarah's other books for sale here.

Please visit our website: www.acukltd.com for more information or go direct to our shop at: www.acukltd.com/shop. If you have any further queries please contact Sarah directly at: sarahlewis@acukltd.com.